When China Ruled the Seas

When China Ruled the Seas

THE TREASURE FLEET OF
THE DRAGON THRONE 1405–1433

LOUISE LEVATHES

OXFORD UNIVERSITY PRESS
New York Oxford

*For Zheng Ziqiang, Zheng Mianzhi, Zheng Zhihai,
and all the members of the Zheng family
in Nanjing and Kunming.*

Oxford University Press

Oxford New York
Athens Auckland Bangkok Bombay
Calcutta Cape Town Dar es Salaam Delhi
Florence Hong Kong Istanbul Karachi
Kuala Lumpur Madras Madrid Melbourne
Mexico City Nairobi Paris Singapore
Taipei Tokyo Toronto

and associated companies in
Berlin Ibadan

First published in 1994 by Simon & Schuster,
Rockefeller Center, 1230 Avenue of the Americas, New York, NY 10020

First issued as an Oxford University Press paperback, 1996

Library of Congress Cataloging-in-Publication Data
Levathes, Louise.
When China ruled the seas :
the treasure fleet of the Dragon Throne, 1405–1433 /
Louise Levathes.
p. cm.
ISBN 0-19-511207-5 (Pbk.)
1. Cheng, Ho, 1371–1435. 2. Explorers—China—Biography.
3. China—Commerce—History. 4. China—History—Ming Dynasty,
1368–1644. I. Title.
DS753.6.C48L48 1996
951'.02'092—dc20
[B] 96-24966

10

Printed in the United States of America
on acid-free paper

Contents

	Pronunciation Guide to Major Figures	13
	Chinese Dynasties	15
	Prologue: Phantoms in Silk	19
1	The Yi Peoples	23
2	Confucians and Curiosities	33
3	The Prisoner and the Prince	57
4	The Treasure Fleet	75
5	Destination: Calicut	87
6	The Strange Kingdoms of Malacca and Ceylon	107
7	Emissaries of the Dragon Throne	123
8	The Auspicious Appearance of the Celestial Animals	137
9	Fires in the Forbidden City	155
10	The Last Voyage	167
11	The Sultan's Bride	183
	Epilogue: A People Called Baijini	195
	Notes	205
	Acknowledgments	233
	Index	237

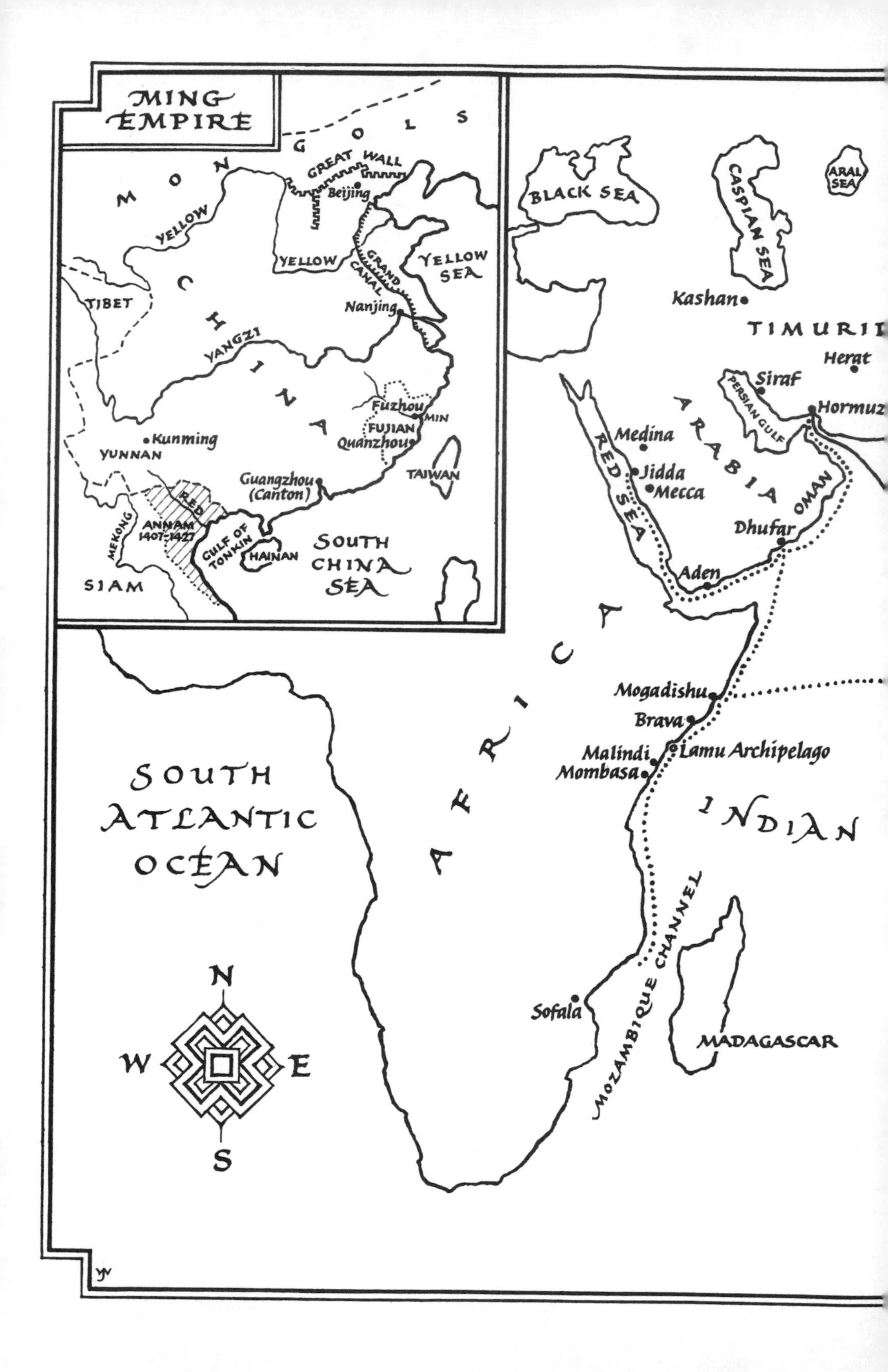
MING EMPIRE
MONGOLS
GREAT WALL
Beijing
YELLOW
YELLOW
GRAND CANAL
YELLOW SEA
TIBET
CHINA
Nanjing
YANGZI
Fuzhou
MIN
FUJIAN
Quanzhou
Kunming
YUNNAN
Guangzhou (Canton)
TAIWAN
RED
ANNAM 1407-1427
MEKONG
GULF OF TONKIN
HAINAN
SOUTH CHINA SEA
SIAM
BLACK SEA
CASPIAN SEA
ARAL SEA
Kashan
TIMURI
Herat
Siraf
PERSIAN GULF
Hormuz
Medina
Jidda
Mecca
RED SEA
ARABIA
OMAN
Dhufar
Aden
AFRICA
Mogadishu
Brava
Malindi
Lamu Archipelago
Mombasa
SOUTH ATLANTIC OCEAN
INDIAN
MOZAMBIQUE CHANNEL
Sofala
MADAGASCAR
N
W
E
S

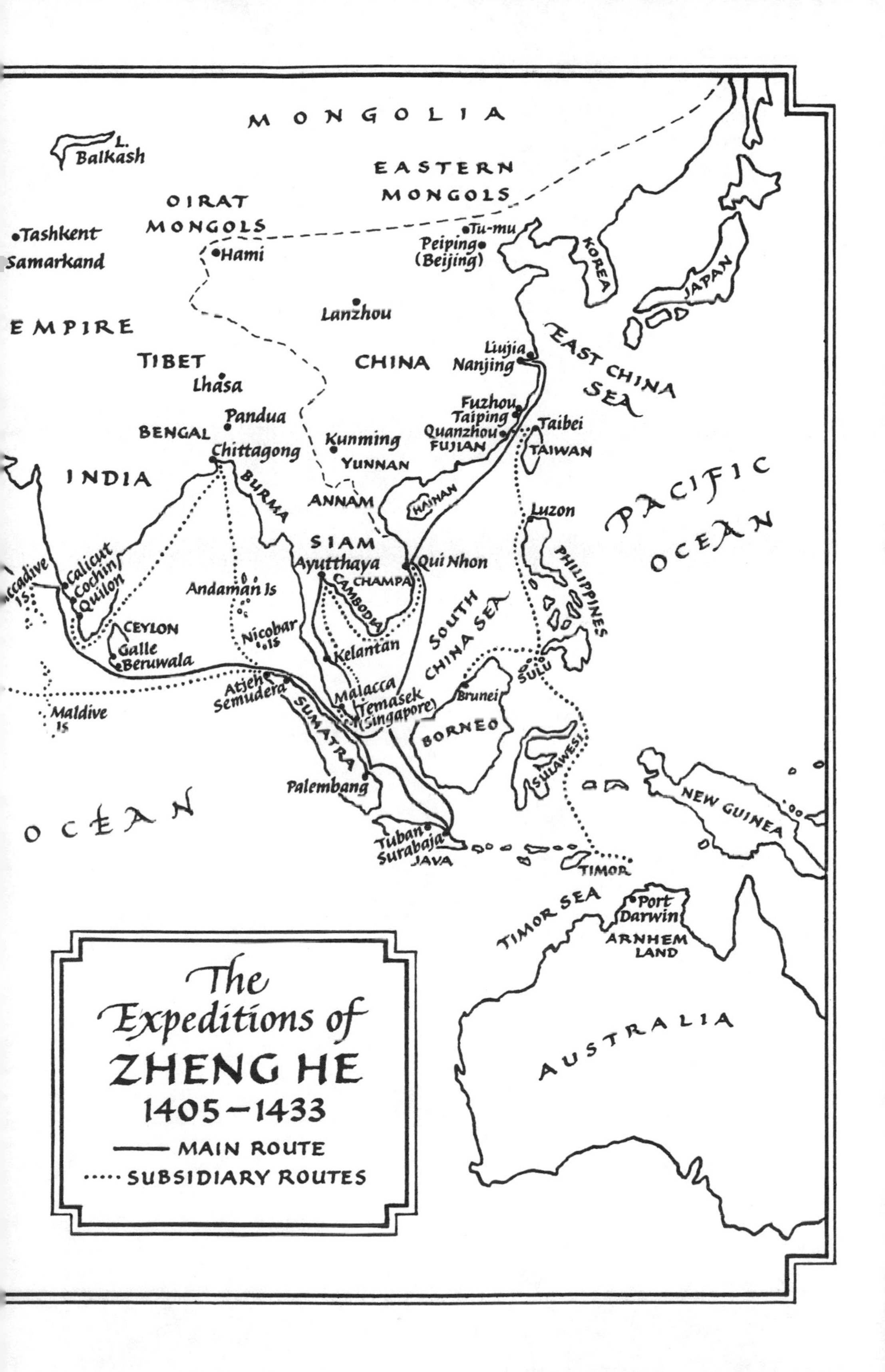

MONGOLIA
L. Balkash
EASTERN MONGOLS
OIRAT MONGOLS
Tashkent
Samarkand
Tu-mu
Peiping (Beijing)
Hami
KOREA
JAPAN
Lanzhou
EMPIRE
Liujia
Nanjing
EAST CHINA SEA
TIBET
CHINA
Lhasa
Fuzhou
Taiping
Quanzhou
FUJIAN
Taibei
TAIWAN
Pandua
BENGAL
Chittagong
Kunming
YUNNAN
INDIA
BURMA
ANNAM
HAINAN
PACIFIC OCEAN
Luzon
SIAM
Ayutthaya
Qui Nhon
CHAMPA
CAMBODIA
PHILIPPINES
Calicut
Cochin
Quilon
Andaman Is
SOUTH CHINA SEA
Nicobar Is
CEYLON
Galle
Beruwala
Kelantan
SULU
Atjeh
Semudera
Malacca
Temasek (Singapore)
Brunei
Maldive Is
SUMATRA
BORNEO
SULAWESI
NEW GUINEA
Palembang
OCEAN
Tuban
Surabaja
JAVA
TIMOR
TIMOR SEA
Port Darwin
ARNHEM LAND
AUSTRALIA
The Expeditions of ZHENG HE 1405–1433
MAIN ROUTE
SUBSIDIARY ROUTES

Pronunciation Guide to Major Figures

Daoyan	[DAOYEN]
Fei Xin	[FAY SHEEN]
Fu Youde	[FOO YOW-DE]
Hou Xian	[HOE SHE-EN]
Hui Shen	[HWEY SHUN]
Ma Huan	[MA HWAN]
Wang Zhen	[WANG JUN]
Xia Yuanji	[SHE-AH YOUANJHEE]
Xu Fu	[SHOE FOO]
Zhang Xuan	[JANG SCHWAN]
Zheng He	[JUNG HUH]

Early Ming Imperial Family

Zhu Di	[JEW DEE]
The Yongle emperor	[YUNG-LE] (1402–24)
Zhu Gaoxu	[JEW GAOSHOE]
Zhu Gaozhi	[JEW GAOJER]
The Hongxi emperor	[HONG-SHE] (1424–25)
Zhu Qiyu	[JEW CHEE-YOE]
The Jingtai emperor	[JING-TAI] (1449–57)

Zhu Qizhen	[JEW CHEEJUN]
The Zhengtong emperor	[JUNG-TONG] (first reign, 1436–49)*
The Tianshun emperor	[TIEN-SHUN] (second reign, 1457–64)
Zhu Yuanzhang	[JEW YOUAN-JANG]
The Hongwu emperor	[HOONG-WOO] (1368–98)
Zhu Yunwen	[JEW YUNWEN]
The Jianwen emperor	[JHEN-WEN] (1398–1402)
Zhu Zhanji	[JEW JANJHEE]
The Xuande emperor	[SCHWAN-DE] (1425–35)

*Reign is divided because he was captured by the Mongols in 1449. His younger brother replaced him on the throne until he was restored to power in 1457.

Chinese Dynasties

商	Shang kingdom	ca. 1600–1028 B.C.
周	Zhou dynasty	ca. 1030–256 B.C.
秦	Qin dynasty	221–207 B.C.
漢	Han dynasty	206 B.C.–220 A.D.
三國	Three kingdoms	220–280 A.D.
晉	Jin dynasty	265–420 A.D.
南北朝	Northern and Southern dynasties	386–589 A.D.
隋	Sui dynasty	589–618 A.D.
唐	Tang dynasty	618–907 A.D.
五代	Five dynasties	907–960 A.D.

北宋	Northern Song dynasty	960–1126 A.D.
南宋	Southern Song dynasty	1127–1279 A.D.
元	Yuan (Mongol) dynasty	1271–1368 A.D.
明	Ming dynasty	1368–1644 A.D.
清	Qing dynasty	1644–1911 A.D.

Dates based on Wan Guoding, *Zhongguo lishi jinian biao* (Chronological tables of Chinese history), Hong Kong, Shangwu, 1958.

We have traversed more than one hundred thousand li of immense waterspaces and have beheld in the ocean huge waves like mountains rising sky high, and we have set eyes on barbarian regions far away hidden in a blue transparency of light vapors, while our sails, loftily unfurled like clouds day and night, continued their course [as rapidly as] a star, traversing those savage waves as if we were treading a public thoroughfare . . .

—Tablet erected by Zheng He, Changle, Fujian, 1432

鄭和

Prologue: Phantoms in Silk

Alarm spread quickly through the East African town of Malindi. Across the sea, beyond the coral reef, strange storm clouds appeared on the horizon. Fishermen hastily dragged their outriggers to safety on dry land. As the clouds gathered, it suddenly became clear that they were not clouds at all but sails—sails piled upon sails, too numerous to count, on giant ships with large serpent's eyes painted on the bows. Each ship was the size of many houses, and there were dozens of these serpent ships, a city of ships, all moving rapidly across the blue expanse of ocean toward Malindi. When they came near, the colored flags on the masts blocked the sun, and the loud pounding and beating of drums on board shook heaven and earth. A crowd gathered at the harbor, and the king was summoned. Work ceased altogether. What was this menacing power, and what did it want?

The fleet moored just outside Malindi's coral reefs. From the belly of the big ships came small rowboats and men in lavish silk robes. And among the faces were some the king recognized. These men he knew. They were his own ambassadors, whom he had dispatched months ago on a tribute-bearing mission. Now emissaries of the dragon throne were returning them home, and they brought wondrous things to trade. But had so many men and so many ships come in peace, or had they come to make the citizens of Malindi subjects of the Son of Heaven?

The year was 1418.

The largest of the ships moored off Malindi were four-hundred-foot-long, nine-masted giant junks the Chinese called *bao chuan* (treasure ships). They carried a costly cargo of porcelains, silks, lacquerware, and fine-art objects to be traded for those treasures the Middle

Kingdom desired: ivory, rhinoceros horn, tortoiseshell, rare woods and incense, medicines, pearls, and precious stones. Accompanying the large junks on their mission were nearly a hundred supply ships, water tankers, transports for cavalry horses, warships, and multi-oared patrol boats with crews numbering up to 28,000 sailors and soldiers. It was a unique armada in the history of China—and the world—not to be surpassed until the invasion fleets of World War I sailed the seas.

In the brief period from 1405 to 1433, the treasure fleet, under the command of the eunuch admiral Zheng He, made seven epic voyages throughout the China Seas and Indian Ocean, from Taiwan to the Persian Gulf and distant Africa, China's El Dorado. The Chinese knew about Europe from Arab traders but had no desire to go there. The lands in the "far west" offered only wool and wine, which had little appeal for them. During these thirty years, foreign goods, medicines, and geographic knowledge flowed into China at an unprecedented rate, and China extended its sphere of political power and influence throughout the Indian Ocean. Half the world was in China's grasp, and with such a formidable navy the other half was easily within reach, had China wanted it. China could have become the great colonial power, a hundred years before the great age of European exploration and expansion.

But China did not.

Shortly after the last voyage of the treasure fleet, the Chinese emperor forbade overseas travel and stopped all building and repair of oceangoing junks. Disobedient merchants and seamen were killed. Within a hundred years the greatest navy the world had ever known willed itself into extinction and Japanese pirates ravaged the China coast. The period of China's greatest outward expansion was followed by the period of its greatest isolation. And the world leader in science and technology in the early fifteenth century was soon left at the doorstep of history, as burgeoning international trade and the beginning of the Industrial Revolution propelled the Western world into the modern age.

In 1498, when Vasco da Gama and his fleet of three battered caravels rounded the Cape of Good Hope and landed in East Africa on their way to India, they met natives who sported embroidered green silk caps with fine fringe. The Africans scoffed at the trinkets the Portuguese offered—beads, bells, strings of coral, washbasins—and seemed unimpressed with their small ships. Village elders told tales of white "ghosts" who wore silk and had visited their shores

Zheng He's treasure ship (four hundred feet) and Columbus's St. Maria (eighty-five feet). (Illustration by Jan Adkins, 1993.)

long ago in large ships. But no one knew anymore who these people had been or where they had come from. Or even if they had really come at all. The treasure fleet had vanished from the world's consciousness.

Zheng He and Vasco da Gama missed each other in Africa by eighty years. One wonders what would have happened if they had met. Realizing the extraordinary power of the Ming navy, would da Gama in his eighty-five to a hundred-foot vessels have dared continue across the Indian Ocean? Seeing the battered Portuguese boats, would the Chinese admiral have been tempted to crush these snails in his path, preventing the Europeans from opening an east-west trade route?

This book will explore how China rose as a maritime power and why, after the wide-ranging voyages of the treasure ships, it systematically destroyed its great navy and lost its technological edge over Europe. At the heart of the matter is China's view of itself and its position in the world, which has changed little to the present day. Today there is still the same ambiguity toward foreigners and foreign influence. The opening and closing of doors. The sullen refuge in isolation.

Far from being the landlocked people they are often portrayed as in history, the Chinese have been skilled and adventurous boatmen since the dawn of their civilization. Even before we can speak of "China" or the "Chinese," Neolithic people from the mainland of Asia were the ancestors of the diverse peoples of Oceania, who conquered both the Indian Ocean and the Pacific in the first millennium B.C. Little doubt remains that there were Asian people in the New World before Columbus, and the evidence points to not one but several periods of contact.

I begin with the land and the sea, with the birth of the concept of the Middle Kingdom and the very early seafaring tradition in southeast Asia that so influenced young China. Here, unsung Columbuses shaped the first oceangoing vessels and made the unfathomable journey across the dark waters to the world's edge and beyond.

1 The Yi Peoples

In the millennium that preceded the rise of the first Chinese empire about 1600 B.C., the diverse Yi (and Yue) peoples of eastern and southern China developed quite independently from the Neolithic tribes centered in the Yellow River valley in north China. Separated by mountains that run parallel to the south China coast, the inland peoples spoke a Tibeto-Burman language most closely related to modern Chinese, whereas the eastern and southern Yi peoples are believed to be linked linguistically to the future Khmers and to the Austronesians who would spread throughout the Pacific and Indian Ocean basins. In the stew of Neolithic cultures from which Chinese civilization would evolve, the Yi had a strong influence.

The inland people were tied to the soil; the Yi, pressed against coastal mountains, were forced to turn to the sea for their livelihood. Thus, the seafaring tradition of China begins with the Yi.

At the height of the last ice age, fifty thousand years ago, the continental shelf of Asia was exposed, linking mainland China with Taiwan and the Malay Peninsula with Sumatra, Borneo, and Java. The forefathers of the Yi peoples were believed to have migrated down from the highlands of central China to the broad shoreline of this exposed shelf. In bamboo rafts, some crossed the narrow body of water from Java to the island of Sulawesi, then no more than thirty-five or forty miles wide, and moved into New Guinea and eventually Australia, where their descendants settled on the shores of an enormous inland sea.

These migrants are believed to be the world's first "boat people," that is, the first people to cross a body of water and settle a new land. Crete was not colonized from the mainland of Greece until about 8,000 B.C., more than forty thousand years after Australia.

Although Australia's inland sea dried up long ago, geologists exploring the ancient dunes of the Willandra Lakes in the late 1960s literally stumbled across the bones of Australia's first-known inhabitants, which simply appeared one day in the shifting sands. Hundreds of settlement sites around the old seabed in western New South Wales have since been identified, indicating that a community of more than three hundred thousand people had flourished there. Examining the skulls of the Willandra Lakes people, the scientists discovered they bore a striking resemblance to skulls of Neolithic people in China's Yangzi River valley thousands of miles to the north. Both were thin and delicate and contemporary-looking in every respect—thus a link between these distant people was first suspected. Recent genetic studies confirm that native Melanesians, Australians, and New Guineans are, in fact, descended mainly from southeast Asians, and, despite appearances to the contrary, bear a closer genetic relationship to them than to Africans.

While southern Asians were moving into Indonesia and Australia, Asians north of the Yangzi River migrated across the then-dry Bering Strait into Alaska and North America. Both early migrations may well have been precipitated by a dramatic shift in the course of the Yangzi River itself. Although the question has not been studied extensively, some geologists believe that at some time during the last ice age, the collision of continental plates that produced the Himalayas also caused tremendous rifting in the Yunnan plateau, which forced the Yangzi to flow from its source in the Tibetan mountains due east into the South China Sea, instead of following its original path south to the Gulf of Tonkin. It was as if the Mississippi had suddenly turned and flowed into the Atlantic instead of the Gulf of Mexico. Such a cataclysmic geological event certainly disrupted life in central China, sending early man on a quest for a stable environment and food source, even if it meant, in the case of the southern Asians, venturing out across an unknown sea.

In time, the glaciers melted and the seas rose, setting off another series of migrations. From 14,000 B.C. to 4000 B.C., a hundred-mile strip of coast off south China was submerged as the sea achieved its current level. Never in recent geological history had the seas risen so fast. The coastal inhabitants were forced to contend with swamped land and rapidly submerging river valleys. Eventually, it is believed, they took to the sea again in large numbers. This second wave of wayward southern Asians became the ancestors of the great seafaring peoples of Indonesia and Polynesia.

In about 9000 B.C., it has been estimated, people from the mainland of Asia crossed the Formosa Strait and settled Taiwan. Then, from 7000 to 5500 B.C., they moved from Taiwan to the Philippines and later, around 4000 B.C., on to the Malay Peninsula and the Moluccas and east to the Bismarck Archipelago. By 1300 B.C. they reached Fiji.

From at least the seventh or sixth century B.C., if not earlier, southeast Asians began to etch pictures of long canoes on the sides of sculpted, barrel-shaped drums. A trail of buried bronze drums has been found from northern Laos and southwestern China to Sulawesi in Indonesia. The etchings depict canoes with cabins or raised platforms and exotic bird's-head ornaments adorning the prows. The canoes also appear to have been steered by large oars or sweeps. The actual boats of the early Pacific seafarers undoubtedly bore some resemblance to the drum pictures.

As time went on and these seafarers ventured farther and farther from the Asian mainland, sails, outriggers, rudders, and other control devices were added to the canoes and rafts to make them more seaworthy and maneuverable. Indonesia, particularly the central island of Sulawesi, became a hub for the design and construction of oceangoing vessels, and the two terms used throughout Oceania for "boat," *waka* (or *vaka*) and *paepae* (or *pahi*) are thought to have a connection to early Chinese words for boats.

The seamanship of the early southeast Asians was so remarkable that they were able to cross the six-thousand-mile expanse of the Indian Ocean to settle Madagascar off the east African coast. There are also strong indications that they sailed in the opposite direction and successfully crossed the Pacific, landing in Central and South America. This was believed to be the first period of contact between Asia and the New World. The vessels that made this extraordinary voyage are believed to be identical to the sailing rafts still used today by fishermen off the coasts of Taiwan, Vietnam, and Peru. They are made of tightly bound balsa logs and employ a complicated steering system that allows them to be maneuvered across the trade winds. Six leeboards or centerboards, three in the stern and three in the bow, can be adjusted to steer a course close to the wind, regardless of the direction or strength of the wind.

Spanish explorers who arrived in South America in the sixteenth century reported seeing many of these rafts, which were then in extensive use. They marveled at large versions with enclosed cabins that could accommodate a hundred people. Others were fitted with

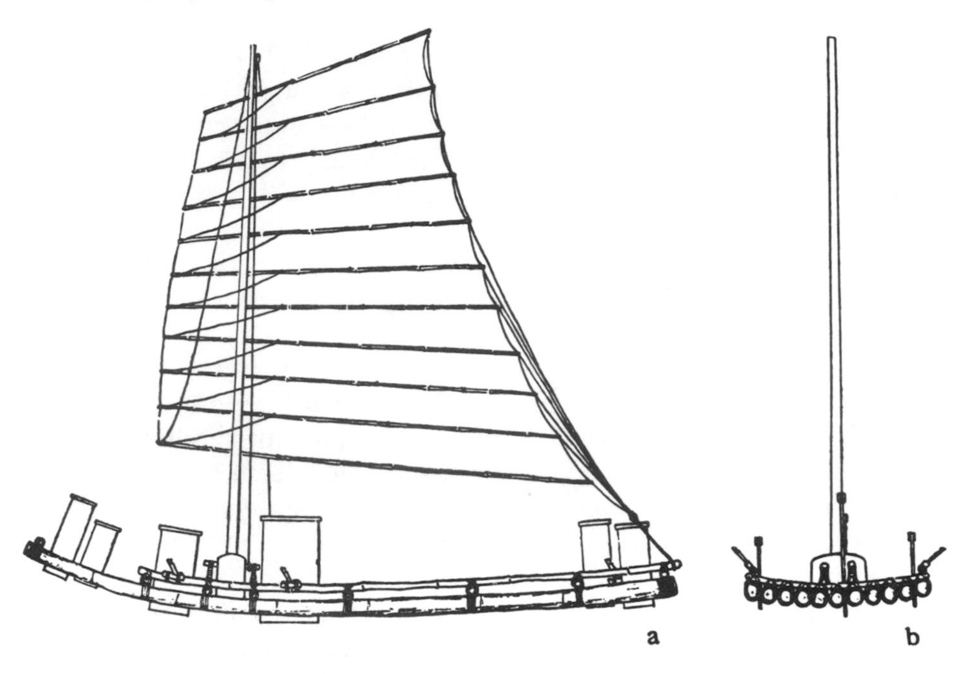

Pacific sailing rafts were believed to have carried Asians to Central and South America in the first millennium B.C. (Courtesy of The Institute of Ethnology, Academia Sinica, Taiwan.)

many masts and could skim the surface of the waves like catamarans, ferrying goods up and down the coast faster, they said, than their own hulled sailing vessels.

Vestiges of the early contact between Asia and the Americas can also be found in the remarkably similiar traditions of bark-cloth making found among two isolated tribes on opposite sides of the Pacific. The upland people of Sulawesi and the Otomi tribes in the central Mexican highlands are both skilled cloth makers. Although styles of bark beaters vary greatly among native peoples around the world, these two tribes use nearly identical beaters—flat stones with crosshatched patterns mounted on flexible cane handles that look like miniature tennis rackets. And, of the seventy separate steps involved in the production of Mexican cloth, fifty are the same in Sulawesi.

Otomi women cut down whole branches from trees, instead of just stripping off the bark. They felt pieces of bark together instead of sewing them, which is easier, and they like to decorate their bark cloth with the sticky gum from rubber plants. They do these things for no other reason than that they have always done them this way.

And (although they don't know it) it was also the way Sulawesi women worked. The chances of such complex traditions and tools evolving independently halfway around the world seem remote.

What first drove early Indonesian people to attempt the long journey across the Pacific is unclear. Sitting on the rim of the Pacific plate, the Malay Archipelago is one of the most volatile volcanic regions of the world, however, and violent eruptions may well have precipitated periodic mass exoduses from the islands in the first or second millennia B.C.

While the Indonesians perfected their sailing rafts and commenced their epic voyages, the maritime traditions of the Yi of Shandong and northern Jiangsu, also called "Dong Yi" or Eastern Yi, were gradually being incorporated with inland cultures, giving birth in 1500 B.C. to the Shang, the first historic "Chinese" kingdom. The Shang rulers established authority over a two- to three-hundred-mile area in the central Yellow River valley. They had chariots, a complex writing system, and sophisticated bronze technology. Priest-kings were guided in the conduct of their daily affairs by divination from cracked sheep bones, and, perhaps influenced by the Yi, the priests also began to use large quantities of turtle shells from south China in their rituals. From the Eastern Yi, the Shang also acquired wet-rice agriculture, irrigation, lacquerware, bamboo, bark cloth, and longboats. The Shang shared the Eastern Yi's reverence for jade and their skill in carving it.

The Shang flourished for five hundred years, until, in about 1045 B.C., a western people, the Zhou, drove them from their cities in the fertile Yellow River valley with a ruthlessness that would come to characterize all changes of power in China. Those Shang not killed in the conquest were subject to harsh military control by the Zhou or were forced to abandon their homes. It is thought that some of these displaced Shang might have turned to the coastal Yi on the periphery of the empire and taken to the sea in their boats.

A later legend associated with the southern coastal people relates the tale of a brother and sister who took refuge in a wooden drum during a flood. The drum floated in the turbulent waters, and, when the flood subsided, an eagle plucked up the two and set them down on dry land. Since there was no food on the flood-ravaged land, the pair offered their own flesh to the eagle in gratitude. They finally survived the trial by planting seeds they had managed to bring with them in the drum. In the myth, the drum is the protector into whose shelter the pair unquestioningly delivered themselves. The legend

Decorative pattern of a voyaging canoe on a Han dynasty bronze drum.

perhaps symbolizes the blind faith that early Asian seafarers had in their own "wooden drums"—their boats—which enabled them to risk long journeys into the unknown.

Mysteriously and unexpectedly, out of primitive societies without highly developed arts, two highly sophisticated civilizations took root in the New World as the Shang empire was crumbling. Nothing seems to be able to account for the sudden ability of the Chavin craftsmen of Peru to fashion stylized bronze figurines of jaguars—which bear, coincidentally, an astonishing resemblance to late Shang miniature statues of tigers. Like the Shang pieces, the Chavin feline forms have projecting teeth, and an intricate pattern covers their bodies. They have distinctive rings on their tails that are realistic for Asian tigers—but are not found on South American jaguars or pumas. A similar coincidence occurred at about the same time in Mexico, where Olmec artists displayed an extraordinary skill in fashioning jade that appears to have had no precedent in local crafts. Like the Shang, the Olmecs used jade as burial offerings in tombs, where it seems to have performed some protective or preservative function.

While stressing the originality of early American cultures, most scholars are generally agreed that there appears to have been at least some Asian influence in the New World before the arrival of Columbus. How much influence and exactly when this influence occurred are the subjects of much debate, but one of the most likely moments of contact seems to be around 1000 B.C. and may have involved the displaced Shang and their Yi boatmen.

By 221 B.C. a local ruler in western China succeeded in defeating the last of the eastern states and created the first unified empire in

China. To protect his people from marauding steppe tribes, the first Qin dynasty emperor began to link the existing fortifications in the north into a defense system similar to the Great Wall of later eras. He held more power over more people than any Chinese ruler to date. He was a man who knew no limits, and toward the end of his life he began an extraordinary campaign—to conquer death itself.

Thousands of miles across the great ocean to the east were reputed to be three islands—Penglai, Fangzhang, and Yingzhou—where immortals lived in palaces of gold and silver, all the birds and beasts were pure white, and magic herbs grew. It was said that anyone who ate these herbs would become immortal, and, if they were laid on the head of a man who had been dead for three days, he would be restored to life. The islands were supposed to be shrouded in clouds, and it was believed that if a ship approached, the islands would sink below the water or a great wind would come up and drive the ship away. Nevertheless, in 219 B.C., the Qin ruler sent a Daoist holy man named Xu Fu on an expedition to find the elusive isles and bring back the miraculous herbs.

After many years at sea, Xu Fu returned. He said that as he approached one of the islands, a dragon had appeared before him.

"Bring me young men of good birth and virgins and workmen of all trades," said the apparition. "Do this—and you will receive the herbs."

The emperor was pleased with this report and gave Xu Fu three thousand young men and women and ample supplies of grain and artisans of every kind. The monk set out again, but after many years he returned, again without the herbs.

"To obtain the herbs of Penglai is quite possible," he said to the disappointed emperor, "but we have had difficulty with great sharks, which is why we have not been successful." He requested archers to deal with them on the next voyage, which the emperor granted.

Some accounts of the story say that the emperor had a dream in which he was fighting a sea god with a human face. He went to sea to patrol the coast of China, and, legends say, he killed a great sea animal. Soon after that, however, in 210 B.C., the emperor died. Xu Fu never returned, and people believed he must have found "some calm and fertile plain, with broad forests and rich marshes, where he made himself king."

About a hundred years later, the Han emperor Wu sent out another search party with a magician named Li Shaochun. At this

Woodcut of a lou chuan *or castle boat with striking poles.*

time, the land south of the Yangzi and the traditional homeland of the southern Yi peoples were incorporated into the empire. The Han domain stretched from the Gulf of Tonkin north to Korea and west nearly to the Oxus River and the Persian empire.

Before Li Shaochun departed on his quest for the magic herbs, young couples chosen for the voyage danced on a high terrace before the emperor to commune with heaven. Torches lighted the festivities, symbolizing a reign of stars. Despite the overture to the heavenly spirits, however, this mission, too, failed. Li Shaochun never returned to China.

Exactly what kinds of rafts or boats were used for these early ocean voyages is not clear. In his military campaign to bring the Yi people into the empire, Emperor Wu had carried soldiers in *lou chuan,* castle or deck ships, that were believed to resemble Greek or Phoenician hulled ships of the first millennium B.C. The boats had many pairs of oarsmen on each side and decks for archers. Some of the boats were said to be a hundred feet high and decorated with flags. River battles during the Han dynasty involved twenty to thirty thousand men and several thousand boats, including *qiao chuan,* or bridge ships, which were used as fighting platforms for men and

The Han navy included a zouke, *a swift, multioared attack boat.*

horses. Han boats also made regular trips to Indonesia, and ships supported the large military operation that brought Korea under Chinese authority.

By the first centuries A.D., the Chinese had some knowledge of the winds and currents of the Pacific, though they thought the waters of the four oceans around them emptied into a great whirlwind or abyss from which no traveler could return. The astronomer Zhang Heng believed the earth floated in space like a yolk in the albumen of an egg, thus understanding even at this early date that the world was round.

What, then, became of the Daoist priest and the thousands of young men and women who went looking for the herbs of immortality?

One theory is that the expeditions landed in Japan and that Jimmu Tenno, the founder of the Japanese empire, was in fact Xu Fu. Another is that the Daoists succeeded in crossing the Pacific, landing in Central America during the rise of the Mayan and perhaps having some perceptible, but small influence on their civilization. Many have remarked at the similarity between Chinese characters and the square-shaped Mayan glyphs, and the astonishing resemblance of the Chinese and Mayan calendars with their complicated, intercepting cycles of days and years.

Whatever became of the Han seafarers at the dawn of the Christian era, China even at this very early point cannot be dismissed as a land-based power with no interest in the sea. And, although the Yi peoples were now absorbed into the Chinese empire, the shipbuilding tradition in China remained largely in the hands of their descendants in the coastal provinces of Guangdong, Fujian, and Zhejiang. The people of these provinces were the empire's future shipwrights and seamen, and remained throughout China's history the most open to foreigners and outside influence.

2 Confucians and Curiosities

To Confucius in the sixth century B.C., China was the entire world. He called it "The Middle Kingdom," "The Multitude of Great States," or simply "All under Heaven." Beyond the borders of the empire lay, as far as he knew, only wilderness and lawless, barbarian tribes. For time and again, out of the steppes and bleak western deserts, came marauding herdsmen, wild men dressed in animal skins who brought destruction and despair. To the east, across the endless oceans, lay only the fantasies and dreams of foolish rulers.

Once, feeling unappreciated in his native Shandong in northern China, Confucius announced to his disciples that he was going to live with the "wild tribes." "How can you do such a thing?" one follower asked. "They are rude." He replied that as the superior man among them, he would tame their rudeness. But, aside from this boast, as his writings make clear, Confucius thought foreign travel interfered with important familial obligations and believed trade was inherently mean and debasing. There was nothing to be gained from contact with foreigners or strange things. He wrote in the *Analects:*

> While his parents are alive, the son may not take a distant voyage abroad. If he has to take such a voyage, the destination must be known.
>
> The mind of the superior man dwells on righteousness; the mind of a little man dwells on profit.

From the second century B.C., with the rise of the Han dynasty, Confucianism became the moral code for the upper classes of Chinese society and the foundation of the emerging feudal bureaucracy. The Han, who incorporated most of southern China into the empire for the first time, embraced Confucianism as a way of strengthening the moral and political authority of the emperor and keeping the powerful nobility in check. Confucius had not only put forth the ancient Shang notion that the emperor was the link between man and the heavenly spirit, but he had said that the true ruler could "transform society with his virtue." The Han emperors set up an academy to transmit the teachings of Confucius formally, and under the influence of the great sage, government service and farming were quickly elevated as the honored professions for virtuous men, while commerce and the barter of goods were shunned as inherently exploitative and corrupt. Merchants were ranked below artisans and were forbidden by sumptuary law to wear the finest-quality silk.

In the chaotic times that followed the downfall of the Han dynasty in the third century A.D., trade in north China was severely limited, if not nonexistent. Whatever curiosity the Chinese may have had about people and places beyond their borders was stifled in a struggle for survival. The fragmented states of the old Han empire remained in an almost constant state of war for four hundred years. Finally, at the beginning of the seventh century A.D., the Li family rose to power and displaced the Sui empire, establishing the Tang dynasty in 618 A.D. The Tang armies went on to conquer the eastern Turks in Mongolia and the kings of southern Manchuria and Korea. The victors then turned west and overran the Turks in what is now the Chinese province of Xinjiang.

Within the borders of this new and enormous empire, there were thus a large number of "barbarians": Turks, Uighers, Persians, Arabs, and Hindus. China was a melting pot, and the Tang ruling family itself was part Turkish. The Chinese could not suppress their fascination with these different peoples, but their curiosity was tempered by a Confucian suspicion of foreigners. The two emotions battled each other like waves in a turbulent sea, shifting without warning. Nowhere was this more evident than at the Tang court in Chang'an, which both imitated foreigners and resented them, lavishly entertained them and ultimately persecuted them.

Though it was sacked several times in power struggles after the fall of the Han, Chang'an emerged in the seventh century as the greatest city in the world at that time—a mighty metropolis covering thirty square miles in the heart of the Yellow River valley in north China with more than a million taxable residents. Surrounding the inner city and its elaborate palace compound was an outer city of 106 separate walled districts, hundreds of temples, and two enormous markets—an eastern market that sold goods from within the borders of the Tang empire and a western market that specialized in exotic goods from India, Persia, southeast Asia, and beyond, to the distant shores of Africa. Near this market, at the edge of the city, were taverns where wine was served in amber goblets and Western girls with green eyes and golden hair danced and whispered flattery into the ears of wealthy patrons.

Down the narrow, winding streets of the western market, one could smell sweet sandalwood from India or Java, which was mashed into a paste and used to cure fevers and intestinal disorders. There were aloes to make soothing salves and cloves to freshen the breath. Frankincense from Somalia could be found there, as well as myrrh, used to treat women who had suffered a miscarriage. There were Persian dates for the complexion, saffron powder for perfume, and pistachio nuts from Persia for sexual vigor. Black pepper from Burma was peddled for stomach ailments and strong mustard from Tibet for use in balms. And some days, there was rare ambergris, a costly incense, which the Chinese believed was "dragon's spittle." The cure for any ailment, from anywhere in the world, could be had for a price in the western market of Chang'an.

For these wonders the Chinese traded their silks and fine porcelains—the world's first true porcelains—with hard, translucent glazes that reflected sunlight brilliantly. Arabs halfway around the globe coveted these miraculous porcelains as decorative objects and also because they believed (though wrongly) that they would show the presence of poisons. Just as silk drove the overland trade routes in the first centuries of the Christian era, it was porcelain that became the impetus for the Indian Ocean trade in the seventh century.

The porcelain route spanned some six thousand miles, from Guangzhou on the south coast of China to the spice ports of Sumatra and Malaya, on to Ceylon and India and finally to Siraf and Oman in the Persian Gulf. The trip took several months, sailing with the aid of seasonal monsoon winds. Although the Tang emperors sent emissaries to Korea, Vietnam, and India in the seventh century, it is unlikely that Chinese traders or junks actually entered the Persian Gulf at this time. Persian merchants, who had long been established as the great middlemen in the overland silk trade, became traders at sea and took control of the porcelain route. They sailed long, narrow Ceylonese ships, which were said to be up to two hundred feet long and capable of carrying six hundred men, or used dhows made by their own shipwrights and held together not with nails but with coconut-fiber lashings. With their triangular lateen sails, they could follow a course close to the direction of the wind. It was the Persians who, navigating by the stars, named important constellations and wind directions, and their language became the universal language of seamen in the seventh century.

The Tang emperor Xuanzong had burned pearls and jade and fine cloth when he first became emperor in 712 A.D. to show that these curiosities meant nothing to him. But four years later, according to the *Zi zhi tong jian* (Comprehensive mirror for aid in governance), the famous annalistic history on the period written between 1067 and 1084 A.D., a foreigner came to his court and told Xuanzong about the riches of the south seas, of enormous pearls and kingfisher birds with glorious feathers, and of medical practices and rare drugs from Ceylon. The emperor was impressed. He ordered his Confucian adviser, Yang Fanchen, to organize an expedition to accompany the foreigner home. Yang objected. He reminded the emperor of his earlier disdain for luxuries.

"That which you now seek is no different from that which you burned," he said. "Besides, is it not unseemly for your trade commissioners to compete for profits with barbarian merchants? Do you want to invite barbarian shamans skilled in medicine to the court? Is it proper? I fear this foreigner is misleading you. [Such an expedition] will not augment your sagacious virtue."

Xuanzong dropped the plan, but other Tang emperors did not hesitate to procure their fancies, initiating foreign trade under the guise of "tribute" to the Son of Heaven. Had not Confucius also recommended "indulgent treatment of men from a distance" if they showed the proper respect, acknowledging the suzerainty of the Middle Kingdom? And was it not the duty of the emperor, ruler of all mankind, to invite the barbarians to come and be transformed by the light of Chinese civilization? Tributes, presented with great ceremony at court, flattered the emperors, reassuring them of their power in the world. It was also clearly a shrewd foreign policy that helped keep restless neighbors and enemies at bay.

The Tang dynasty imperial gardens were said to be filled with exotic birds—herons, tufted ducks, and glorious peacocks from India and fine hunting hawks brought by emissaries from Korea, Manchuria, and Mongolia. The palace complex also had warehouses of ice, where fruits—peaches, melons, and figs—from the far corners of the empire and beyond were kept fresh for the emperor. Horses for imperial cavalries were imported by the thousands from Fergana in central Asia. More necessity than luxury, these strong, swift creatures were essential for China's ongoing struggles with the northern nomadic tribes. The Chinese bred the horses for such special color combinations as white horses with black manes or yellow horses with red manes, and military units prided themselves on having matched pairs.

The Tang emperors were also great admirers of Korean women, who were demanded as tribute for imperial harems. Dwarfs and pygmies (whether they were true Pygmies from southern Africa or New Guinea is unclear) were prized human cargo, as were black slaves from a land called "Zangi" or "Zenj" somewhere on the east coast of Africa. Zhou Qufei, a Guangzhou customs official, noted in his personal record entitled *Ling wai dai da* (Information on what is beyond the passes) that slaves came from a distant western island, which might have been Madagascar:

> [In the west] there is an island in the sea on which there are many savages. Their bodies are as black as lacquer and they have frizzled hair. They are enticed by [offers of] food and then captured and sold as slaves to Arabic countries, where they fetch a very high price. They are employed as gatekeepers, and it is said that they have no longing for their kinfolk.

From the ninth century A.D., there are excellent descriptions of Africa in Chinese sources, suggesting that if indeed Chinese junks never traveled to Africa, the Chinese were at least getting reliable information from Persian and Arab traders. Duan Chengshi, who died in 863 A.D., relates his account of what appears to be an early encounter with African herdsmen in the *Yuyang za zu* (Miscellany of Yuyang mountain), a compendium of various kinds of knowledge.

> The country of Bobali [thought to be Berbera in Somalia] is in the southwestern ocean. [The people] do not eat any of the five grains but eat only meat. They often stick a needle into the veins of cattle and draw blood which they drink raw, mixed with milk. They wear no clothes except that they cover [the parts] below the loins with sheepskins. Their women are clean and of proper behavior. The inhabitants themselves kidnap them and sell them to strangers at prices

many times more than they would fetch at home. The country produces ivory and ambergris.

The extent of the China slave trade is difficult to determine. Enslavement had been a form of punishment since Han times, so there was no shortage of men and women in bondage in China. Nevertheless, it was said, "most of the wealthy people" in Guangzhou "kept devil slaves" as gatekeepers. African slaves were treated little better than beasts of burden. They were made to lift heavy weights and, because the Chinese believed they swam "without blinking their eyes," were employed as divers to repair leaking boats. Many certainly must have died soon after their arrival in China. The Chinese described the intestinal disorders they suffered, which they believed were caused by cooked food, to which they were unaccustomed. But "if they do not die, one can keep them, and after having been kept a long time they begin to understand the language of human beings, though they themselves cannot speak it."

Tang court women followed Persian and Turkish fashions, wearing dresses with tight-fitting bodices, pleated skirts, and hats with enormous veils. And it was apparently imitation of foreign toe-dancing groups that originally led upper-class Chinese women to bind their feet. At first it was just palace dancers who bound their feet slightly, like ballet dancers, to stand on their toes. Later, in the Song dynasty, the practice spread beyond the palace because small feet were admired and considered aesthetically pleasing. Mothers bound the feet of their young daughters so tightly, however, that the girls became virtually crippled and confined to their houses for the rest of their lives, which presumably had the added virtue of ensuring conjugal fidelity.

Men's clothing styles also reflected foreign influence. Chinese nobility sported leopard-skin hats. And the Tang poet Bo Juyi was supposed to have erected Turkish tents of blue felt on the grounds of his house for parties. Fondness for foreign objects touched every class—even simple household objects used in the most humble dwellings were decorated with figures of bearded, long-nosed foreigners.

Carefully monitoring the flow of goods in and out of China was the Bureau of Merchant Shipping, set up in the eighth century in Guangzhou on China's southern coast. Its commissioners changed the amounts of import duties seemingly without reason, sometimes sending frustrated merchants to Vietnam to do business. As much as a quarter of all foreign goods had to be surrendered to Chinese officials. Export cargos were double-checked to make sure that contraband—Chinese coins, concubines, and slaves—did not fall into the hands of the barbarians, although some certainly did. Corrupt officials exacted additional duties and sometimes conducted an illicit trade with their own private fleets.

Some two hundred thousand Persians, Arabs, Indians, Malays, and others lived in seventh-century Guangzhou as traders, artisans, and metalworkers. Though they lived and worked side by side with the Chinese, tensions flared from time to time, perhaps provoked by discriminatory laws. In 628 A.D., for example, the government tried to discourage casual contact between foreigners and Chinese women by mandating that if a foreigner took a Chinese woman as his wife, he was obliged to remain in China. In 799 A.D., Uighurs were forbidden to court Chinese women or pass themselves off as Chinese and were compelled to wear their native costume. And in 836 A.D., foreigners were banned from owning land and houses and living with Chinese.

The Chinese must occasionally have resented the success and wealth of the foreigners living among them; and the foreigners in Guangzhou, it must be assumed, were unhappy with the arbitrary tariffs and laws imposed upon them. But precisely what sparked the mayhem of 758 A.D., when Arabs and Persians began looting warehouses and burning the homes of Chinese, is not clear. The rioters forced the governor of Guangzhou to leave the city, after which they themselves fled to Hainan Island, just south of the Chinese mainland. How many Chinese died in the episode is unknown, but in the bitter aftermath the emperor closed the port to foreigners for fifty years.

In 878 A.D. the Chinese unleashed their own torrent of animosity. Forces of a rebel named Huang Chao, discontented with heavy taxes and corrupt officials, sacked Guangzhou, killing, along with a number of Chinese residents, an estimated 120,000 Jews, Christians, Moslems, and Magians. Abu-Zayd of Siraf, a tenth-century Arab writer, described the ensuing chaos, when Chinese bandits took the law into their own hands, butchering people at will and persecuting Arabs and Persians; "disaster reached [even] the ship captains and pilots in Siraf and Uman." Huang Chao was eventually captured, but his rebellion marked the end of the Tang dynasty, and a period of strife between competing petty kingdoms in China followed.

In the busy shops of Siraf and Ubullah, sailors gathered after their long journeys and spun tales of their adventures across the seas that were eventually preserved as the Sinbad legend. "I have seen oceans where the sun rises," the story begins, "and have trod atolls that are like giants' rings fallen from the sky. I have plied trade from sandbanks to deltas and from islands to archipelagos, from Salahat to Serendib and from Comari to Kela. I have traded fabrics for ginger and camphor; cinnamon and spiked cloves for ambergris, ivory and pearls."

The Chinese spun their own tales, one of which suggests that Buddhist monks reached the shores of America in the fifth century A.D. The story, as recorded in the *Liang shu* (History of the Liang dynasty), describes the voyage of Hui Shen and five Afghan monks to a strange place called Fusang guo—the Country of the Extreme East—that seems to bear a strong resemblance to Mayan Mexico. Hui Shen said he found people there who made cloth and paper from bark and wrote with characters. Like the emperor of China, the king of this place, he reported, was preceded and followed by drummers and heralds, and he changed the colors of his robe (as did the Son of Heaven) in accordance with a ten-year cycle. Like China, Fusang guo had a severe judicial system in which not only a criminal but also his children and grandchildren were punished.

It would be easy to dismiss the possibility that Hui Shen visited Central America if it were not for a strong influx of Buddhist and Hindu elements that appear in Mayan art at this time. Suddenly, Mayan bas-relief figures are depicted on lotus thrones, sitting cross-legged like meditating Buddhas. There also appear multiheaded deities similar to the multiheaded gods of India. Moreover, the detailed bas-reliefs at Copán, Honduras, show priests dressed in diamond-patterned ceremonial robes that bear an astonishing resemblance to traditional Tibetan Buddhist robes. Stone statuary at Xculoc, Mexico, shows a distinctive hand gesture—right hand lowered, palm out; left hand raised, palm out—that appears to be a classic Buddhist stance called *shi yuan wu wei,* meaning "the granting of a wish." Some outside Buddhist-Hindu influence on Mayan civilization seems likely, whether it is attributable to Hui Shen and his Buddhist companions or to other Asian seafarers. This is thought to have been the last period of contact between Asia and the Americas before the arrival of Columbus.

> In former times [the people of Fusang guo] knew nothing of the Buddhist religion, but in the second year of Da Ming of the Song dynasty [485 A.D.], five monks from Chipin [Kabul, Afghanistan]

> traveled by ship to that country. They propagated Buddhist doctrines, circulated scriptures and drawings, and advised the people to relinquish worldly attachments. As a result, the customs of Fusang changed.
>
> —*Liang shu,* seventh century A.D.

The next burst of seafaring activity in China occurred during the beleaguered Song dynasty (960–1279), when the empire was under siege by strong, aggressive states to the north. In 1127 the Song court was forced to abandon its northern capital at Kaifeng and move to the port city of Hangzhou, just south of the Yangzi River. With half the income-producing lands of the empire in foreign hands, the emperor turned to overseas trade to finance the needs of the state. Necessity demanded a reexamination of Confucian texts to put trade and profit into a more favorable light.

Emperor Gao Zong (1127–1162) expressed the new attitude toward commerce: "Profits from maritime commerce are very great. If properly managed, they can amount to millions [of strings of coins]. Is this not better than taxing the people?"

The emperor sought the help of merchants in building a fleet of vessels that would challenge the long-standing supremacy of Persian and Arab traders in the Indian Ocean. Government funds were used to improve harbors on the southern coasts, widen canals to accommodate oceangoing junks, and build warehouses for merchants. A costly system of navigation beacons to guide merchant and government ships was also built every thirty *li* (about ten miles) along the coast.

Revenues from overseas trade jumped from a half-million strings of coins at the end of the eleventh century to one million in the early twelfth century and two million by the middle of the twelfth century. (A thousand small copper coins tied together with a cord or "one string" was the official unit of exchange in the Song empire.)

Song philosophers reviewed the classical texts of the sages and began to discuss the merits of profit as a way of encouraging men to work for the good of the state. "Goods and wealth are needed for a livelihood and cannot be omitted," wrote Chen Chun in *Beixi zi yi,* a twelfth-century glossary of neo-Confucian terms. "So long as one engages in profit-making when the business is proper and acquires a thing when the acquisition is correct, that is righteousness. If one employs devious means and deceit to engage in profit-making when the business is improper or acquires a thing when the acquisition is wrong, that is for profit."

The outlook of the Chinese was fundamentally altered after the fall of the northern capital obliged them to start new lives in southern China. Uprooted from their ancestral homeland, these refugees felt freer, more open to change and travel. And, since there was little land available for cultivation, they embraced commerce, crowding into busy port cities and the new capital at Hangzhou.

By the end of the thirteenth century, Hangzhou had close to a million people and had become a city "greater than any in the world," as Marco Polo observed on his visit there. "It has twelve principal gates," noted Polo, "and at each of these gates . . . are cities larger than Venice or Padua." Although the residences of the rich at the southern end of Hangzhou were surrounded by large, walled gardens and magnificent groves, people in the center of the city lived in multistoried bamboo and wood houses on narrow streets, crowded together, with sometimes as many as ten families under one roof. To feed these masses, hundreds of pigs were slaughtered every night in the central market and barges brought tons of fresh vegetables, rice, and salted fish to the city daily. As the people of Hangzhou used to say, "vegetables from the east, water from the west, wood from the south, and rice from the north."

On every street corner at any hour of the day or night were jugglers and storytellers. Flat-bottomed pleasure boats lounged in the canals. This was a carnival city, a city of excesses. Novelty shops sold false hair, crickets in cages, and fumigated powders to repel mosquitoes. All along the Imperial Way were teahouses where wealthy men sipped aromatic teas and plum-flower wines and, if they wished, wandered upstairs to rooms lit by crimson and gilt lanterns where "singing song girls" danced and indulged the men in sensual pleasures.

Even after abandoning its northern provinces, the Song empire was not safe from the powerful states that pressed on its western and northern borders. Hangzhou was considered vulnerable to attack from the sea, and in 1132 the emperor ordered the establishment of China's first permanent navy. The sea became China's new "Great Wall," its defense against a powerful land-based enemy.

"Our defenses today are the [Yangzi] River and the sea, so our weakness in mounted troops is no concern," explained Finance Minister Zhang Yi at the time. "A navy is of value . . . to use our navy is to employ our strong weapon to strike at the enemy's weakness."

The internal system of rivers and canals that supplied goods throughout the empire was now viewed as its western defense network. The Yangzi River was the northern line of defense, and the eastern line was the coast. The Song navy grew rapidly from a patchwork force of merchant vessels and coastal patrol boats to an effective fighting fleet. In 1130 there were 11 squadrons and 3,000 men; in 1174, 15 squadrons and 21,000 men; and in 1237, 20 squadrons and 52,000 conscripted men. By the early thirteenth century the Song navy controlled the East China Sea from Fujian province to Japan and Korea, and patrolled China's main rivers. The total number of ships reached six hundred, the largest of which were twenty-four feet wide and carried a crew of forty-two. All warships were equipped with battering rams, catapults, various incendiary weapons thrown from catapults, protective screens, and fire equipment.

The emperor offered cash rewards to spur innovation in ship design, and a variety of new boats, as well as naval gunpowder weapons, were created. Ten different oceangoing junks evolved and ten types of warships, as well as ferryboats, water tankers, floating restaurants, horse transport ships, manure boats, and a dozen other specialty craft. Along with creativity came open-mindedness. Abandoning their superior stance toward other cultures, Chinese scholars studied Arab and Hindu contributions in navigation and geography and in turn created their own star and sea charts and studies of the tides and currents of foreign countries. They also invented the floating mariner's compass. And the birth of the explorer's sense of wonder can be detected even among such strict Confucians as Mo Ji, director of the National Academy during the reign of Gao Zong. He took periodic leaves from his duties and sailed the seas for no other purpose, it seems, than to satisfy his own curiosity.

By the early thirteenth century the Chinese had the best boats in the Indian Ocean and had captured the bulk of the sea trade from the Arabs. The average oceangoing merchant junk was about 100 feet long and 25 feet wide at the beam, and carried 120 tons of cargo and a crew of 60. The largest ships carried three hundred tons and five to six hundred people and towed lifeboats. The underside of the ship narrowed to a knife edge to cut through ocean waves, and the prow and the stern were left empty to increase the ship's speed. There were three separate holds in the center of the ship: the foremost was undecked and contained the kitchen and water caskets; the center hold was divided into four compartments for cargo; and the rear hold was fitted with windows and sleeping quarters for the officers and merchants. The ship was fitted with a stern-post rudder, a hundred-foot mainmast, and an eighty-foot foremast. Pine from Fujian and Zhejiang provinces in southern China was used throughout the ship, except in the rudder, which was made from a particularly hard wood from Guangdong called *wulan*. The ship was caulked with silk rags dipped in a mixture of tung oil and lime, and the sails were made of fine bamboo matting. On a good day, with strong winds, the junks could travel three hundred miles.

Life at sea was unpredictable but not without such amenities as fresh meat and fermented wines. Song seamen had little fear of rough waves on high seas. As Zhou Qufei reported in *Ling wai dai da*, hidden shoals and shallow water where their ships could get hopelessly stuck were far more terrifying:

> The ships which sail the southern sea and south of it are like houses. When their sails are spread they are like great clouds in the sky. Their rudders are several tens of feet long. A single ship carries several hundred men, and has in the stores, a year's supply of grain. Pigs are fed and wine fermented on board. There is no account of dead or living, no going back to the mainland when the people have set forth on the azure-blue sea. When the gong sounds at daybreak aboard ship, the animals can drink their fill, and crew and passengers alike forget all dangers. To those on board, everything is hidden and lost in space—mountains, landmarks, and foreign countries. The pilot may say, "To make such and such a country, with a favorable wind, in so many days, we should sight such and such a mountain, [then] the ship may steer in such and such a direction." But, suddenly the wind may fall, and may not be strong enough to allow the sighting of the mountain on the given day. In such a case, the bearing may have to be changed. Then again, the ship may be carried far beyond [the landmark] and lose its bearing. A gale may spring up, blowing the ship off course, or the ship may encounter shoals or hidden rocks and be broken apart to the roofs [of the cabins]. A great ship with heavy cargo has nothing to fear in high seas, but in shallow water it will come to grief.

Among the variety of warships and patrol boats created for the Song navy were two particularly extraordinary craft. The "sea falcon" actually looked like a flying waterbird with a low prow and a high poop deck. Floating leeboards in the shape of birds' wings were attached to the gunnels. These leeboards, or regulating rudders (*fuban*), stabilized the ship in high seas and may possibly have been descended from the steering leeboards of the Pacific sailing rafts.

Increase in Yellow Sea trade by the Song produced a flat-bottom junk, dubbed a "sea falcon," with floating rudders to stabilize the ship in high seas.

"Flying tiger warships" were paddle-wheel boats, driven by manpower and extremely effective in naval battles on rivers and lakes. The idea for a paddle wheeler may have come from the waterwheels commonly used before and during the Song era to irrigate fields.

In 1131 the Song navy tried, using paddle-wheel boats, to wipe out a nest of pirates on Dongting Lake in the center of China. Their boats had eight wheels, which were powered by forty-two men on treadmills. The wheels were covered so that the boats appeared to move "like a dragon," floating effortlessly over the water. Terrified onlookers thought supernatural powers were at work. On the top deck of the paddle wheeler were archers and a kind of battering ram that would come crashing down on the deck of any enemy ship that came within close range. The navy had a few successful skirmishes until the pirates managed to capture the engineer and designer of the boats. The pirates then quickly built their own, larger paddle-wheel boats, and a great battle of these flying tiger ships seemed inevitable.

A Song commander, however, came up with a plan to foil the

A secret weapon of the Song navy was the terrifying paddle-wheel boat or "flying tiger warship."

enemy's paddle wheelers. In 1135 he lured the pirates onto a part of the lake into which his men had thrown logs and rushes. The blades of the pirates' boats became hopelessly caught in the logjam and could not move. With conventional, flat-bottomed river junks, the government forces then destroyed the trapped paddle wheelers. The humiliated pirate leader, it was reported, drowned himself.

It would not be long, however, before the Song navy faced a more formidable challenge. In 1161 the Jin empire, which had overrun the Liao in north China, launched a three-pronged attack against the Song. The Jin attacked with cavalry forces from the western province of Sichuan; with other troops they tried to cross the Yangzi near Nanjing; and from the sea they attempted to seize the capital with a fleet of six hundred warships and seventy thousand men.

Song naval battles also included the first use of gunpowder weapons, which were sometimes loaded on the front end of a special boat that could then be unhitched—leaving it to blow up and destroy enemy boats.

The Jin cavalry was successfully repulsed. Then the Jin forces at the Yangzi faced Song commander Yu Yunwen with a fleet that included twenty-four paddle-wheel boats. Like the pirates, the Jin soldiers had never seen these frightening contraptions that moved without sails or oars. From the paddle wheelers, the Song hurled gunpowder bombs launched from catapults—the first time, it is believed, that gunpowder was ever used in battle. The gunpowder, along with lime and broken bits of iron, was packed into earthenware pots or paper cartons and ignited. These primitive grenades exploded when they landed on the water or on enemy ships, "making a noise like thunder" and scattering the lime in a smoky fog that blinded and terrified the enemy and their horses. The Song forces then easily boarded the enemy ships and defeated them. It was said that all of the Jin men and horses drowned.

On November 16, 1161, the main fleet of the Song navy went out to meet the formidable Jin armada off the Shandong Peninsula. The Song were vastly outnumbered—they had just one hundred twenty warships and three thousand men—but they were able to pick off the Jin boats one by one with their gunpowder weapons because the enemy was strung out in a long line.

The four decades that followed that great victory (1164–1204) marked the height of the Song navy. But in the early years of the thirteenth century the command of the navy shifted from the commissioner of coastal defense to an official in the imperial court. Gradually, the government began to deploy sailors to work on other state projects. In 1239, when an official was sent to inspect the naval base at Zhenjiang on the Yangzi just east of Nanjing, to his dismay he found only five hundred out of five thousand men fit for fighting. "The rest of the men were weary, dispirited, deaf, moronic, emaciated, short, and frail," he reported. "They cannot ride the waves and thrust their spears."

The Song were soon faced with the possibility of an attack from the north. The charismatic and ambitious Genghiz Khan had taken control of the Mongols and quickly overran the Jin Tartars. He moved into Beijing in 1215, and his successors took Kaifeng in 1233. After that, the Mongols set their sights on bringing the Song empire under their authority, a campaign that would occupy them for the next forty-six years. In the process, Genghiz and his grandson, Khubilai Khan, added to their army of horsemen a formidable navy capable of launching large-scale assaults against the Song fleets. It was one of the most spectacular creations of a powerful navy in history, but it was accomplished in part with the help of defecting Song commanders and merchants.

"Our strength rests in cavalry which is unbeatable, but we are inferior to the Song in naval warfare," said Liu Cheng, one of the Song commanders who went to the Mongols. "We can nullify their superiority by constructing warships and training men in naval warfare."

With the help of Liu and others, the fledgling Mongol navy captured Song towns along the Han and Yangzi rivers and confiscated over three thousand of the enemy's boats for use in their own fleet. By the end of 1275 the Mongols controlled the Yangzi. Two opportunistic Song merchants, Zhu Qing and Zhang Xuan, perhaps hoping for better trade agreements under the Mongols, secretly supplied them with another five hundred boats and several thousand crewmen for the final assault on the Song capital at Hangzhou.

The capital fell in 1276, and the Song emperor, a young boy, was taken prisoner. But the Chinese continued to fight. The emperor's brothers were smuggled out of the capital to Fuzhou in Fujian province, where one was proclaimed emperor. Three years later, near Guangzhou, eight hundred Mongol warships finally captured the large junk of the renegade Song court because the ship was too slow and heavy to make a successful escape. Cornered, the boy emperor and many of his courtiers leaped from the decks, drowning in the sea.

Thus, in 1279, Khubilai Khan became master of an empire that stretched four thousand miles across the plains of central Asia from the Adriatic Sea to the south China coast. The Mongols punished resisters severely, and in China they massacred entire towns, sparing only artisans and others the khan thought could serve him. The early khans took what they wanted from the peasants, and when they needed more, they took all that the people had. They had little use for Confucians and their methodical means of counting populations and levying taxes so that dynasties would last "ten thousand years." Instead, the Mongols appointed many foreigners to powerful positions. Khubilai Khan himself resisted assimilation, conducting business in Mongolia and vacationing at Shangdu (Coleridge's Xanadu) across the border. More than at any other time in their history, the Chinese found themselves in a position of servitude to an occupying power, and Confucian influence fell to an all-time low.

According to Yuan dynasty regulations, there were four layers of society: the Mongolian conquerors; *se mu,* that is, all central Asians; *han ren,* northern Chinese, who had been ruled before by other non-Chinese people; and, at the bottom of the social scale, *nan ren,* southern Chinese, who made up the vast bulk of the population. Confucians were stripped of their special tax exemptions. In bitterness at the humiliation they suffered during this period, Confucians later said that, in terms of their usefulness in Mongol society, they believed they were ranked next to the bottom, between prostitutes (no. 8) and beggars (no. 10).

Khubilai Khan was called "ruler of rulers," and "overlord of mankind," but this hunger for power remained unsatisfied. Having built a formidable fleet to conquer the Song, why not use it? He sent emissaries to Sumatra, Ceylon, and southern India to establish influence in the area while Yuan merchants gradually snatched the lucrative spice trade from the Arabs. The merchants sailed giant junks that by all accounts far surpassed Song vessels in size and grandeur as well as any sailing ship that Europeans could build at the time.

At the port of Quanzhou on the Fujian coast, Marco Polo, who stayed at the khan's court from 1275 to 1292, saw four-masted oceangoing junks with no fewer than sixty individual cabins for merchants. Depending on their size, the ships carried 150 to 300 crewmen, and they had watertight bulkhead compartments, which would not be introduced into European shipbuilding for another six hundred years. Fifty years after Marco Polo's visit, the Arab traveler Ibn Battūtah described gardens aboard Mongol vessels on

which vegetables and herbs were cultivated in wooden tubs, and he said the captain of the ship would disembark at ports "like a great emir . . . the archers and Ethiops [slaves] march before him bearing javelins and swords, with drums beating and trumpets blowing."

Even before his final victory over the Song, Khubilai Khan had set his sights on Japan, launching an invasion in 1274 with a com-

As depicted in this reproduction of a thirteenth-century Japanese illustrated scroll, Mōko shūrai ekatoba, *Chinese exploding ''fire'' weapons, thrown over the heads of their archers, decimated the Japanese cavalry and brought initial success to Khubilai Khan's forces in the 1274 invasion of Japan.*

bined force of nine hundred junks, some forty thousand men, and fifteen thousand horses. The fleet sailed from Korea across the narrow strait to Japan. The Mongols easily took possession of the islands of Tsushima and Iki, then moved on to Kyūshū, Japan's large southern island. There the khan's soldiers seized Japanese women and, piercing their hands with wires, tied them to the sides of their ships.

This enraged the Japanese, who assembled an army of 120,000 to meet the Mongols. But their archers were no match for the Mongols' noisy gunpowder weapons. Terrified Japanese retreated as the Mongols moved rapidly up the coast, taking towns and villages. Even so, the Mongols were worried. They knew they were outnumbered.

"To drive on fatigued troops into the enemy's ground is not safe tactics," advised Mongol general Hu Tun. "It is better to draw back our forces."

As the Mongols retreated, a great storm hit the Japanese coast. The captains tried to steer their ships out to sea, away from the shallows, but it was too late. Strong winds dashed the ships against the rocks, and men were thrown helplessly into the raging sea. It was said that so many soldiers washed ashore on Kyūshū that there were mounds of bodies in the sand. More than three hundred ships were lost, and twenty thousand men were killed or drowned.

Upon hearing of the disaster, Khubilai Khan seized several Jap-

Typhoons assisted the Japanese in ultimately repelling both the 1274 and 1281 invasions of Khubilai Khan's navy. The Moko shurai ekatoba *(Illustrated text of the Mongolian invasion) depicts Japanese soldiers in a skiff boarding a Mongolian warship in a successful raid.*

anese envoys who were in the Chinese capital, promptly executed them, and put their heads on display. Unable to accept defeat, he immediately ordered a second invasion. It would take seven years to assemble the new armada, even larger than its predecessor. This force of 4,500 ships and 150,000 men was the largest ever brought together anywhere in the world up to that time. In 1281 Khubilai Khan's mighty fleet set sail from Korea in fair winds, a sea of ships extending to the horizon and beyond.

As before, the Mongol fleet initially did well, retaking the island of Iki and achieving victories on Kyūshū. But while the Mongols were preoccupied with land battles, small Japanese boats edged out into the bays, setting fire to the large junks on the fringe of the fleet. Again the Mongols decided to retreat in the face of strong opposition, and again a typhoon of exceptional strength struck the islands unexpectedly. The hastily departing junks collided with one another.

Masts snapped, and ships were dashed apart on the rocks. The Japanese stalked the beaches, striking down Mongol and Korean soldiers who staggered ashore. More than four thousand ships were supposedly lost in the shallow gulf off Kyūshū, creating a rubble of wreckage a man could walk across. It was said that more than 130,000 Mongols and Koreans perished. After the great victory, the Japanese believed for many centuries their islands were protected by divine winds they called *kamikaze.*

The ambitious khan also sent fleets into the South China seas to attack Annam (north Vietnam) and Java, whose leaders both briefly acknowledged the suzerainty of the dragon throne. The khan's envoys traveled farther afield than any official Chinese emissaries had ever gone before, and, according to Marco Polo, even reached Madagascar. At the same time, the khan initiated plans to reopen the two-thousand-mile Grand Canal—badly damaged during the long war with the Song—to transport grain from the breadbasket of the Yangzi River valley to the new capital at Beijing, which—because of the narrow margin of agriculture in north China—could not feed itself. While repairs on the canal were under way, the emperor made the decision to initiate large-scale grain transports up the coast. It was a mammoth undertaking, a testament to the extraordinary sea power of China during the Mongol dynasty.

In 1282, 6 million pounds of grain were transported in 146 large, flat-bottomed barges north to a seaport in Hebei province near the modern city of Tianjin. Ten years later, that figure reached 16.8 million pounds, and by 1329, at the height of the grain transport, 420 million pounds.

As the Mongols were losing their grip on the empire, this vital project fell into the hands of two Chinese merchants, Zhu Qing and Zhang Xuan. They reaped enormous profits from the grain transport and soon extended their trade operation into southeast Asia. It was said that the members of their households were so wealthy that all of them wore gold and silver badges. The merchants traveled with a personal garrison of a thousand men who terrorized local people, condemning to death anyone who defied their authority. Their greed knew no bounds. Not only did they charge the government exorbitant prices for grain, they also accepted tribute gifts from foreign merchants, a privilege reserved for the emperor. It was a fatal mistake. In 1302 the two were charged with treason. Zhu took his own life, and Zhang was executed in Beijing along with his son and grandson.

The behavior of these two scoundrels confirmed the low opinion of trade and merchants held by Confucians, who were beginning to reassert their influence in the weakened Mongol empire. They took over the grain trade and established strict policies—called *guan du shang ban* ("government supervision and merchant operation")—over merchants and overseas ventures. By the 1330s most of the grain going north was transported by the restored inland canal system, which was safer and more reliable than the coastal transport, which gradually diminished.

If you kill the hen, it will give you no eggs. Confucian bureaucrats knew that regulation could smother capitalist ventures. People must be allowed to prosper if the tax rolls were to increase. But from this point on China never relaxed its policy of *guan du shang ban* for very long. The hen was kept in a cage and watched closely. This profound Confucian mistrust of merchants and overseas ventures would have a direct bearing on the fate of the Ming treasure fleet and China's future economic development.

3 The Prisoner and the Prince

From the Himalayas of Tibet, a high plateau extends eastward hundreds of miles through southern Sichuan to Yunnan. It is a rough, mountainous land with snowcapped peaks rising over fifteen thousand feet and unnavigable rivers snaking through steep, walled canyons. The plateau is surrounded by dense rain forests and traversed by narrow, muddy roads and rickety bamboo bridges that for hundreds of years have made travel arduous and unsafe, isolating Yunnan and its people.

Khubilai Khan lost half his army to malaria in Yunnan during an unsuccessful invasion of Burma, and the last remnants of Mongol forces retreated there after the Chinese succeeded in toppling them in 1368. In 1374 the new Chinese ruler, Zhu Yuanzhang, sent an envoy to Yunnan, urging the Mongol prince Basalawarmi to accept Ming rule. The Mongols defiantly killed the envoy, and subsequent diplomatic efforts ended in failure. Finally losing patience in 1381, the emperor ordered one of his most capable generals, Fu Youde, and an army of three hundred thousand to invade Yunnan and subdue the Mongols. The Chinese took the provincial seat at Kunming in 1382, and before being captured the rebel leader and his commanders committed suicide.

The Ming army showed no mercy, butchering an estimated sixty thousand Miao and Yao tribesmen during the Yunnan campaign, as well as countless Mongols. As was the custom since the first millennium B.C., young sons of prisoners were castrated. Thousands of young boys—some no more than nine or ten years of age—were stripped naked, subjected to one brutal stroke of a curved knife that cut off both penis and testes, and left with a plug in the urethra. Hundreds never recovered, dying of infection and exposure. Those who did were taken to the capital to serve as court eunuchs.

A Muslim boy from a family named Ma was among those captured by the Ming army in Yunnan. General Fu Youde and his troops encountered the ten-year-old by chance on a road and questioned him about the whereabouts of the Mongol pretender to the Chinese throne.

"He jumped into a pond," the boy replied.

"Is that so?" asked the general.

Fu Youde thought the boy was clever to conceal the truth if he knew it and brave to dare to say such a thing to the general. He took him prisoner. Three years later, in 1385, the boy was castrated and placed in the household of the twenty-five-year-old Prince of Yan, Zhu Di, the fourth son of the emperor, who was General Fu Youde's aide-de-camp.

The formalities of palace life usually established a distance between members of the imperial family and the eunuchs. But during the next decade, as they followed the trail of the renegade Mongols, the prince and his eunuch servant, the young Zheng He, spent much time together in tented military camps on the fringes of the empire, developing a friendship that would last a lifetime.

The Yunnan campaign was Zhu Di's first taste of battle. Strong, handsome, and energetic, the young prince had recently taken up residence at the old Yuan palace in Beiping (or Daidu, as the Mongols called it) and was charged by the emperor Zhu Yuanzhang with protecting the northern frontier. The Beiping guard units were officially under the command of the emperor's top general and old friend, Xu Da, under whom Fu Youde and the prince served.

Xu had been the emperor's closest companion in his struggle to overthrow the Mongols and had once been his proxy when Zhu Yuanzhang had been captured by hostile forces. The emperor himself was an orphaned peasant from Anhui in the center of China. He had spent several years in a Buddhist monastery, where he had learned to read and was exposed to the Confucian classics. He was tall with a large, flat nose and protruding jaw and had a serious, intense demeanor that commanded immediate respect. Later, as a rebel, Zhu Yuanzhang distinguished himself from other emerging Chinese leaders by not plundering or killing civilians and by seeking the advice of learned men.

Zhu Yuanzhang credited a large part of his military success in the rebellion to the spirits of the mountains and rivers, to whom he prayed conscientiously. He believed his grandfather was a shaman who had the power to persuade water spirits to send rain. Later, when he became emperor and took the name Ming (meaning "bright" or "enlightened") for the new dynasty, he made belief in spirits a state religion above Buddhism and Daoism. But just as he believed there were spirits everywhere—in the moats and walls and rivers—he also believed that someone, somewhere, was always plotting against him. He trusted no one, not even his closest associates. One of his first acts upon ascending the dragon throne was to set up a network to spy on his subordinates and to register the entire population of China for the first time. Every household was required to list the names, ages, and professions of all who lived there; neighboring households were instructed to keep watch on one another.

Empress Ma, who married Zhu in the midst of the rebellion, tempered her husband's paranoia, arguing for an equitable treatment of prisoners and encouraging him to keep grain reserves to help the people in emergencies. Once, when he rebuked her for caring about the peasants, the empress replied, "I am as much the mother of the people as you are the father." Indeed she was. She sewed clothing for Zhu's soldiers, and in 1360, during a crucial battle, she took her husband's gold and silver reserves and distributed them to the men at the front as a reward for their loyalty and bravery.

As Zhu Yuanzhang rose to power, he took dozens of concubines and consorts, some Mongolian and some Korean, fathering in all twenty-six sons and sixteen daughters. The empress Ma bore no more than four of the sons, although it was rumored that she was barren and may not have given birth to any of the emperor's children. She was certainly not the mother of Zhu Di, who would eventually usurp the throne. According to one legend, he was the son of the last Mongol emperor. When Zhu Yuanzhang entered Daidu, the Mongol capital, the story went, he found a young princess, one of Toghon-temur's wives, who had been abandoned or forgotten by the Mongols when they fled. He took her as his wife, and she did not tell him she was already pregnant. When she gave birth to Zhu Di, the emperor accepted him as his own son. In fact, Zhu Di was probably the son of one of the emperor's lesser consorts who gave birth prematurely. For that unfortunate happenstance, an insult to the emperor, she was subjected to a Chinese torture called "the iron skirt." Immobilized out in the cold by a suit of iron clothes, the young woman, already weakened from her difficult labor, eventually died of exposure.

Determined to overcome his humble beginnings by establishing a proper imperial court, Zhu Yuanzhang invited four eminent Yuan scholars to Nanjing to serve the fledgling rebel government and to supervise the instruction of the princes and court officials. A Daoist temple was temporarily converted into a miniature palace, where officials learned court etiquette and were tested for three days before an examiner posing as the emperor.

Zhu asked one of the scholars, Song Lian, "What is the most important work to understand the task of ruling?" Song replied that it was a commentary on the Daxue (Great learning) called *Da xue yan yi* by the Song scholar Zhen Dexiu. The emperor had passages from the book copied on the palace walls of the Forbidden City and sometimes gathered his officials around a particular inscription and asked Song to comment on it. Imperial princes also studied the *Shi jing* (Book of poetry), a collection of folk songs that were read as guides to moral behavior, as well as the *Shu jing* (Book of documents), a collection of pronouncements from the sage kings of antiquity that was regarded as a guide to proper conduct of rulers, and the *Chunqiu* (Spring and autumn annals), a history of the ancient dukedom of Lu (present-day Shandong province) edited by Confucius and said to reflect his moral judgments on political behavior.

The strong Confucian principle of filial obligation was taught to the princes through such parables as the story of the stepmother who repeatedly berated her stepson in front of his father. Though the son was mistreated, he nevertheless made every effort to please his stepmother. One day in the middle of winter he took off his clothes and lay down on a frozen lake so that he might melt the ice and obtain fresh fish for her.

Once the emperor became very angry when he discovered that one of his sons had been struck on the head by his tutor for not being attentive. The emperor was on the verge of taking action against the tutor when Empress Ma intervened. She advised her husband that "as brocade in the process of weaving needs shearing, so do children, undergoing instruction, require punishment." Reluctantly, Zhu let the matter drop.

Zhu's unpredictable temper was sometimes directed against his concubines, on whose behalf the empress also intervened. On one occasion she pretended to be more angry at a concubine than her husband was and sent the girl off to a palace official to be punished.

"Why did you interfere with this?" the emperor asked her.

"When you are in a temper, your punishments tend to be excessive," she said. "The staff officials will deal justly with her case. Even a criminal should not be judged by you but should be turned over to the proper authorities."

"And why were you angry with the woman?" he asked.

"To reduce your anger," she replied.

After the death of his oldest son in 1392, the emperor hesitated in appointing his bookish fourteen-year-old grandson, Zhu Yunwen, as his successor over Zhu Di, then thirty-two, whom he considered the most capable of his sons. From an early age, it was said, one could see the difference between the two, but it cannot be determined whether the tales of Zhu Di's superiority are true or simply products of his later attempts to alter official histories. One day, the emperor was supposed to have asked both Zhu Yunwen and Zhu Di to write the second line of a couplet modeled after his opening line: "Wind blows the horse's tail into a thousand strands of thread."

Zhu Yunwen's response was drab: "Rain beats the sheep's wool into a flat piece of felt." But Zhu Di said, "Sun reflects off the dragons' scales into ten thousand bits of gold." If poetry can reveal the soul, a strong, optimistic spirit shone through these lines and impressed the emperor.

But Zhu Yuanzhang's Confucian advisers counseled against favoring Zhu Di. They said it would cause a rift among his other sons and plunge the country into civil war. Still worried about the capabilities of his grandson, Zhu Yuanzhang launched on a campaign in the final years of his life to rid the empire of anyone who might conceivably be a threat to his successor. Fifteen thousand civil officials and loyal military commanders were summarily executed in the emperor's mad purge. Even the faithful Fu Youde came under suspicion and was charged and summoned to Nanjing. According to some accounts, Fu Youde presented the heads of his two sons to the emperor before he slit his own throat in the presence of the astonished court.

After the executions, Zhu Yuanzhang was said to have placed a thorny stick in front of the heir and told him to pick it up. Zhu Yunwen hesitated. "I'm getting rid of the thorns before giving you the stick—is there anything more I can do?" said the emperor.

Ma He was the second son of a Muslim family from Kunyang, just south of Kunming in central Yunnan. His father and grandfather were both known by the name Hajji, indicating they had made a pilgrimage to Mecca. Just when the family came to Yunnan is uncertain, but it was believed they were part of a large influx of Muslims at the beginning of the Mongol or Yuan dynasty. The family claimed to have been related to an officer in the army of Genghiz Khan who had helped the khan occupy Yunnan and had been appointed its provincial ruler in 1274.

Although Muslims had entered China in the eighth century, both by overland routes and by sea into the port cities of Guangzhou and Quanzhou, there was an influx of Muslims of all nationalities in the early Yuan. Arabs, Persians, converted Turks, and Uighurs spread out into all areas of the country as never before. As Genghiz Khan swept through Samarkand, Balkh, Herat, and other central Asian cities, he enlisted men of learning into his service, and many Muslims served the Yuan court.

Whether Ma He's father, Ma Hajji, was serving with or aiding the Mongol army in Yunnan or was simply caught up in the confusion of the dying dynasty is not known. What is clear is that he died or was killed at age thirty-seven in 1381, the same year his second son, Ma He, was captured. Ma Hajji was buried outside Kunming by his eldest son, Wenming, and years later, when Ma He had risen to power in the emperor's service, he had a memorial tablet engraved in his father's honor:

> The title of this gentleman was Hajji. His surname was Ma. He was originally from Kunyang prefect, Yunnan. His grandfather's surname was Bayan; his grandmother's surname was Ma. His father was called Hajji; his mother's surname was Wen. The gentleman was by birth tall, husky, and unusually good-looking, of imposing and redoubtable demeanor and bearing, unwilling to compromise himself [or] toady to others; when a person was at fault, straightaway [he] castigated him to his face and held nothing back. By nature being especially fond of doing good, [on] encountering those who were impoverished or distressed—including widows, orphans, and others with no one to rely on, he routinely [offered them] protection and aid, [and] never did he appear to be bothered [by this]. [It was] for this reason that there was no one in the local community who did not look up to [this] gentleman. He took in marriage [a woman] surnamed Wen, [full] of wifely virtues. He had two sons, the eldest [named] Wenming, the other, He, and four daughters. He had been since childhood talented and ambitious; and in the service of the [Yongle] emperor was granted the surname Zheng and served as director of the Directorate of Palace Eunuchs. The gentleman was diligent, clear-headed, and

> sharp-witted; modest, respectful, strict, and close-mouthed; [he] did not avoid working hard and exerting [himself]; the local gentry all praised him for this. Verily, by observing his offspring one surely can see what the father accomplished during his life and taught by his righteous ways. This gentleman was born on the ninth day of the twelfth [lunar] month of the *jiashen* year [January 12, 1345] and died on the third day of the seventh [lunar] month of the *renxu* year of Hongwu [August 12, 1382], having enjoyed [a life of] thirty-eight *sui* [about thirty-seven years]. [His] eldest son, Wenming, carried the coffin with reverence and set up a gravestone on the plain of the village of Hedai in the community of Baoshan. . . . As a person, [Ma Hajji] dwelt in the border region yet respected the practice of ritual and righteousness; in his station, [he] was content as an ordinary commoner yet cherished the bestowal of extraordinary favors; it is fitting that the good fortune he leaves behind be [both] profound and enduring and that he [should have] had offspring illustrious in their own times.
>
> By Imperial decree—composed on the day of the Dragon Boat Festival in the third year of Yongle [June 1, 1405] by . . . the president of the Ministry of Rites . . . Li Zhigang.

Living in the prince of Yan's household in Beiping, Zheng He probably received more of an education than he would have at the imperial capital in Nanjing. There he was called "San Bao," meaning "Three Jewels." The emperor mistrusted eunuchs and once said, "They should not be given responsibility and their numbers should not be large." In 1384 he was said to have hung a sign on the palace gate that read, "Eunuchs should not intervene in government affairs. Those who disobey will be beheaded." He also believed it was better to keep eunuchs illiterate.

Eunuchs had become established at court in the Han dynasty to run the imperial household and to prevent confidential matters from being revealed to the general public. As in Turkey, eunuchs were entrusted with guarding the harem and ensuring that the imperial bloodlines were not compromised. As the custodians of imperial custom and court etiquette—though unable to read in the early Ming—they advised the princes about such things as protocol, table manners, and sexual conduct. Before the prince of Yan was married at the age of sixteen to the fourteen-year-old daughter of General Xu Da, he may have been led by a eunuch into the imperial gardens, where there were graphic Buddhist statues of men, women, and beasts in the act of lovemaking.

Under Zhu Yuanzhang, the eunuchs were organized into twelve directorates or divisions in charge of such things as food and provisions, archives, construction of warehouses and temples, imperial stables, and munitions. The top post was the Directorate of Ceremonial, which consisted of three eunuchs who made the appointments to all other offices and also sent eunuchs on special missions. Ultimately, Zhu Yuanzhang found it too inconvenient to keep all the eunuchs illiterate and disobeyed his own directive so that there could be a few competent eunuch clerks in the Directorate of Palace Servants, which kept the staff documents.

Eunuchs like Ma He who were castrated before puberty were called *tong jing*, meaning "pure from childhood." They were especially favored by court ladies and tended to behave like young girls themselves. As adults, they were said to have shrill, unpleasant voices, and they were often temperamental and emotional, quick to anger and cry. Ma He clearly departed from this stereotype. Family records report that he was "seven feet tall and had a waist about five feet in circumference. His cheeks and forehead were high but his nose was small. He had glaring eyes, teeth as white and well-shaped as shells, and a voice as loud as a huge bell. He knew a great deal about warfare and was well accustomed to battle." Given some exaggeration in the account (and the fact that Chinese *chi*, or feet, are somewhat smaller than the western measure), one nevertheless gets the impression of an exceptionally large, commanding presence. He was also said to have read the works of Confucius and Mencius. And, from the Yunnan campaign on, he accompanied the prince of Yan on all of his military expeditions, learning the art of war, fighting side by side with his master, and eventually playing a significant role in the 1390s campaign against the Mongols in the northern steppe.

Like his father before him, Zhu Di was an able soldier, and as it had for his father, this skill would prove essential to his gaining and retaining the throne. Zhu Di's abilities were evident in his very first command, when the emperor entrusted him to stem the southward advance of the elusive Mongol leader Naghachu in the winter of 1390.

Fragments of the outcast Mongol armies expertly launched lightning-fast guerrilla raids on Chinese towns and outposts, followed by equally swift retreats into the security of the endless steppes of Mongolia, where their tracks vanished with the wind. They could live for months off their herds of sheep, moving camp frequently to find pasture and hustling their sturdy ponies from oasis to oasis. The Ming troops, burdened by long trains of supply wagons, were slow, and they frequently exhausted themselves before they had even seen the enemy or engaged in combat. A winter campaign was particularly dangerous and seldom attempted.

When Zhu Di, accompanied by the twenty-year-old Ma He, moved his army out of Beijing on March 2, he knew Naghachu would think he was secure. It was unseasonably cold, and the Mongols would not expect to be pursued. Indeed, as Zhu Di's troops moved through Gubeikou pass in what is now the Great Wall, uncertainty about the undertaking spread through the ranks. Officers and soldiers alike were reluctant to continue when they saw the barren, windswept plains laid out before them, from horizon to horizon and beyond. It was madness to proceed in such weather, they thought.

The Chinese cavalry wore a Mongolian style of dress: high leather boots, loose trousers, and short red jackets open at the front to facilitate riding. They had tight-fitting steel helmets with red tassels like horsetails and wore triangular-shaped breastplates of iron or copper over their jackets. Their leather shoulder and knee pads and wide leather belts were fashioned in the shape of large animal heads, making them look as if they were possessed by fierce beasts.

Zhu Di pulled his horse to a halt and, gathering his commanders around him, revealed his plan to send scouts ahead to find Naghachu and gather information about his campsite. They would not wander aimlessly looking for him; they would go directly to him—with a carefully planned attack.

As the scouts departed, galloping quickly out of sight, the army pushed on. Before long, the scouts discovered the Mongol chief camped at a place called Yidu, just across the Mongolian border. Zhu Di hastened toward Yidu as snow began to fall heavily, covering the desert with a silver patina. Again the soldiers were apprehensive.

"The weather is so bad the enemy would not dream of our coming," Zhu Di exhorted them. "If we advance quickly in the snow, we can surprise them and win a big victory."

They rode on, and, when they were near the Mongol campsite, Zhu Di ordered his men to hide in the dunes. He had something of a secret weapon, a Mongol officer named Nayira'u, who had been captured by the Chinese some months before and was a close friend of Naghachu's. Zhu Di sent the Mongol officer out to meet the Mongol leader. Naghachu was astonished to see his old friend and wept. As the two embraced and began to talk, Zhu Di ordered his men to close in on the camp.

When Naghachu realized the deception and jumped onto his horse to flee, he was stopped by Nayira'u, who told him of Zhu Di's plan. Seeing no way to escape, Naghachu surrendered. The prince graciously received the Mongol leader like an honored guest and that night prepared a banquet for the entire army and their families. The Mongols feasted, and on the following day many decided willingly to join Zhu Di's army. His bloodless victory won the prince both admiration and apprehension in Nanjing. Proudly, the emperor announced that his worries about the security of the northern border were finally over. Silently, advisers to the heir worried about the prince's growing military power.

Seven years later, in 1398, Zhu Yuanzhang, who had named his reign "Hongwu," meaning "Vast Military Prowess," died at the age of seventy-one. Fearing that his sons might undermine the authority of the heir and fight among themselves if they gathered in the capital for his funeral, he issued orders before his death that they were all to stay in their respective fiefs and not, under any circumstances, to attend his burial. The location of his tomb had been chosen with great care early in his reign. It was finally placed just east of Nanjing, on a slight rise halfway up Purple Mountain, where a small stream flowed in front of it on its way around the mountain. The spirit of the emperor was thus trapped between the mountain and the stream and would not be able to wander after his death, creating insecurity and trouble for his descendants.

Rows of large carved stone animals, soldiers, and civil officials were placed around the base of the mountain leading to the tomb and arranged in double pairs so that one set would always be "on guard." The mile-long path wove and turned to discourage evil spirits, who were believed to travel only in straight lines. His pallbearers were entombed with him along with forty-two of his concubines. The concubines were either buried alive or had their throats cut. Sheep and pigs were also skinned, cooked, and buried as offerings to the spirit of the emperor, who was believed still to have worldly needs.

There is much debate about whether Zhu Di was forced into a civil war by his scholarly nephew, now twenty-one years old, or whether he himself provoked a rebellion by increasing the size of his garrison illegally. The truth perhaps lies somewhere in between. Official histories do report that upon ascending the throne, Zhu Yunwen adopted a policy called *xiaofan*, meaning "reducing the feudatories," that is, eliminating the guard forces of his uncles. One by one, Zhu Di's brothers were placed under house arrest and stripped of their powers and military forces. In a rage, Zhu Bo, the prince of Xiang, one of the ablest of Zhu Yuanzhang's sons, refused a summons to appear before the emperor and answer trumped-up charges of impropriety. He set his palace at Jingzhou on fire, burning his family to death, then rode his terrified horse into the flames, killing himself.

By the summer of 1399, a year after Zhu Yunwen acceded to the throne, five of the most powerful princes had been eliminated and two others had died of natural causes. None of the other remaining princes was old enough or influential enough to be of concern to Yunwen, except, of course, the prince of Yan in Beijing. Zhu Di, who had obeyed his father and had not left his fief since the funeral, was now isolated. To give himself time to decide what to do, he feigned madness. He ran through the streets of Beijing screaming and yelling, stealing food and wine, and sleeping in gutters. For days at a time he sank into apparently deep depressions and would see no one. In warm weather he sat by the stove, shivering and complaining of the cold. But it was all a smokescreen, meant to deceive the emperor into thinking he was ill and harmless.

Early that summer Zhu Di asked that his three sons, who were at the emperor's court in Nanjing, be returned to him. So as not to arouse Zhu Di's paranoia, the emperor permitted the sons to travel home. It was Zhu Yunwen's most serious mistake. With his sons by his side, Zhu Di would not hesitate to act if he were provoked. And he was soon provoked.

In July the emperor sent a small force to Beiping to arrest two of Zhu Di's commanders, who were supposed to have been involved in suspicious activities. At first Zhu Di agreed to turn his officers over to Zhu Yunwen's agents, but then, in a daring plan, he convinced the arresting officers to enter his palace alone and seized them, executing them on the spot. Before the court could formally protest this action, the prince of Yan took the initiative and declared his intention to *feng tian jing nan*, that is, "accept Heaven's [command] to quell the troubles [at court]." He spoke not of rebellion but rather of removing the "treasonous" officials around his nephew. He was especially wary of two Confucian advisers, who, he charged, had changed the policies of Zhu Yuanzhang, the founder of the dynasty by leading this attack on the princes.

In an address to the people and soldiers of Beiping, he appealed to the emperor, saying:

> The treasonous official Qi Tai and Huang Zicheng harbor destruction in their hearts: my five young brothers, Su, Fu, Bo, Gui, and Bian, have all in the space of a few years been stripped of rank and forcibly removed [from their positions]. Bo is the most pitiable, having burned himself to death with his entire family. [Were] a benevolent and sagely [ruler] on the throne, how could he endure this? . . . It is like chopping down a great tree; first cut off the appended branches; once the princes of the blood have been eradicated, the court will be isolated; the treasonous officials [shall have] achieved their aims and the altars of soil and grain (i.e., the empire) will be in certain danger. . . . Your servant [I, the prince of Yan] reverentially reads that it says in the *Ancestral injunctions,* "[If] the court has no upright ministers, [and] within there is treason and malfeasance, then the princes of the blood must drill their troops and await the command: the emperor shall secretly order the princes to jointly lead their troops to put down and settle this [matter]." Your servant reverentially bows low and awaits the command.

Such noble motives masked the prince's true ambitions well. Yes, he thought he was a worthier choice than Zhu Yunwen to succeed his father. Certainly he was more capable. Had not fortune-tellers told him he had the walk of a dragon and the stride of a tiger? And yes, the thought of rebellion had crossed his mind and the minds of others, particularly his adviser the monk and military strategist Daoyan, who mocked the emperor, saying he was "born with a weak and soft-hearted nature." Secretly, Daoyan had already begun training a special strike force of eight hundred in the palace park. He cleverly filled the park with flocks of honking geese and ducks to mask the noise of their military maneuvers. But, the prince wondered, was this the right moment to strike, or was he acting too hastily?

A bad storm had struck Beiping the night Zhu Di seized the emperor's officers. Tiles were blown off the prince's palace, and Zhu Di thought this was a sign from heaven that he would be defeated. But Daoyan reassured him that it was instead a bad omen for the emperor.

"Has my Lord not heard," he said, "that when dragons fly in heaven, wind and rain accompany them. The falling tiles mean that heaven will change your residence to a yellow-tiled house"—the imperial palace.

At first the emperor did not take the rebellion seriously and went about his business as usual. He was determined to decentralize the government and free it from some of the terrors of his grandfather. Political prisoners held since the early days of the dynasty were released, and some punitive taxes were repealed. But because all of the capable military leaders who could have come to the aid of Zhu Yunwen had been killed in Zhu Yuanzhang's last, frantic purge, the emperor really had no potential allies in his mission to quash the rebellion. The first imperial troops sent to fight Zhu Di in the north suffered defeat at every turn, despite their vastly superior numbers. Out of humanity or naiveté, the emperor ordered his troops not to kill the prince. Zhu Di knew this and took advantage of it.

Again Zhu Di stunned his enemy with surprise raids. Once, in the middle of the night, while the emperor's troops were drinking and celebrating the autumn festival in Hebei province, several thousand of Zhu Di's forces struck and slew eight thousand imperial soldiers. Another ten thousand were captured soon after, when Zhu Di's men, hiding underwater near a bridge and breathing through reeds, surprised the imperial army crossing overhead. Such attacks ultimately crippled and defeated what had been a mighty army of 130,000.

In the late fall, however, a second, larger army of an estimated five hundred thousand men was sent north by the emperor to capture Beiping. But the troops marched out of Nanjing in their summer uniforms and were caught unprepared by the northern snows. Imperial soldiers, freezing in their straw sandals, attacked Beiping, raining arrows over the walls. The prince and his army were on maneuvers outside the city, so the women of Beiping mounted the walls and bravely threw pots down on their attackers until the men arrived to help them. The city stood, and the imperial casualties numbered almost two hundred thousand.

The imperial army regrouped in the spring of 1401 and launched a crushing offensive in which they used devastating gunpowder grenades. Several of Zhu Di's commanding officers were killed, and thousands of troops narrowly escaped capture, including the prince himself. In Shandong, Zhu Di found himself completely surrounded by enemy cavalry, his horse wounded, only to be rescued by a daring charge of Mongolian units who had joined his army. On Daoyan's advice, the prince withdrew to Beiping to rest his troops. It was the low point in the rebellion. Neither side now underestimated the other. A stalemate ensued.

Help came to Zhu Di from an unexpected source—the court eunuchs. The emperor had forbidden the eunuchs to go on official business outside the Forbidden City to keep them from abusing their positions of power. Furious, the eunuchs had fled Nanjing for the prince's court in Beiping. There they revealed to him the secrets of the defense of the capital, which was in fact quite poor. They also advised him that the cities of Fengyang in Anhui and Huai'an in Jiangsu should be avoided because they were well fortified. The prince was elated. This gave him the encouragement he needed to march south and try to take Nanjing.

This bold campaign began in January 1402. With Ma He as one of his commanders, Zhu Di followed the route of the Grand Canal south, capturing grain barges and disrupting the flow of supplies to important cities. He avoided the heavily defended points, taking only the weak towns and cities, sometimes without a fight. A final victorious encounter with imperial troops in Anhui province, in which confusion over a cannon signal sent the emperor's men and horses out from protective trenches and into enemy fire, cleared the way for Zhu Di to cross the Yangzi River and surround the capital city at Nanjing.

Nanjing was surrounded by enormous walls, measuring fifteen miles around, thirty-six feet high, and twenty-one feet wide at the top. It had four tiers of gates, defended by troops who actually lived in long, narrow chambers in the walls. The discipline of the Ming soldiers on the walls was usually very strict. Guards could move only five paces in either direction, and anyone who left his post on the wall was decapitated on the spot. A deserter was killed, along with the other four men in the deserter's combat group, who had failed to stop him. Anyone caught in idle talk had his ears cut off.

However well prepared Zhu Di was to storm the city, the siege of Nanjing would have taken months. However, the loyalty of the officials around the emperor began to crumble. Shortly after Zhu Di arrived at the outskirts of Nanjing, two imperial commanders went to the prince's camp to discuss a peaceful settlement and negotiated a secret deal to surrender the city. On July 13, 1402,

Zhu Di and his army marched in triumph through the Jinchuan Gate.

He found the imperial palace already in flames. The prince ordered a eunuch to investigate, and the charred bodies of the empress and her eldest son were found. Another body, burned beyond recognition, was believed to belong to the emperor. Yet, even before the three bodies were buried on July 18, rumors spread that Zhu Yunwen was still alive.

When Zhu Di was approaching the city, one rumor had it, Zhu Yunwen was urged by one of his officials to open the vermilion chest left by his grandfather. The late emperor had stipulated that it should be opened only in time of crisis. In the box were ordination certificates for three monks bearing the names Yingwen (meaning "Should Be Literate"), Yingneng ("Should Be Capable"), and Yingxian ("Should Be Worthy"). A message directed Yingwen to leave "through Demon's Gate; the rest will go along the water gate of the imperial moat; at twilight, meet on the west side of the Shenle [Divine Joy] Temple." The box also contained a monk's robes, hat, and shoes, and a razor to shave his head.

According to the tale, the emperor dressed as a monk and, with a few loyal followers, went to Demon's Gate, where they saw a skiff tied at the water's edge. Wang Shen, the Daoist master of Shenle Temple, was awaiting there and said that the first Ming emperor had appeared to him in a dream and asked him to aid them. Thus the emperor escaped. It was said that three monks never left his side and that twenty people in various disguises traveled back and forth along the road to procure food and clothing for the emperor.

Before the city fell, the emperor's two Confucian advisers, Qi Tai and Huang Zicheng, who had so strongly fought to reduce the power of the prince, managed to flee undetected. Qi Tai painted his white horse black with ink, but the ink eventually wore off with the horse's perspiration, and he was recognized and caught. Huang tried to organize a resistance in Suzhou that was quickly crushed by the prince's troops. After denouncing the prince to his face, Huang was condemned to a particularly gruesome execution for high treason known as *ling chi,* or "death by one thousand cuts." Cuts were made on his chest, abdomen, arms, legs, and back, so that he very slowly bled to death over a period of time, perhaps as long as three days.

Zhu Di picked the name Yongle, meaning "lasting joy," as the name of his reign.

Zhu Di's first act upon ascending the throne on July 17 was to execute those officials and military officers who refused to recognize him, along with their relations to the ninth and tenth degrees and their neighbors, teachers, servants, and friends. Many Confucians who had served Zhu Yunwen were among them. In the wake of this horrible purge, reminiscent of his father's 1393 massacre, Zhu Di picked the name Yongle, meaning "lasting joy," as the name of his reign. He publicly announced that the years his nephew had occupied the throne simply had not existed, and he changed the historical record, officially extending the rule of his father to 1402.

From the beginning of his reign, Zhu Di did not place his trust in the Confucians but instead gave unprecedented power to the eunuchs who had helped him in the rebellion. Zhu Di rewarded his loyal servant and eunuch commander Ma He by bestowing on him the name Zheng. He chose that name, it is believed, because in the early days of the rebellion his horse had been killed just outside Beiping at a place called Zhenglunba. Zheng He had particularly distinguished himself in the 1399 defense of Beiping and in the final campaign south in 1402 to capture Nanjing.

As Zhu Di tried to justify his rebellion and to suppress the facts of Zhu Yunwen's reign, legends spread of an emperor-monk in hiding. Some accounts said the emperor lived out the rest of his days in Yunnan in a place called White Dragon Mountain. Others said he went to Guangxi, where, it was reported, he sold his precious jade belt to obtain food. Still another version recounted how he fled to Fujian, where he took a mistress and had four more sons.

On the road to Yunnan, it was reported, a court official named Yan Zhen came across the emperor. The two recognized each other and wept.

"What are you going to do with me?" Zhu Yunwen asked.

"Your Majesty may do as you wish," said the official. "Your subject will take care of himself."

That night, it was said, Yan hanged himself in an inn.

Other rumors insisted that, although he traveled widely around the country at first, Zhu Yunwen eventually settled in a large Buddhist monastery called Pu Ji nestled in the Gonglong Mountains outside Suzhou, where he lived until he died at the age of forty-five in 1423. He was supposed to have been assisted by Daoyan, who quickly became disillusioned with the prince of Yan after he seized the throne. Even in severe drought, local people say, the spot on the temple grounds where the emperor is supposed to have been buried is always green.

Yet another rumor suggested that the emperor had actually fled overseas.

In 1403 Zhu Di issued orders to begin the construction of an imperial fleet of trading ships, warships, and support vessels to visit ports in the China seas and Indian Ocean. Bearing all the treasures the empire had to offer, such a grand fleet had never been assembled before, and soon every province became absorbed in the mammoth effort. Part of the purpose of the undertaking, at least according to the *Ming tong jian*, an unofficial history of the period, may have been to comb the seas and either find Yunwen or dispel the unsettling rumors of his exile abroad.

> Regarding the Jianwen emperor's escape, there are some who say he is abroad. The emperor ordered Zheng He to seek out traces of him.

Certainly the magnificence of the so-called treasure fleet seemed to have been designed to convince any foreign ruler who might be harboring the deposed emperor just who the rightful occupant of the dragon throne was. And it probably wasn't far from the emperor's mind that the imperial treasury, depleted by a long civil war, was in need of replenishment by foreign trade.

4 The Treasure Fleet

A branch of the Qinhuai River meanders through the southern end of Nanjing. In the gentle curves of the lazy river were moored flat-bottomed boats with luxurious cabins like miniature palaces, where men used to come day and night to be entertained by young girls with cheeks the color of ripe peaches. Occasionally, at their clients' request, the boats would leave the banks, moving slowly upstream, and the sound of soft music and high voices would waft over the still water like morning fog.

But downstream, to the east of the city where the main branch of the Qinhuai joins the mighty Yangzi, a steady stream of barges shuffled busily back and forth from inland ports, bringing lumber and building materials of every kind to the Longjiang shipyards. Men and horses hauled the goods up the muddy banks to large warehouses. The drumbeats that marked the hours heightened the impatience of supervisors too often behind schedule. Ships were barely completed before yet another imperial order was issued, demanding more.

In the reign of the Yongle emperor, Longjiang nearly doubled in size, covering several square miles from the east gate of Nanjing to the Yangzi. It surpassed the Suzhou shipyards near the mouth of the Yangzi as the country's largest shipbuilding center and was perhaps the largest shipyard in China's history. Until 1491, Longjiang was actually two separate shipyards, near each other, and at one, most of the treasure fleet was built.

In May 1403 the emperor ordered Fujian province to produce 137 oceangoing ships. Three months later Suzhou, and the provinces of Jiangsu, Jiangxi, Zhejiang, Hunan, and Guangdong, were instructed to produce 200 more vessels, and in October 1403 the court sent

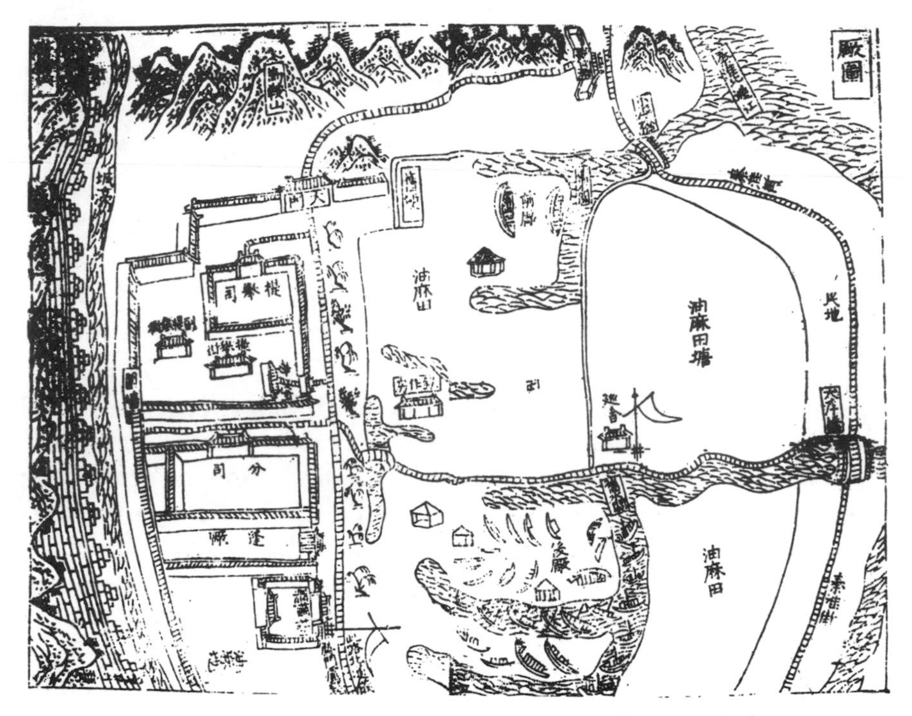

Woodcut of Longjiang shipyard outside Nanjing showing workshops (left) for carpenters, sail makers, and ironsmiths and drydocks (center) leading into the Yangzi River.

orders to the coastal provinces to promptly refit 188 flat-bottomed transport boats for service on the high seas. A frenzy of shipbuilding activity followed from 1404 to 1407, with the construction or refitting of over 1,681 ships for the emperor's various emissarial missions. The coastal provinces alone could not supply all the necessary wood, so large inland lumbering operations were hastily mobilized around the outer reaches of the Yangzi and Min rivers. Timbers were floated downstream to the shipyards, which had easy access to the sea. Most of the empire became involved in this mammoth effort.

In the reigns of Hongwu and Yongle more than four hundred households of carpenters, sailmakers, and shipwrights from Jiangsu, Jiangxi, Zhejiang, Fujian, Hunan, and Guangdong were transferred to Longjiang, and at its height twenty to thirty thousand people worked and lived at the yards. The skilled craftsmen were organized into four basic workshops: carpenters, ironsmiths, caulkers, and sail and rope makers. Each workshop had about a hundred households. In addition, there were timekeepers, specialists in the construction of scaffolding and bridges, and men who took care of the dozens of imperial horses used in hauling materials around the yards. The shipwrights generally could not read, and therefore they instructed the artisans in their craft by whittling miniature demonstration models, whose meticulously crafted pieces fit together perfectly without nails.

There is a Chinese saying: "In order to obtain the pearl necklace from the dragon, it is first necessary to find the man to slay the dragon." In shipbuilding, as in other important ventures, the Longjiang master shipwrights placed great emphasis on doing everything in the correct way and in the proper sequence.

At the center of the shipyard were seven 1,500-foot-long drydocks. They ran nearly perpendicular to the Yangzi and were separated from the river by high dams. When the ships were finished, gates in the dams were opened, flooding the rectangular docks and enabling the ships to be moved easily into the mainstream of the Yangzi. Guards patrolled the gates of the dams so that no harm would come to the unfinished ships.

Drydocks first came into European shipbuilding in Portsmouth, England, at the end of the fifteenth century. In China they date to at least the tenth century, when a plan for the repair of two large "dragon" or pleasure boats outlined the concept:

> In the Xining reign (1068–77 A.D.), the eunuch official Huang Huaixin offered a plan [for repairing the hulls of the imperial pleasure boats]:
>
> Excavate a large basin at the north end of the Qinming Lake capable of containing the dragon ships; set up columns on the bottom of it and put large wooden crossbeams on top of them. Then, open a breach to let in the water and tow the ships over the crossbeams, after which water can be removed from the basin with waterwheels. The ships will be suspended in the air. Once the repairs have been completed, the ships [can] again be floated on the water; take apart the crossbeams and columns, and use a large building to cover them; then [there will be] a hangar for storing the ships and they will never be endangered by exposure.

Construction of wooden ships at Longjiang began with the hull and placement of bulkheads at regular intervals. The hull was then covered with longitudinal planks in overlapping and multiple layers. The mast was secured in front of one of the bulkheads, called the *mao tan* (or "anchor altar"), and then the joints between the planks were caulked with jute fibers and covered with a mixture of sifted lime and tung oil. The iron nails that joined the planks were also covered so rust wouldn't damage the wood fibers. The tung oil mixture had to be boiled and cooked before it would harden into the excellent waterproofing material that had been in use on Chinese ships since the seventh century. Mud and lard, which held together the sewn boats commonly used on the Indian Ocean, often disintegrated in open seas, resulting in serious leaks.

The masts of Chinese sailing ships were usually made out of a strong fir, *shanmu,* and the hull timbers and bulkheads were fashioned from elm, camphor, sophora wood, or *nanmu,* a special cedar from Sichuan. The rudderpost was usually of elm; the tiller, of oak. Oars were made from fir, juniper, or catalpa wood. Longjiang had ten rows of sixty rooms used for storing materials for the treasure fleet, including old planks salvaged from other ships.

In the reign of Zhu Di's father, Longjiang had been engaged in building *shachuan,* or "sandboats," used for travel between China and Korea in the comparatively shallow Yellow Sea, where there was a danger of shifting sandbanks. This type of boat was first built in the seventh century on Chongming Island in the Yangzi estuary and was then known as *fang sha ping di chuan,* or "flat-bottom-boat-that-prevents-running-into-sand." It had a flat bottom, a small, squared-off prow, a high stern, and a shallow draft. Its long, flat hull had low water resistance, so if the junk unexpectedly encountered shallow waters, it wouldn't get hopelessly stuck. *Shachuan,* however, were unstable in high seas and would not have been suitable for travel in the stormy South China Sea and Indian Ocean, to which the treasure fleet was assigned.

The Fujian shipwrights whom Zhu Di transferred to the Longjiang shipyard built another kind of junk specifically for travel in the southern oceans. These boats had sharply pointed hulls, "sharp like a knife," which could cut through large waves, and wide, overhanging decks. A keel ran across the bottom of the V-shaped hull for stability. Both the prow and the stern were high, and the boats had four decks. The lowest deck was filled with earth and stones for ballast; the second deck had living quarters for the men and a storage area; the third or top deck was a combination outdoor kitchen, mess hall, and operations bridge; and the fourth deck was a high fighting platform that sometimes interfered with the function of the sails. The prow was very strong and was used to ram small boats. It could also withstand contact with hidden reefs, which were

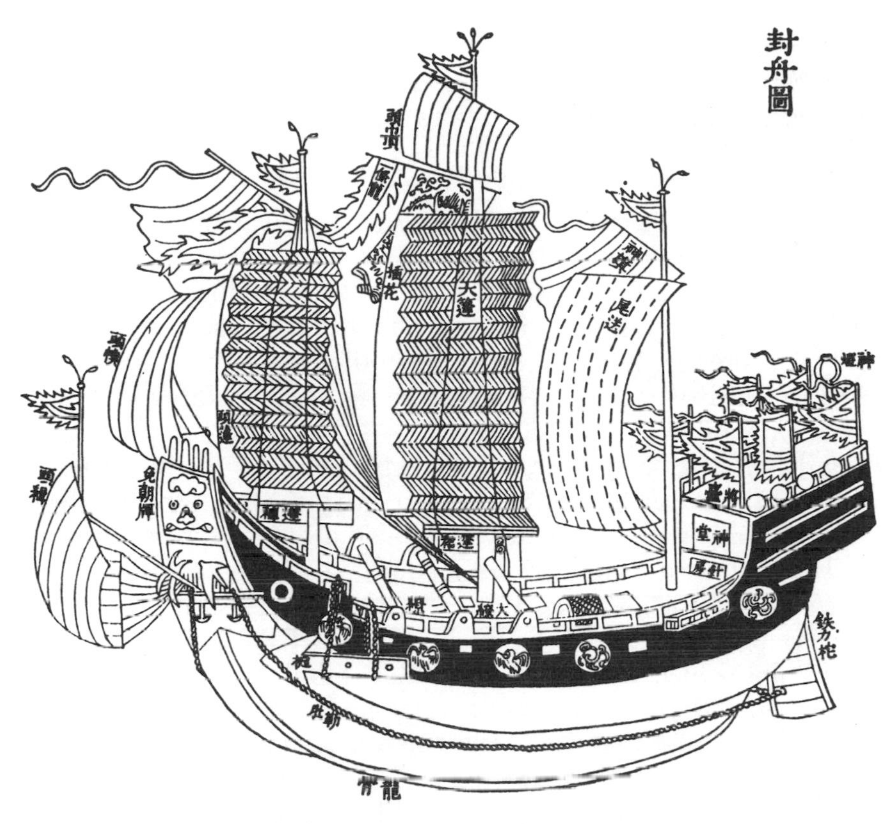

Ocean-going fuchuan *with their high prow and keel or "dragon bone" running the length of the hull provided a model for the treasure ships.*

a danger in the South China Sea. King Fuchai of the Spring and Autumn Period (770–476 B.C.), who built a shipyard on the Min River near Fuzhou, gave his name not only to Fujian province but also to these graceful, locally built sailboats, which became known as *fuchuan.* When Marco Polo left Quanzhou, Fujian, in 1292 to accompany the lady Cocotin (Kuka Chin) to the court of the khan of Persia, he took with him fourteen *fuchuan,* each having four masts, nine sails, and a crew of 250 to 260 men. All Ming warships and coastal patrol boats were *fuchuan.* It was the custom that large "dragon eyes" be painted on the prows of *fuchuan* so that the boats could "see" where they were going.

The shipwrights at Longjiang created a new vessel for the treasure fleet, combining these two boat designs. In keeping with the enormity of the emperor's desire to show the world the greatness of his reign and the righteousness of his claim to the throne, the grandest of the treasure ships in the fleet was—enormous. Some historical records give its dimensions in complicated accounting characters 肆拾肆 rather than simplified ones 四十四, leaving no doubt as to the exact figures. The *bao chuan* (treasure boat) or *long chuan* (dragon boat) were "44 *zhang* 4 *chi* long and 18 *zhang* wide." However, the official length of a *chi,* or Chinese foot, varied considerably throughout the Ming Dynasty, from 9.5 inches to over 13 inches. Moreover, the *chi* varied depending on what it was being used to construct and where it was being used; building standards in the empire were not uniform.

Early calculations of the size of the treasure ships were based on a *chi* of 12.129 inches (*Ming gong bu chi*) or 13.338 inches (*Huai chi*), which were the standards in Jiangsu province for the building of *shachuan.* Based on these *chi,* a ship of 44 *zhang* (1 *zhang* equals 10 *chi*) would be 448.8 to 493.5 feet long. A wooden sailing ship of this length would be very difficult to maneuver, if indeed it were seaworthy, which seems doubtful. Most scholars now believe that the treasure ships, though built in Nanjing, were *fuchuan* in their basic design, and that the Longjiang shipwrights, the majority of whom were from the coastal provinces, would have brought their tools with them. Based on actual shipbuilding *chi* unearthed in Fujian province, which varied in length from 10.53 to 11.037 inches, the largest of the treasure ships is now thought to have been between about 390 and 408 feet long and 160 to 166 feet wide—still one of the largest wooden sailing ships ever built anywhere in the world.

The number "444" (44 *zhang,* 4 *chi,* or 444 *chi*) prescribed for the length of this important imperial ship was certainly no accident. Four was the symbol for the earth, which was thought to be "four-cornered." The Middle Kingdom was imagined to be in the middle of four seas. There are four cardinal directions, four seasons, and, according to Confucian philosophy, *si wei,* "four bonds" or virtues: propriety, integrity, righteousness, and modesty. All were auspicious associations for the treasure ships.

The treasure ships were longer than any oceangoing boat previously built in China but not inconsistent with the style and stature of early ship models. In the Tang dynasty ships were 20 *zhang* long, and in the Song they approached 40 *zhang.* The *ke zhou* (guest ships) of the Song emperor Huizong were 10 *zhang* long and 2.5 *zhang* wide; and the *shen zhou* (spirit ships) he sent on emissarial missions were reported to be three times as big. The ships of Khubilai Khan each had more than ten sails and were said to hold a thousand men. On the large lake west of Hangzhou, grand pleasure boats from the Song dynasty called *Xihu zhou chuan* (West Lake ships) were presumed to be more than 50 *zhang* long. They "were skillfully made with engraved railings and painted pillars. They moved through the water with great stability and made the passengers feel as if they were on dry land."

To the Yongle emperor, size seems to have been equated with grandeur, and, at the same time he was building the treasure fleet, he also ordered the construction of a huge stone stele for his father's tomb. The tablet was supposed to be 135 feet high, 45 feet wide, and about 12 feet thick. But before the work was finished at the imperial quarry at Yanmen, about eight miles east of Nanjing, the emperor was informed that it was too big and heavy to be moved. Had it been erected, it would have been the largest stone tablet in the world. Today, however, the giant tablet stands majestically in the abandoned quarry—almost free of the huge boulder from which it was carved—a monument to the monumentality of Zhu Di.

Most of the drydocks at Longjiang were 90 to 120 feet wide, but two of them were 210 feet wide, big enough to accommodate a ship 160 to 166 feet wide. The treasure ships were quite wide for their length, but, like typical *fuchuan*, they were "balanced like a scale" with stability created by the V-shaped hull, the long keel, and the heavy ballast. The keel consisted of long pieces of wood bound together with iron hoops. In rough weather, holes in the prow would partially fill with water when the ships pitched forward, lessening the violent rocking motion of the waves. Floating anchors cast off the side of the ship also increased stability in turbulent seas. In the stern were two eight-foot iron anchors, weighing over a thousand pounds each, for mooring offshore. Each anchor had four flukes set at a sharp angle against the main shaft, a shape characteristic of Chinese anchors since the beginning of the Christian era.

The strength of the treasure ships was created by another Chinese innovation, watertight bulwark compartments modeled after the multichambered structure of a bamboo stalk. The treasure ships also used a balanced rudder that could be raised and lowered, creating additional stability like an extra keel. A "balanced" rudder placed as much of the rudder forward of the stern post as behind it and made such large boats as the treasure ships easier to steer. Neither bulwark compartments nor stern posts and balanced rudders were introduced into European shipbuilding until the late eighteenth or early nineteenth century.

In their rigging and grand appointments, however, the treasure ships resembled *shachuan*. The ships had nine staggered masts and twelve square-shaped sails made of red silk cloth. They were thus better able to make full use of the wind and so were faster than typical *fuchuan*. Although the treasure ships carried twenty-four cast-bronze cannon that had a range of up to eight or nine hundred feet, they were not considered fighting ships and did not have the *fuchuan*'s raised platforms or extended planks for combat. Rather, the treasure ships were appointed for luxury. There were grand cabins for the imperial envoys, and the windowed halls and antechambers were festooned with balconies and railings. The ships' holds were filled with expensive silks and porcelains for trade with foreign countries. The ships' bodies were brightly carved and painted, their prows adorned with carved animal heads and glaring dragon eyes and their sterns with dragon and phoenix patterns or eagle and ball designs that symbolized auspiciousness. The bottoms of the vessels were whitewashed, and near the red waterline was a sun-and-moon frieze.

It is not clear just how many large treasure ships were among the fleet of 317 ships that the emperor assembled in Nanjing in the spring of 1405. As Ming novelist Lou Maotang suggests in *San Bao taijian Xiyang ji tongsu yanyi*, his sixteenth-century novel about Zheng He's voyages, there may have been only four such splendid boats for the eunuch commander and his principal deputies. And, as verified in historical records, the bulk of the treasure fleet consisted of other types of vessels of various sizes. The second-largest boats were eight-masted "horse ships," some 339 feet long by 138 feet wide. These ships did, in fact, carry horses, which were an important part of the tribute trade, as well as other tribute goods and all building materials necessary to repair the fleet at sea. The large holds of the seven-masted "supply ships"—about 257 feet long and 115 feet wide—were packed with food staples for the crew, who numbered 28,000 on some voyages. Six-masted "troop transports"—approximately 220 feet long and 83 feet at the beam—were used to carry the treasure fleet's large contingent of soldiers. The fleet had two kinds of warships, five-masted, 165-foot-long *fuchuan* and smaller eight-oared patrol boats, some 120 or 128 feet in length, that terrorized pirates.

Special water tankers built specifically to accompany the treasure fleet were able to supply fresh drinking water to the men at sea for a month or longer, the first such convenience for a large armada anywhere in the world. Usually, however, the fleet tried to stop at ports every ten days to refill the tankers, thought to number as many as twenty on the larger expeditions.

Communication at sea between the various vessels of the treasure fleet was made possible by an elaborate system of sound and sight signals. All ships were equipped with one large flag, signal bells, five banners, one large drum, gongs, and ten lanterns. Sound signals were used to issue commands on board, and drums loud enough to be audible between neighboring ships warned the fleet to seek safe harbor if a storm was approaching. Lanterns were used to convey signals at night or in foul weather, and carrier pigeons were employed for long-range communication. Each ship could be identified by its special color and a black flag with a large white character indicating to which squadron it belonged.

While the treasure fleet was being built, the crews were assembled. Under the eunuch commander in chief were seven eunuch directors who served as imperial representatives and ambassadors on the voyage. Ten eunuch assistant directors worked under the ambassadors, followed by fifty-two eunuchs of unspecified rank. The military command, which was under eunuch supervision, included two regional military commissioners in charge of all the troops accompanying the fleet, 93 military commanders in charge of regiments, 104 battalion commanders, and 103 company commanders. Each of the boat captains was specifically appointed by the emperor and was given the power "to kill or let live" to maintain order on board. In addition, the fleet had two secretaries to prepare official documents; one senior secretary from the Ministry of Revenue, who was in charge of grain and fodder supplies; two officials from the Ministry of Rites, who would have been in charge of protocol at official receptions; and one official astrologer and geomancer assisted by four student astrologers and geomancers, who would have been responsible for making astronomical observations, forecasting the weather, keeping the calendar and interpreting natural phenomena. Ten instructors, whose official title was *tong yi fan shu jiao yu guan,* literally, "teacher who knows foreign books," were on board to serve as translators. Arabic speakers and those knowledgeable in central Asian languages would certainly have been among them.

The fleet also had 180 medical officers and pharmacologists to collect herbs in foreign countries. There was one medical officer for every 150 men. The majority of the regular seamen and soldiers were banished criminals. Finally, specialized workmen such as ironsmiths, caulkers, and scaffolding builders were included on the mission in the event that the ships needed repair at sea. All personnel, from the lowest to the highest, would be rewarded for their service to the emperor with money and cloth when they returned. Should they be injured or killed during the voyage, they or their families would receive extra compensation.

As imperial orders were issued around the country for materials to build the treasure fleet, so too were provinces commanded to supply the ships with goods to be traded abroad. They included thousands of bolts of silk and cotton cloth as well as large supplies of iron, salt, hemp, tea, wine, oil, and candles. Suzhou and Hangzhou were traditional centers for silk making. Cottage industries and textile factories were under strict imperial orders to produce specific quantities and qualities of fine silks and brocades for the treasure fleet. Greatly coveted abroad were ceremonial robes with the imperial dragon or phoenix motif done in a fine tapestry weave called *kesi* or "cut silk," which showed the design on both sides. In *kesi,* a needle was used as a shuttle, creating twenty-four warp threads per centimeter, as compared with the eight to eleven found in the finest French Gobelins tapestries. Silk makers who failed to meet the strict imperial specifications were fined or imprisoned.

The imperial porcelain works at Jingdezhen in Jiangxi province increased from twenty kilns at the beginning of the Ming dynasty to fifty-eight in the reign of Xuande (1426–35), producing for export mainly white porcelain and the bluish or greenish Qingbai, a delicate, thin-walled porcelain. The treasure ships were also certainly laden with Cizhou, a northern Chinese stoneware with painted or incised decoration under a clear glaze; Dehua, a Fujian-made porcelain with a lustrous brownish glaze; and pale green celadons, which were considered to possess magic qualities. Ample quantities of all types of Chinese porcelains have been found from the Philippines to East Africa. Ironworks in Nanhai county, Guangdong, expanded as well, making nails, needles, pots, and iron wire not only for the Longjiang yards but also for foreign trade.

So great were the needs of this enormous fleet that almost immediately it began to be a strain on the population. To ease the burden on the people in supplying the all-important tung oil and hemp for the ships, the emperor created large orchards outside Nanjing with more than ten thousand tung trees to meet the needs of the Longjiang yards. But wealth from foreign trade would flow back mainly to the court. For ordinary subjects the voyages would become associated with heavy taxes and corrupt officials who squeezed counties for even more than their share.

One tale about an official named Peng Bailian demonstrates that even if a scam were discovered, there was often little an honest man could do about it. According to historical accounts, county supervisors in a remote part of Jiangxi province had been instructed by the court to order three wealthy men to collect lumber for the treasure ships' masts, or to pay a certain sum in silver if they could not. By accident, Peng discovered that the supervisors had tapped not three wealthy men but some 280 for the required timber and so collected for themselves an enormous sum of money. He reported this to higher authorities and then found himself imprisoned on false charges trumped up by the corrupt supervisors. Peng was finally released, but not before losing his position and suffering greatly for his forthrightness. A favorite ploy of the eunuchs who were dispatched around the country to gather supplies for the fleet was to find fault with an imperial porcelain order and "reject" it. They would later sell it for their own personal gain. One such corrupt eunuch was discovered and summarily executed, but such disciplinary action may have been more the exception than the rule.

But if in the glory of these wondrous ships were the seeds of discontent, it did not particularly concern the Yongle emperor—if indeed it had ever been brought to his attention. The ships were launched, one by one, from the docks of Longjiang into the Yangzi. Looking out over the fleet as it prepared for its mission, he knew the glory of his reign had been made manifest and soon the whole world would see it.

5 Destination: Calicut

With the work at Longjiang going well, the emperor faced the decision of who would command the great treasure fleet. Was Zheng He at thirty-five, he wondered, too old for the dangerous journey?

"Let not Your Imperial Majesty forget the saying 'the old horse knows the way,' " counseled a court official. "Indeed, like ginger and dates, there are things which become better with age."

The official went on to enumerate the eunuch's virtues, which, he said, could be seen in his face. Zheng He's skin was "rough like the surface of an orange," indicating he had experienced hardships in his life and could tolerate the rigors of the two-year mission. The space between his eyebrows, a predictor of personal happiness, was "narrow," suggesting his energies would be focused on his professional life and service to the emperor. "His eyebrows were like swords and his forehead wide, like a tiger's"—both signs of Zheng He's strength of character and aptitude as a military commander. His mouth was "like the sea," words flowed eloquently from his lips, and his eyes "sparkled like light on a fast-moving river," evidence of his energy and vitality, despite his advanced years.

Whatever Zhu Di's faith in physiognomy, he did finally appoint Zheng He principal envoy and commander in chief of the treasure fleet. It was the first time in Chinese history that a eunuch had been appointed to such an important military command. As a sign of trust in this longtime companion, the emperor presented Zheng He with blank scrolls stamped with his seal, so that the commander could issue imperial orders at sea.

In autumn of 1405, the fleet of 317 brightly painted junks with a total crew of more than 27,000 men was ready to depart from Nanjing. As the ships assembled in formation in the center of the

Yangzi, the sculpted "eyes" on the majestic bows looked anxiously downstream toward the open sea.

The destination of the treasure ships was Calicut—the powerful city-state in Kerala on the west coast of India that had a market for spices and rare woods that attracted traders throughout the Indian Ocean. Here, in this isolated coastal region west of the Ghat range, grew cardamom, cinnamon, ginger, turmeric, and precious pepper, worth its weight in gold. After the flooding of the ancient Indian harbor of Muziris in 1341, Calicut had emerged as the most important port not only in India, but in all of south Asia.

If the mission of the treasure fleet was to track down rumors of the last emperor's escape overseas, was Calicut the best place to begin the search? Would the emperor, fleeing the flames of his burning palace in monk's robes, have boarded a ship for this distant port? It seems unlikely. Was the purpose of the expedition primarily diplomatic? This, too, is hard to believe, since two years earlier Zhu Di had dispatched a flurry of envoys to Japan, Thailand, Indonesia, Malaysia, and the Indian state of Cochin to announce his accession to the Ming throne. What, then, was the emperor's intention in sending out this extraordinary fleet of more warships than the Spanish Armada and tons of the Middle Kingdom's finest silks, porcelains, lacquerware, and art objects?

Part of the explanation can perhaps be found in Zhu Di's immediate repudiation of his father's strict tribute and trade policies upon becoming emperor. He allowed private trade and lifted the restrictions on pepper and gold. To the horror of his Confucian advisers, who subscribed to the ideal that China's prosperity rested in agriculture and agriculture alone, Zhu Di threw China's doors open to foreigners and foreign merchants, saying, "Now all within the four seas are as one family." The emperor decreed, "Let there be mutual trade at the frontier barriers in order to supply the country's needs and to encourage distant people to come."

After thirty years of barely more than a trickle of foreign goods into China, was the purpose of Zheng He's first voyage thus to reopen the Indian Ocean trade, to renew old commercial ties, making up for lost time with the ships' vast treasures? Immediately upon Zheng He's return from Calicut in 1407, Zhu Di ordered a second mission to India, and during that voyage (1407–9) the Chinese envoys helped install a new king of Calicut and erected a tablet celebrating the close relationship between the two countries.

China's retreat from commerce under Zhu Yuanzhang had created havoc among the small city-states in Indonesia and the Malay peninsula. Their principal source of income had been abruptly cut off. Lured by the lucrative profits of the spice trade, roving bands of pirates and bootleggers entered the vacuum. The Chinese coasts were hounded by Japanese *wako;* the south Vietnamese coast was controlled by bandit slave traders; and Palembang in southeastern Sumatra became the center of the illicit China trade, ruled by renegades from Guangzhou. The impressive array of warships that accompanied the giant treasure-laden junks was more than mere show. Zhu Di undoubtedly wanted to protect the fleet's precious cargo, thus opening the sea routes to legitimate trade.

The evening before the fleet's maiden voyage, the emperor hosted a sumptuous banquet for the crew with more delicacies and wine than could possibly be consumed, as a sign of his boundless generosity and wealth. Officers and common seamen alike were presented with gold, silver, and silks in varying amounts, each according to his rank. The gathering had a serious purpose as well: To ensure safe passage and success on the journey, prayers and sacrifices were offered to Tianfei, the Celestial Consort, the patron goddess of sailors.

The emperor eventally built a magnificent new temple to Tianfei on a hill overlooking the Longjiang shipyard and the Yangzi, and Zheng He brought back rare and exotic trees for the temple's orchards and lavish gold and silver ornaments to grace the statue of the goddess. Murals inside both new and old temples depicted scenes from Tianfei's life, beginning with her birth in 960 A.D. to a Fujian fisherman named Lin. It was said when she was fifteen or sixteen, she received enlightenment while gazing into a well, after which she had the power to foresee the future and to heal the sick. According to legend, she was able to convey a warning to her brother at sea, which saved him from drowning. After she died in 987, her spirit was believed to wander above the sea in a red dress, guiding sailors in danger. Her cult grew in Fujian and all along coastal China, and she was credited with many miraculous rescues and healings.

With burning of incense and repetition of prayers, Zheng He and his men honored Tianfei and asked for her guidance. Goats, pigs, and cattle, parboiled with their feet bound as if kneeling, were presented at her altar, and fake paper money was burned to encourage *gui shen,* "spirits," to treat her spirit kindly. Even in the remote regions of the four oceans, Tianfei could respond to trouble because she was assisted by two spirits: one with a thousand eyes who could see everything, the other with sensitive ears who could hear as far as the winds blew. The goddess also had the power to peer into men's hearts. Prayers had to be sincere and inspired by pure motives. To risk a long voyage on the ocean—where it was believed giant dragons lived beneath the surface—without the goodwill of the goddess was the most unthinkable madness.

"Our one fear is not to be able to succeed," Zheng He later wrote on a tablet. "[But], if men are able to serve their ruler with the exertion of all their loyalty, then all things will be successful. If they are able to serve the gods with utmost sincerity, then all their prayers will be answered."

After boarding, each captain said additional prayers before the ship's compass—prayers to the ancient geomancers, to the great mathematicians and astronomers of past dynasties, who had used the water compass with skill. They had braved the oceans and returned safely. Their wisdom was sought in using this most miraculous device with its floating needle. Zheng He and his men bowed before the compass, which was to be their guide and salvation for the many months ahead, and prayed:

> "As the divine swirling smoke rises, with hearts pure and true, we bow down and beseech the messengers of merit to convey by means of the incense in this burner that in this year, in this month, on this day, at this hour,
>
> "WE RESPECTFULLY ENTREAT the patriarchs of the imperially created compass throughout the ages:
>
> "Yellow Emperor, Duke of Zhou, immortal masters of former ages divinely knowledgeable about yin-yang, Dark Raven, immortal White Crane master . . .
>
> "[And] patriarchs of the ages who have traversed the sea; who know the mountains, the sandbanks, the shallows, the depths, the isles, the shoals; who are conversant with the sea lanes, the mountains, the mooring waters, the constellations and guiding stars; those from past times to the present day, those who first transmitted it and those who later taught it.
>
> "[And] the great guardian spirit generals of the 24 directions; the great guardian spirit generals of the 24 azimuth points of the patriarch of books, the compass classic; the page boy who sets the compass di-

> rections, the spirit of the water basin, the lord of the water changing, the strongman who sets down the compass needle, the spirit soldiers who move the compass needle, the guardian spirits of the direction of the needle, the master of the lookout, and all the other immortal masters and spirit soldiers and divine emissaries—All the efficacious spirits of the incense burner.
>
> "[And] the protectress of our ships, the Celestial Consort, brilliant, divine, marvelous, responsive, mysterious force, protector of the people, guardian of the country.
>
> "[And] the all-seeing and all-hearing spirit soldiers of winds and seasons, the wave quellers and swell drinkers, the airborne immortals, the god of the year, and all the local tutelary deities of every place.
>
> "COME DOWN ONE AND ALL to this incense feast, partake of this sagely vessel,
> "Come riding on auspicious clouds from the ends of the earth,
> "Come down and grace our incense table,
> "Let us seat you in your respective places and carefully prepare a pure goblet that we might reverentially offer the immortal masters a flagon of wine, beseeching them to protect our ships and valuables."

As the smoke from the burning incense drifted upward, the priests offered vessels of wine to the gods. Would the smoke carry their supplications to heaven? Would they be well received? The chanting continued. Prayers described the enormous dragons who dwell in the seas and cause storms when they are angry, churning up huge waves and spitting torrents of spray. The priests asked the dragons to be still and not disturb them on their voyage, and they prayed for favorable winds:

> "When this day at an auspicious hour we set down the compass needle,
>
> "LET THE DARK WATER DRAGONS go down into the sea and leave us free from calamity.
>
> "Humbly, respectfully, piously, we offer up this flagon of wine, offer it once and offer it again, pouring out this fine, fragrant wine. . . .
>
> "Your servants, pure of heart and pious, respectfully lift up the wine to make a secondary offering: reverentially, we take three cups of excellent wine and fill the golden beaker, to call up the winds,
>
> "THAT OUR SAILS MAY meet favorable winds,
> That the sea lanes be peaceful and secure,

That our coming and going be auspicious,
That gold, pearls, wealth, and valuables fill our ships full with glory,
with pious hearts we do offer up this excellent wine. . . .

"WE HOPE AND WISH that when the compass needle is set in the bowl,
it will always point true north and south and east and west,
That from dawn to dusk the ship's captain will be protected,
That crossing the seas, coming and going, we follow the correct route,
That men and ships both be content and at peace, That the sea crossing is fine and uneventful, and that hidden shoals not be met, and sails hang high forever without worry. . . .

"THEN, in the rising smoke of burnt offerings of paper money and valuables, depart our meager feast.

"Having respectfully invited you, we received you bowed at the waist offering incense; we see you off on our knees, bowing to the ground, foreheads touching the floor in pious respect, prostrate in grave attentiveness."

In their prayers, the mariners evoked the great geomancers of the Han dynasty because it was from the brass divining boards they had used to determine auspicious locations for buildings that the compass had evolved in the first century A.D. Geomancers studied land features and river courses in order to place such important buildings as imperial tombs in locations where they would be in harmony with the spirits of the earth and water. Their divining boards had a magnetized ladle or needle that was allowed to align itself in a north-south direction on the polished surface. A thousand years later, mariners took magnetized needles on their ships to guide them when weather prevented them from reading the sky. Because level surfaces could not be found on a rocking ship, the needles were floated in small stone basins of water. With these water compasses, pilots could stay the course over long distances. The "south-pointing needle" took the fear out of a starless night.

The mariners had placed themselves in the hands of the gods, trusting in their virtue and the virtue of the Son of Heaven, who had sent them on this mission. The fleet proceeded slowly down the Yangzi from Nanjing to Liujia, a port near the mouth of the river. A sleepy, rice-growing village in the Yuan dynasty, Liujia was now an important harbor with masts "as thick as a forest." Here, additional sacrifices were made to Tianfei, and Zheng He organized the fleet for the ocean voyage.

Although the treasure ships moved easily out of Liujia into the East China Sea, on return voyages it was often difficult for the pilots to locate the entrance to the harbor because the terrain had no prominent landmarks. In 1412, before the fourth expedition, Zheng He supervised the building of an artificial mountain at Liujia, some thirty-three feet high and almost a mile in circumference, named Bao Shan (Treasure Mountain) to help guide the treasure fleet into the Yangzi. At the base of the mountain Zhu Di erected a tablet that read: "By day, smoke rises from the mountain. By night, a fire glows bright," indicating just how the hills aided ships at sea. By the mid–eighteenth century, however, the mouth of the Yangzi had shifted, and Shanghai, farther to the east, succeeded Liujia in importance.

From Liujia, the fleet then traveled four hundred miles down the China coast to a large harbor by the entrance to the Min River south of Fuzhou on the Fujian coast. In the third century the harbor had been the chief shipbuilding area for the king of Wu and was hence known as Wu's Head. Zheng He changed the name to "Taiping," meaning peace, and waited here several months for the favorable northeast monsoon in late December or early January to take the fleet across the South China Sea. Final repairs were made to the ships with the aid of the excellent local shipwrights, and additional provisions were taken on board. On a mountain south of the harbor there was a cluster of three temples where Zheng He and his men again made offerings to Buddha and Tianfei; one, the Pagoda of the Three-Peak Temple, was used by Zheng He as a signal tower for the fleet. From the top of the pagoda he had a commanding view across the harbor to Fafeng Mountain, then an island in the Min River. Signals were given by means of torches or colored flags, as they were when the fleet was at sea.

When the winds began to blow steadily and strongly from the northeast, the treasure fleet left the safety of the Min River and sailed past an outcropping of prominent rocks in the ocean known as Five-Tiger Mountain. The fleet then headed south-southwest through the Formosa Strait and across the South China Sea toward the ancient state of Champa, now south Vietnam. Special care was taken to avoid the hazardous reefs and islands in the South China Sea. On later voyages some of the treasure ships were lost there in storms.

At sea, the ships' pilots navigated principally by means of the water compass and measured time by burning graded incense sticks. A small basin in the center of the compass was filled with "yang"

The sixteenth-century reproduction of Zheng He's twenty-one-foot-long sailing map is known as the Wu bei zhi *chart (1621), after the military treatise in which it is preserved. The center portion of the map (above) shows the west coast of India along the top, the island of Ceylon at the right, and the African coast along the bottom. Proper scale and north-south orientation have been ignored; the chart served mainly as a compendium of*

sailing directions between important ports. Thus, to navigate from the Maldives (above, center) to India the instructions read: "steer exactly 75 degrees; after 45 watches the ship makes Quilon." Skilled pilots would have been necessary to direct the large fleet in and out of harbors.

water, seawater taken from the upwind side of the ship, and the magnetized needle, in the shape of a flat fish, was then gently placed on the water, where it slowly drifted into a north-south direction. A day was broken into ten "watches" of 2.4 hours each. Under good conditions the treasure fleet traveled about twenty miles during a watch at a speed of about eight knots. Speed was checked by throwing an object overboard at the bow and then walking along with it to the back of the boat and measuring, by chanting a rhyme, how long it took for the vessel to pass it.

Pilots determined latitude by measuring the altitude of Polaris or the Southern Cross above the horizon with a simple measuring board called a *qianxingban*, which was used for the first time during the treasure fleet voyages. The board consisted of twelve pieces of square wood; pilots aligned the *qianxingban* with the horizon and then used the length of their arms to calculate the position of the stars, in much the same way Western navigators employed a cross staff with string and board. Before and after the voyages of the treasure ships, Chinese pilots used a *liangtianchi*, a vertical ruler. Following the Arab system, degrees were roughly measured in *zhi*, or finger widths.

Zheng He's captains also regularly consulted a twenty-one-foot-long sailing chart, unrolled in sections as the fleet progressed on its journey. The chart was a compendium of sailing directions—given in terms of compass bearings and lengths of watches—from port to port across the Indian Ocean. It had neither grid nor scale and only the shorelines of countries were shown, but the chart carefully depicted important landmarks and geographic features, such as mountains, river mouths, bridges, beaches, shoals, rocks exposed at low tide, and the depth of channels. Simple pictorial symbols also indicated the location of outlooks, pagodas, military bases, storage areas, forests, and areas of flatland that were easy to traverse.

For long, frequently traveled routes, star maps augmented the sailing chart, showing the succession of stellar positions throughout the voyage. The Chinese created their own pantheon of constellations in the sky, so they navigated not by the Southern Cross, Centauri, Circinus or Lyrae, but by the Lantern, the twin stars in the Southern Gate, and the rising of the Weaving Girl in the northeast sky.

Approaching the coast of Champa, soundings were taken with a lead and line and samples from the bottom were brought up to help pilots identify by the type of sediment their distance from shore and

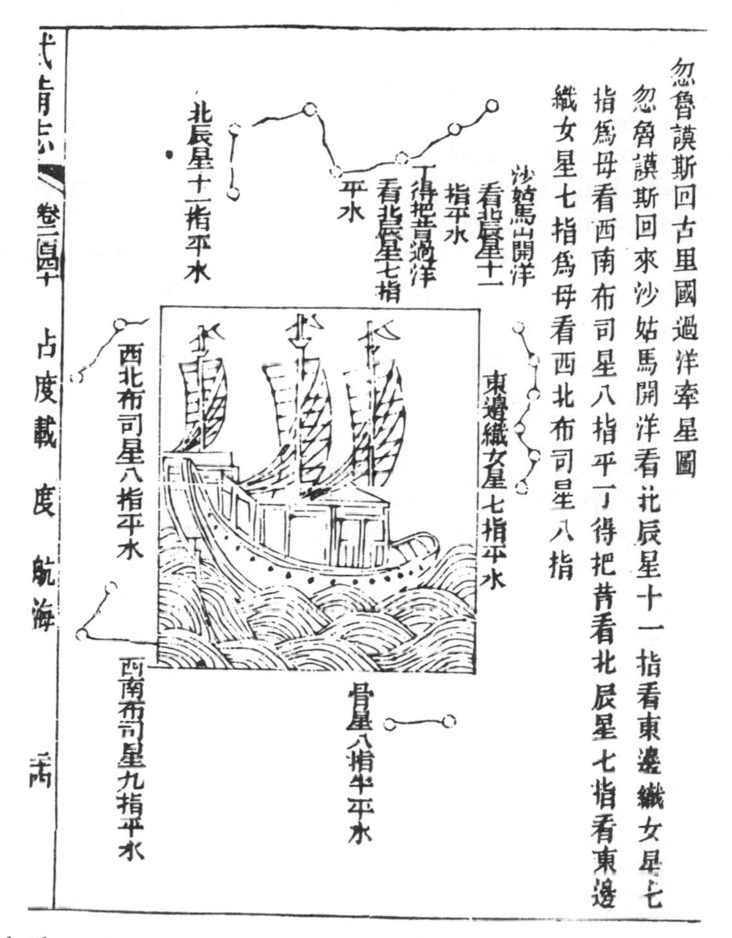

Although Zheng He's captains navigated primarily by compass bearings and time, they measured the altitudes of stars close to the horizon to check their latitude during voyages. The Wu bei zhi *(Records of military preparations) (1621) contained reproductions of Zheng He's stellar diagrams, including the one shown above to help the fleet navigate from Hormuz in Persia back to India. Captains were advised to keep the* Bei chen, *''Northmorning'' star (Polaris) ''11 fingers'' or about 17 degrees above the horizon when setting out on the journey. To the east the* zhi nü, *''Waving girl'' star (Lyra) is ''7 fingers'' or about 11 degrees ''above the level [of the water]'' and, to the south, the ''*Gu, *'bone' star (Cross) is 8½ fingers'' or about 13 degrees above the horizon.*

how best to direct their ships into the harbor. Very likely, Zheng He landed near the modern city of Qui Nhon. Champa was a loose confederation of communities that hugged the river valleys and depended on plunder from military raids and a lucrative slave trade in prisoners of war. It was, therefore, continually at war with its neighbors: the now north Vietnamese state of Annam, the Khmer kingdom, and the emerging Siamese state. In 1402 Annam invaded Champa, taking possession of Champa's northern border provinces. The Cham harbors were the slave traders' dens and notoriously unsafe.

What interested the Chinese in Champa was ebony, lakawood, an unusual black bamboo, and especially a rare aloe wood, from which they made an expensive incense. Zheng He believed this aloe wood grew on only one mountain there—and nowhere else in the world—and was worth its weight in silver. From the Chinese, the Chams purchased blue-and-white Ming porcelains and silks. The coveted aloe wood, along with rhinoceros horn, elephant ivory, and other products, was offered to Chinese envoys as tribute for the emperor.

The treasure fleet moved on, sailing south to Majapahit on Java and three independent townships on the north coast of Sumatra: Semudera, Deli, and Atjeh. It is interesting that Zheng He sailed right by the most important city-state on Sumatra, Palembang, on the northeast coast. This was perhaps a calculated oversight. Zheng He had heard of trouble in Palembang. A Chinese pirate, Chen Zuyi from Guangzhou, had taken control of the city and was now plundering ships that passed through the narrow Strait of Malacca. Thus, this first visit to Sumatra may have been a reconnaissance mission for Zheng He, to gauge the strength of the pirate band. The seamen of Palembang had a reputation as fierce fighters in naval battles. Whereas the Chinese navy favored ramming in sea fights, the Malays tried to board enemy boats with bands of armed soldiers. How many of these local fighters had Chen Zuyi recruited for his raiding parties? Clearly, something had to be done about the pirates, but Zheng He must have determined that this was not the best time to do it.

China was partly to blame for Palembang's woes. Because of Palembang's position at the entrance of the Strait of Malacca, it became an early entrepôt for a vast Indonesian trading monopoly in spices. In 1017, writing to the Song emperor, the maharaja of Palembang called himself "the king of the ocean lands." In the fourteenth century, however, the island of Java was gaining influence and the Siamese were extending their control down the Malay Peninsula. China's restrictive trade policies under Zhu Yuanzhang intensified the rivalry between Sumatra and Java, which by that time claimed sovereignty over Palembang. In 1377 Java kidnapped and killed Chinese envoys who were on their way to Sumatra to recognize Palembang as an independent state.

This barbarous act was such an affront to the *de* (virtue) of the dragon throne that Zhu Yuanzhang imprisoned the Javanese trade envoys in China and refused to receive any tribute missions from Palembang. Both city-states suffered as their trade with China dwindled. In 1397 Java attacked Palembang and appointed a Javanese ruler to govern the city. The Sumatrans promptly threw him out and installed one of their own leaders. In this weakened state, the city was taken control of by Chinese pirates a few years before Zheng He's arrival.

On his visit to Java, Zheng He found large colonies of wealthy Chinese merchants, who had arrived at the end of the fourteenth century despite Zhu Yuanzhang's strict ban on private trade and foreign travel. The town of Gresik on the northwest coast of Java was governed by a man from Guangdong province, and a thousand Chinese families lived there; Surabaja in the northeast also had "many Chinese." Under Zhu Di, who encouraged trade, these communities flourished. The Chinese seemed to have kept apart from the other island people—Muslims, Malays, and an upland aboriginal people whom Zheng He's men described as devil worshipers who consumed "snakes" and "all kinds of insects."

While trading porcelains and silks for spices and copper coins on Java, Zheng He's men witnessed wayang performances, in which an actor improvises a narrative from a picture before an audience. They thought it was very much like their own tradition of storytelling:

> Each time he [the performer] unrolls and exposes a section of the picture, he thrusts it forward toward the audience, and speaking with a loud voice in the foreign language, he explains the derivation of this section; [and] the crowd sits around and listens to him, sometimes laughing, sometimes crying, exactly as if the narrator were reciting one of our popular romances.

The Chinese saw a jousting contest, still played in eastern Java though in a less lethal form. In Zheng He's time, two Javanese men would advance toward each other and retreat to the beat of drums, brandishing and thrusting sharp bamboo spears. The men's wives or slave girls would stand nearby and yell "*larak!*" (draw back) to end the match, but often not before one or the other had been stabbed to death. The victor would give a gold coin to the dead man's family—then keep his widow or slave as a prize. Zheng He's men also observed cremations and the Hindu tradition of wives joining their husbands in death. Dancing and wailing on a platform above the burning funeral pyre, "wearing grasses and flowers all over their heads, their bodies clad in kerchiefs with designs of the five colors, . . . they [then] cast themselves down into the flames, and are consumed in the fire with the corpse of their lord, in accordance with their rite of sacrificing the living with the dead."

From Java and Sumatra, the treasure fleet sailed on to the island kingdom of Ceylon, where Zheng He received a cool reception from its ruler and did not linger. The king "proved arrogant and disrespectful and wanted to harm [Zheng] He. He heard about this and went away." The treasure fleet hastily departed, but not, it seems, before Zheng He made careful note of both the country's strong religious undercurrents and its immense wealth in gemstones and pearls. On the high mountain in the center of the island was a curious impression in the rocks, a giant "footprint" that Buddhists identified with the Buddha, Muslims with Adam, and Ceylonese Hindus with the god Siva. Buddhists washed themselves in the water that collected in the footprint, which they believed never evaporated. When it rained on the holy mountain, water rushed down the gullies, bringing with it a shower of precious stones—rubies, deep blue sapphires, and yellow oriental topaz—said to be the crystallized tears of Buddha. Zheng He had brought offerings for neither Buddha nor Allah. Had this unconscious oversight affronted the king? The priests on the treasure ships pondered this problem as the fleet set sail again and traveled around the southern point of India to Calicut on the west coast.

The Chinese called *Kuli,* or Calicut, "the great country of the Western Ocean." It lay on the sea, north of its rival city-states Cochin and Quilon, with whom the emissaries of the dragon throne also traded. The ruling zamurin of Calicut had declared it a free port, and even vessels headed for other destinations could stop there for water and provisions. Although the Chinese referred to most other people in the Indian Ocean as "barbarians," they treated the zamurin as an equal and had the utmost respect for this highly structured society with an efficient civil service, a well-trained army and navy, and a harsh system of justice. Like the Chinese emperors, the zamurins were patrons of literature and the arts.

"The people are very honest and trustworthy," wrote Ma Huan, a Muslim translator who traveled with Zheng He on his later voyages. "Their appearance is smart, fine, and distinguished."

Zheng He probably stayed in Calicut to barter and trade from December 1406 until April 1407. The bartering had a ritual of its own. First, one of Zheng He's officers and an Indian broker would set a date to discuss prices for the goods from the treasure ships. On that date the men would go over the cargo piece by piece. When the prices had been decided, all involved would join hands and the broker would say, "In such and such a moon, on such and such a day, we have all joined hands and sealed our agreement with a hand-clasp; whether [the price] is dear or cheap, we will never repudiate it or change it."

The same thing was then done with the Indian articles of trade—precious stones, pearls, coral, and pepper. While the Chinese made their calculations on an abacus, the Indians counted on their fingers and toes, but, according to Ma Huan, they did "not make the slightest mistake . . . [which is] extraordinary." If done quickly, the bartering took a month; if not, it could take two to three months. Then the goods were exchanged at the prices that had been decided, without "the slightest deviation." The zamurin collected duty on all trade.

While the trading went on, the Chinese heard for the first time the curious story of a holy man called Moses and the incident involving Aaron and the golden calf, which they wrongly assumed had taken place in Calicut and was linked to the Hindu veneration of the cow. The tale, as understood by Zheng He and his crew, nevertheless has the thread of the Old Testament version:

> There is a traditional story that in olden times there was a holy man named Mouxie [Moses], who established a religious cult; the people knew that he was a true [man of] heaven, and all men revered and followed him. Later the holy man went away with [others] to another place, and ordered his younger brother named Samoli [the Samaritan] to govern and teach the people.
>
> [But] his younger brother began to have depraved ideas; he made a casting of a gold calf and said, "This is the holy lord; everyone who worships it will have his expectations fulfilled." He taught the people to listen to his bidding and to adore the gold ox, saying, "It always excretes gold." The people got the gold, and their hearts rejoiced; and they forgot the way of Heaven; all took the ox to be the true lord.
>
> Later Mouxie the holy man returned; he saw that the multitude, misled by his young brother Samoli, were corrupting the holy way; thereupon he destroyed the ox and wished to punish his younger brother; [and] his younger brother mounted a large elephant and vanished.

In the spring the monsoons shifted to the southwest. Their trading done, the Chinese headed back across the Indian Ocean, carrying with them envoys from Calicut, Quilon, the Sumatran states of Semudera and Deli, and Malacca on the Malay Peninsula. The ambassadors bore messages from their kings and tribute to present to the emperor. The trip home for the treasure fleet, however, was anything but uneventful.

In the Strait of Malacca, Zheng He finally fought the pirate chief Chen Zuyi. Official Ming histories record that at first Chen indicated he wanted to surrender in the face of the treasure fleet's superior forces, but Zheng He's informants warned him it was a trick. As the two fleets sailed out to meet each other, it was Zheng He who lured Chen into an ambush and one by one burned ten of the pirate's warships and captured seven others. No details of the battle were written down, but Ming naval tactics stressed the importance of gaining the upwind position in combat to better facilitate hurling explosive and incendiary weapons at the enemy. Crows nests were manned day and night, and scouts won handsome rewards for spotting the enemy first, thus enabling the fleet to maneuver into an advantageous position.

Zheng He's warships had an array of many so-called fire weapons. By the mid-sixteenth century, military treatises describe two to three hundred incendiary weapons. *Fei tian pen tong* ("sky-flying tubes") sent a spray of gunpowder and flaming bits of paper to set fire to the enemy's sails, while *huo yao tong* ("gunpowder buckets") and *huo zhuan* ("fire bricks") were compact gunpowder-and-paper grenades soaked in poison. Half of the men on later Ming warships were specialists in deploying such explosives. Some incendiary devices were packed with noxious fumes, human waste, and smoke-producing chemicals and were intended merely to frighten and blind the enemy. Other, more lethal, grenades, were filled with metal pellets and powerful explosives that could maim or kill soldiers and cause severe damage to ships. Zheng He would certainly have employed skillful archers who would send showers of flaming arrows at the enemy's sails to set them on fire and cripple the boats. Despite these weapons, or perhaps because Chen Zuyi's ships had their own, it took Zheng He several months to capture the pirate and his principal lieutenants. He then took them back to Nanjing, where they were executed.

On the long stretches of open sea, the navigators of the treasure fleet did their best to avoid bad weather. The cumulative wisdom of the diviners and astrologers was collected into forecasting proverbs, which the ships' meteorologists memorized. They studied the sky, the sea, and the currents for the slightest changes:

> At dawn, look to the southeast. If it is dark,
> there will be rain before noon.
> At dusk, look to the northeast. If it is dark,
> there will be rain at midnight.
> If there are clouds in the sky like flowing silk,
> you can expect a fine day.
> But, if in the morning clouds rise from the sea,
> soon there will be wind and rain.

At some unknown point on the long journey home the sky was read, but there was no escaping its ominous portents. The fleet was caught in a violent storm. Perhaps the ships had begun their northward tack through the treacherous South China Sea, where typhoons materialize without warning. Wherever they were, the frightened crew believed they had come upon a giant dragon beneath the ocean, a furious beast who churned the high seas with its powerful claws and spit showers of spray and foam. Afraid the ships would capsize and they would be lost in the deep, the sailors called out the name of Tianfei, the Celestial Consort, and, "as swiftly as an echo," their prayers were answered. "Suddenly, there was a magic lantern in the mast and as soon as this miraculous light appeared, the danger was becalmed. Everyone on the fleet, set at rest, felt assured that there was [now] nothing to fear."

The men had witnessed Saint Elmo's fire, an electrical phenomenon well known to Western sailors. But to Zheng He it was a miracle, and so grateful was he upon the fleet's safe return to Nanjing that he appealed to the emperor to give the goddess an honorary title. The emperor granted his request and bestowed the name of "protector of the country and defender of the people" on Tianfei. But to Zheng He this was not sufficient tribute. Though the emperor immediately ordered a second expedition to return the ambassadors home and assist Calicut in the installation of its zamurin, Zheng He did not accompany the ships, which departed in late 1407 or early 1408. He remained in China to repair the Tianfei Temple at Meizhou, Putian, in Fujian, the birthplace of the goddess. He may also have had something to do with the establishment of a school for translators in Nanjing, a portent of future voyages to lands in the Persian

Gulf and beyond. And apparently he had a conversation with the emperor about the whereabouts of Zhu Yunwen.

Whatever Zheng He said, the emperor was still very worried that his predecessor was alive, but he did not involve the treasure fleet any further in the search. The focus of his concern was now China itself. In November of 1407 he ordered a court official named Hu Ying to look for Yunwen throughout the Middle Kingdom. It was a mission that would occupy the next twenty years of his life and almost the entire reign of Zhu Di. Zhu Di did not even allow Hu Ying to return from his wandering for his mother's funeral. Periodically, Hu Ying was asked to send large-character reports to the nearsighted emperor so that he could read them himself.

While the treasure fleet was at sea on its second expedition, the king of Brunei, on the west coast of Borneo, visited China. He was the first king to personally pay his respects to the emperor and acknowledge the suzerainty of the dragon throne. Three years earlier, Zhu Di had recognized Brunei as an independent state no longer under the authority of Java and had agreed to trade directly with its ruler. The forests of Brunei had camphor, gums, and resins, which the Chinese were eager to obtain for their medicinal properties.

Landing in Fujian province with his family and an entourage of 150 officials, the king of Brunei was escorted to Nanjing and well received at court. Shortly after that, however, he became very ill and the concerned emperor reportedly sent his personal physician to attend him.

"In my illness I have been the recipient of the Son of Heaven's concern and thoughtfulness," the king told his wife. "If I should pass away, it is fate. From a remote region and desolate frontier, I have had the good fortune of coming to pay homage at court, to look upon the brilliance and reputation of the Son of Heaven; if I die, it is without regrets. And if in death my body and soul are put to rest in China, I will not be a barbarian ghost. I regret only that having received the great favor of the Son of Heaven, and having not been able to repay him in this life, I truly shall be beholden to him in death."

Not long after that the king's condition worsened, and he died at age thirty-eight. To show his respect, the emperor stopped business at court for three days and assigned officials to attend to his burial. The emperor commissioned the inscription on the tablet that marked the king of Brunei's tomb outside Nanjing. It reads:

Alas, tributary king! Outstanding and exceptional.
In all the countries of the southwest,
No one can be compared to him.
Faithful and sincere in life, ennobled in death,
Granted the title of king to pass on to his descendants,
Given a grand tomb with halls, [offered] sacrifices
To comfort his royal spirit
For an eternity beyond reckoning.
Though he did not return home,
The king is greatly renowned
[For] the Son of Heaven's magnificent favor
Shall shine [on him] for ten thousand generations!

The emperor also commissioned a pair of life-sized stone warriors, clad in armor and holding swords, to guard the tomb. The statues are accompanied by a pair of solemn stone scholars and pairs of carved stone rams, tigers, and horses with saddles beautifully etched in an Indonesian motif, all to create a sacred path to the burial mound.

Weeping as she knelt before the emperor's envoy, the queen of Brunei said, "[The king] left an order that the Son of Heaven should always be remembered."

The imperial envoy then presented her with jewelry, gold, fine fabrics, clothes, and household objects as a parting gift. The king's son received a crown and belt befitting his rank, clothing, and a saddle and bridle. No measure was spared to secure favorable trade relations with Brunei.

Meanwhile, on the way to Calicut, the treasure fleet made a stop in Siam. It suited Zhu Di's policy of "fragmentation" of the barbarians to seek relations with the Siamese and aid them in their struggle with the Khmers, whom the Siamese princes had been fighting constantly since 1350. Also, in 1408, China invaded and annexed the unruly Annam, and it certainly did not need another unfriendly neighbor near its southern border.

The fleet probably returned the Siamese ambassador and his party home. In 1407, at its own initiative, Siam had sent envoys to the Ming court with tribute of elephants, parrots, and peacocks, which pleased the emperor very much. He responded in turn with generous gifts of money, Chinese court costumes, and fine writing materials. China valued trade relations with Siam for its rich supply of hardwoods, aloes, incense, ivory, kingfishers' feathers, tin, cardamom, and chaulmoogra-seed oil, which was used as a treatment for leprosy. In Siam women were the traders. In fact, women seemed to make all the decisions and, according to Chinese sources, enjoyed a rather liberated lifestyle.

"It is their custom that all affairs are managed by their wives," wrote Zheng He's translator, Ma Huan. "Both the king of the country and the common people, if they have matters which require thought and deliberation—punishments light and heavy, all trading transactions great and small—they all follow the decisions of their wives, [for] the mental capacity of the wives certainly exceeds that of the men."

Ma Huan goes on to note that sometimes the married Siamese women were very intimate with the Chinese envoys—eating, drinking, and sleeping with them. Their husbands did not mind. Rather, they took it as a compliment, saying, "My wife is beautiful and the man from the Middle Kingdom is delighted with her."

The Chinese were also shocked to discover that when the Siamese men moved, they made a tinkling noise like tiny bells. This was because, at age twenty, upper-class men had a dozen tin or gold beads partly filled with sand inserted into their scrotums. It looked "like a cluster of grapes," wrote Ma Huan, "a most curious thing," but the vain Siamese considered it "beautiful."

The second expedition concluded with the installation of Mana Vikraman as the new zamurin of Calicut. In Zheng He's place, eunuchs Wang Jinghong and Hou Xian, who were in command of the treasure fleet, erected a stone tablet and pavilion in the Indian city, commemorating the warm relationship between the two countries. The inscription reads:

> Though the journey from this country to the Middle Kingdom is more than a hundred thousand *li*, yet the people are very similar, happy and prosperous, with identical customs. We have here engraved a stone, a perpetual declaration for ten thousand ages.

The second expedition of the treasure ships had only sixty-eight ships, perhaps because some of the warships had been deemed unnecessary and left at home. With the pirate nest in Sumatra eliminated, the seas were certainly safer. Together, the two voyages had reestablished China's trade links in southeast Asia. A steady influx of foreign goods and information resumed, and China's formidable presence would be felt in the coming years from Japan to the east coast of Africa. The treasure ships cast long shadows across the seas.

6 The Strange Kingdoms of Malacca and Ceylon

In the fall of 1409, a treasure fleet had again been assembled at Liujia harbor at the mouth of the Zangzi for a third voyage to the Indian Ocean. This time, Zheng He was personally in command of the forty-eight ships and thirty thousand men. Eunuchs Wang Jinghong and Hou Xian were his principal deputies. The fleet made a brief stop in Taiping on the Fujian coast, then sailed on to Champa, arriving ten days later. Temasek (the future Singapore) was reached in a fair wind in eight days, and Malacca, farther up the Malay Peninsula, two days later.

In 1405 the Malaccan ruler Parameswara had visited the Ming court and sworn his alliance to Zhu Di, for which he was rewarded with a Chinese seal of investiture recognizing the fledgling city-state of Malacca as an independent kingdom. Enraged at this gesture, the Siamese, who claimed authority over Malacca, snatched the seal away from Parameswara on his way home. Zhu Di learned of the theft in October of 1407. One of the purposes of the third expedition of the treasure ships was to give Malacca a new seal and thus support its status as a power on an equal footing with the Siamese and the powerful Javanese to the south. The Chinese wanted to keep both of their ambitious trading partners in check, and Parameswara was a convenient and very willing foil.

Parameswara, a young Palembang prince, had managed in a short period of time to alienate both his neighbors, so he very much needed the protection of the Chinese. The history of his hasty departure from Palembang on the east coast of Sumatra and subsequent founding of Malacca is shadowy and entwined with myth, but it seems clear that he was a "very warlike man" who had openly rebelled against the Javanese overlord of Palembang in 1391 or 1392.

He and his followers were driven out of Sumatra and fled to Temasek, which Parameswara hoped to make the new Malay capital. While he was there, however, he killed a Siamese vassal and was expelled from the city. Parameswara and his band then wandered up the west coast of Malaysia, finally settling sometime around 1400 in a small fishing village that had a good harbor free of mangroves and a hill that could be easily defended.

As legend relates, while Parameswara was resting beneath a tree near the village during a hunt, he happened to see a mouse deer, barely a foot tall, kicking one of his hunting dogs. He was astonished at the boldness of the small creature.

"This is a good place, if even the mouse deer are full of fight!" he said. "We would do well to make a city here."

And so he decided he and his renegade followers would stay there, and he ordered his chiefs to begin building a city.

"What is the name of the tree under which I was standing?" he asked the chiefs.

"It is called 'malacca,' " they responded.

"Then Malacca shall be the name of this city," Parameswara said.

Three years later, Malacca's population had swelled to two thousand. A royal compound was built on the prominent hill near the harbor, and thatched wooden houses on stilts clustered at the base of the hill and on the other side of the Malacca River, which meanders into the interior. A covered bridge connected the two residential areas and served as a marketplace for both the citizens and the growing overseas trade. With little to offer in the way of natural resources, Malacca's survival depended on overseas trade and its location midway between the spice islands of Indonesia and the Malabar coast of India. In time the city's marketplace became well known throughout the Indian Ocean. Cloves, nutmeg, and other island spices, along with seed pearls, bird plumes, and batiks were exchanged here for Indian textiles. Malacca also bartered its own tin. Parameswara soon came into conflict with rival Sumatran trading ports just across the strait, and, in a brazen move, he sent out patrol boats to force passing foreign vessels to call on Malacca.

Zheng He was probably not aware of Parameswara's aggressive trade practices when he arrived in Malacca, and he certainly would not have approved of them. The point of recognizing the sovereignty of Malacca, from China's point of view, was to enhance the stability of the region. Zheng He presented Parameswara with two silver seals, an official hat, and a royal girdle and robe and set up a stone tablet officially declaring the city and its environs a country. Zhu Di had personally overseen the composition of the text for the Malaccan stele—an unusual gesture for a Chinese emperor and one he would repeat three more times during his reign in efforts to secure closer relations with Japan, Brunei, and Cochin in south India.

In the Malaccan tablet inscription Zhu Di described the role of "sagacious and virtuous rulers" in aiding "the workings of heaven, earth and humanity." His deceased father, "the Supreme Ancestor, sagelike and divine," had been such a ruler. Moreover, it was because of the first Ming emperor's "overflowing favor and good blessings" that Malacca was now enjoying such peace and prosperity. Zhu Di acknowledged Malacca's wish "to be treated as a subject state of the Middle Kingdom in order to excel and be distinguished from the barbarian domains" and formally designated the city-state's west mountain as "Guardian Peak of the Kingdom," thus elevating Malacca to the status of vassal state. A commemorative plaque included a poem praising Malacca and its king:

> Its righteous king, paying his respects to imperial suzerainty, wishes his country to be treated as one of our interior domains and to follow the Chinese way.

Whatever "the Chinese way" was, Parameswara did not seem to give it much thought. His primary concern was to free himself immediately from Siamese authority—which he did by refusing to pay the Siamese ruler the expected annual tribute of forty-eight ounces of gold. This angered the Siamese, who continued to harass Malacca, but they knew there was little they could do. An outright invasion of Malacca was now out of the question and would have endangered their own trade with the Middle Kingdom.

In Malacca Zheng He obtained ebony, aloes, and a native tree resin called dammar, used as a caulking material and lighting fluid. Historically, the Malay Peninsula was known as an ancient source of gold, which had attracted Indian merchants in the early centuries of the Christian era, but there is no mention of gold in Ming records. Malacca was nonetheless a valued trading partner to the Chinese because it was the gateway to the Indian Ocean. On future expeditions there, Zheng He established an entrepôt where goods from throughout the Indian Ocean and south seas could be collected and stored before the final leg of the journey home. He built a stockade with towers and four gates near the harbor. Inside the stockade were granaries and warehouses that were carefully guarded both day and night. It is unclear whether this facility was abandoned completely between voyages or if it was maintained as a permanent Chinese colony in Malacca for the duration of Zheng He's later expeditions. Fei Xin, an officer who traveled with Zheng He on those voyages, seems to suggest the latter and also the possibility that the transplanted Chinese took Malay wives and raised families in Malacca.

Writing in *Xing cha sheng lan* (Marvelous visions from the star raft) in 1436, Fei noted in his description of the Malays that "their skin resembled black lacquer, but there were [some] white-skinned people among them who are of Chinese descent."

Like many of the southern Chinese, the Malays were descended from early Yi peoples. In later centuries the population had mixed with darker-skinned colonists from India. The stylized motifs on the early southeast Asian bronze drums—spiral bands, longboats, and men in feather headdresses—have survived in Malay textile patterns, bamboo carvings, and traditional house designs. Although Buddhism and Hinduism came to the Malay Peninsula in the first centuries A.D., much of the ancient religion and folk beliefs remained. Zheng He and his men noted them with curiosity on their many visits.

They discovered that the Malays believed in a soul, *semargat*, that inhabited all things—men, animals, boats, houses, trees, rivers. (The Melanesians and Polynesians called it *mana*.) If the spirit of the tin mine was offended, the mine would produce no tin. If rice grains realized they were being severed from the mother plant, the seeds would not germinate. The Chinese observed special Malay customs associated with mining and reaping, and they learned from the Malays that of all the spirits, kind and malevolent, the most feared were the spirits of people who had been grievously wronged in life.

Zheng He's translator, Ma Huan, spoke of the terrifying "corpse-head barbarian," which was supposed to be the wandering soul of a woman who had died in childbirth. The spirit appeared at night, a ghastly apparition of a disembodied head with dangling entrails that preyed on helpless newborns.

"The head," wrote Ma Huan, "eats the tapering faeces of human infants; the infant, affected by the evil influence which invades its abdomen, inevitably dies." Malays often planted thorns beneath their houses to snare the entrails of the vampire spirit so it would do them no harm.

Malaccans also greatly feared men who could turn themselves

into menacing tigers and stalk their enemies. In the interior highlands of the Malay Peninsula, there were thought to be villages where these were-tigers lived in huts thatched with women's hair. Zheng He's officers reported the strange coming and going of these "black tigers . . . with dark stripes." Upon entering towns, they thought that the tigers turned into men and mixed with the people. "After they have been recognized," wrote Ma Huan, "they are captured and killed." Women in their first pregnancy were supposed to have been particularly vulnerable to were-tiger attacks. It is said that tigers can smell the sweet blood of such women across seven hills and seven valleys. One could, however, keep the tigers away with special chants.

> Ho! mighty Brahma,
> Lord of the earth,
> Take away thy cat!
> Harm not nor destroy my body!
> May my teacher be strong to free me
> Ho! mighty and powerful Ali!
> Bow low and love me
> Have love and affection for me!
> May my teacher be potent.

Fear of the were-tigers perhaps kept Zheng He's men close to their ships in Malacca harbor. They did not seem to be adventurous explorers in foreign lands. After the Portuguese took Malacca in 1511 and introduced Christianity to the Malays, were-tigers were combated with exorcisms, but the belief never died and in rural communities lingers to this day.

Before departing, Zheng He provided Parameswara with an escort and a ship to take him and his family to China. The new vassal wished to express his gratitude to the Yongle emperor with tributes and gifts.

From Malacca the treasure fleet sailed on to Sumatra, stopping at Semudera and another place on the east coast near Tamiang, where Zheng He's men, according to Fei Xin, "cut wood." Because rudders were easily damaged on long voyages, Zheng He was always on the lookout for hardwoods suitable for emergency replacements. In the forests of Siam he discovered mahogany, which is extremely hard and heavy and makes excellent rudders. For this remarkable wood, he paid the Siamese in gold. The forested interior of Sumatra and other Indonesian islands also yielded such precious tree resins as camphor, frankincense, and gharawood, used in making incense, and pepper, ginger, and healing herbs. Sulfur, another important medicine, was found in abundance near Sumatra's active volcanoes.

The dramatic population rise in China in the early Ming dynasty was coupled with frequent outbreaks of infectious diseases, particularly measles and smallpox. In 1407, 78,400 died from epidemics in Jiangsu and Fujian provinces alone. Epidemics struck China again in 1410, 1411, and 1413. The restrictive trade policy of the Hongwu emperor also meant that there was an extreme shortage of foreign medicinal herbs on the eve of the voyages of the treasure fleet. The desperate need for medicines must have been on Zheng He's mind in recruiting the 180 physicians and pharmacists who served on the fleet, more than would have been necessary simply to take care of sick men on board. Kuang Yu from Changshu in Jiangsu province, for example, was a specialist in collecting medicinal plants and joined the fleet at the Taiping anchorage.

The most important medicines he and the other pharmacists would have been seeking were rhinoceros horn, used as an antitoxin for snake bites; deer antlers, believed to strengthen bones and restore sexual potency; sulfur, also valued in Western medicine as a skin ointment and cure for rheumatism and lung ailments; and chaulmoogra oil, used to treat leprosy. Aromatics, such as frankincense, myrrh, camphor, pepper, cloves, cardamom, gharawood, putchuck, storax, and benzoin, were also used in large quantities because, although they did not cure infections, they provided relief when inhaled or applied to the skin as a paste. Incense was also used to drive away mosquitoes, thus preventing the spread of disease. Many of the herbs Zheng He's men collected had to have been processed immediately on the treasure ships—steamed, boiled, soaked, or dried—to retain their effectiveness for later use.

From Sumatra the fleet sailed on to the island of Ceylon, where a curious sequence of events took place. Zheng He carried with him an unusual trilingual tablet in Chinese, Tamil, and Persian, which he hoped to erect on the island. The tablet bore the date February 15, 1409, indicating that it had been inscribed in Nanjing before the treasure fleet departed for the third voyage. The Chinese portion of the tablet praised Buddha and offered thanks for his protection of the treasure fleet on its two previous voyages:

His Imperial Majesty, Emperor of the Great Ming, has dispatched the Grand Eunuchs Zheng He, Wang Jinghong and others, to set forth his utterances before the Lord Buddha, the World-Honored One, as follows:

Deeply do we revere Thee, Merciful and Honored One, of bright perfection wide-embracing, whose Way and virtue passes all understanding, whose Law pervades all human relations, and the years of whose great *kalpa* rival the river-sands in number; Thou whose controlling influence ennobles and converts, inspiring acts of love and giving intelligent insight [into the nature of this vale of tears]; Thou whose mysterious response is limitless! The temples and monasteries of Ceylon's mountainous isle, lying in the southern ocean far, are imbued and enlightened by Thy miraculously responsive power.

Of late we have dispatched missions to announce our Mandate to foreign nations and during their journeys over the oceans they have been favored with the blessing of Thy beneficent protection. They have escaped disaster or misfortune, journeying in safety to and fro, ever guided by Thy great virtue.

Wherefore according to the Rites we bestow offerings in recompense, and do now reverently present before the Lord Buddha, the World-Honored One, obligations of gold and silver, gold-embroidered jeweled banners of variegated silk, incense-burners and flower-vases, silks of many colors in lining and exterior, lamps and candles with other gifts in order to manifest the high honor of the Lord Buddha. May His light shine upon the donors.

The Tamil portion of the tablet offered similar praise to the Hindu god Tenavarai-Nayanar, perhaps a local form of Siva, and the Persian inscription praised the glory of Allah and the saints of Islam. To each god the Chinese gave equal tribute so none would be slighted: 1,000 pieces of gold, 5,000 pieces of silver, 100 bolts of silk, and more than 3,000 pounds of perfumed oil, as well as gilded and lacquered ecclesiastical ornaments. On the surface, this appears to be a respectful and generous gesture on the part of the Chinese, showing Zheng He's awareness of the religious tradition of the island.

Ceylon held a special place in the minds of ancient and medieval travelers. So beautiful was the island that the Arabs thought it was God's compensation to Adam and Eve for the loss of paradise. According to legend, Ceylon was settled by an Indian prince, Vijaya, on the day Buddha died in 483 B.C. The Sinhalese believe they have a special destiny as defenders of the faith.

"In Lanka, O lord of gods, will my religion be established," Buddha said. "Therefore, carefully protect him [Vijaya] and his followers and Lanka."

A branch of the Bo tree under which Buddha received enlightenment was supposed to have come to Ceylon. In the sixth century, a relic believed to be the tooth of Buddha was brought to the island from India and became the symbol of authority for Sinhalese kings, who were themselves considered semidivine bodhisattvas, that is, those who would become buddhas. Sinhalese kings took great care to keep the *dalada,* as the tooth relic was called, in their possession. And when the capital changed, as it frequently did, the kings would build a new container and building, called the *dalada maligava,* to house the sacred tooth.

On the eve of Zheng He's arrival in Ceylon, the once unified island was divided into three warring states. The principal Singhalese authorities in the center of the island were fighting both the Hindu Tamils, who had a foothold in the north, and a Muslim usurper who was trying to make Islam the state religion. Nissanka Alagakkonara (or Alakeswara), a local chief, having successfully rebuffed a large Tamil invasion, now harbored ambitions of seizing power from the legitimate Singhalese ruler in Kotte. It was a troubled time in the country, making the Singhalese mistrustful of one another and especially leery of foreigners. Greeks, Romans, Persians, Jews, and Arabs had all come to their shores, each wanting something, and Singhalese history told of constant battles with the dark-skinned Tamils from southern India, who periodically controlled the island. To survive in their own land, the Singhalese were forced to become masters of guerrilla warfare and deceit, and sometimes they turned their special skills on each other.

It was Alakeswara, the skillful warrior and hero in the war against the Tamils, not the legitimate rulers of the capital cities of Gampola or Kotte, who met Zheng He upon his arrival in Ceylon. And it was Alakeswara who flatly refused to pay tribute to the Chinese emperor or to erect the tablet, which he thought was some symbol of Chinese sovereignty. He handily beat the Chinese in a brief skirmish and drove them back to their ships.

After sailing on to India and conducting their trading in Quilon, Cochin, and Calicut, the Chinese returned to Ceylon to avenge this ingratitude and disrespect to the dragon throne. What happened after that is the subject of considerable debate. The Chinese and the Singhalese recorded two very different versions of the events.

According to *Ming shi lu,* the veritable record of the period, Alakeswara sent his son to demand gold, silver, and precious things from Zheng He. When Zheng He refused, he ordered fifty thousand troops to seize the treasure fleet. The soldiers cut down trees to block Zheng He's way back to the coast.

When Zheng He discovered this, he said, "Since most of the barbarian forces are heading toward the ships, there must be only a few to defend the capital."

Zheng He marshaled the forces at hand, who numbered about two thousand, and easily seized Alakeswara in the capital. After fending off the Singhalese army, which by now had surrounded the capital, Zheng He made an escape back to the ships with Alakeswara as prisoner.

He took Alakeswara back to Nanjing, where the emperor and court officials considered his fate. Zhu Di, it was reported, finally decided to pardon "the king" for his ignorance and ordered "one of his wise followers" to rule in his place. The account is unclear about the identities of both the king and the wise follower. The wise follower could well have been the legitimate ruler of Ceylon, who may have been taken captive along with Alakeswara by the Chinese. Indeed, the Ming sources seem confused about the local power structure.

Nevertheless, the bravery of Zheng He and his men in this incident is celebrated in verse. The victory is considered the most glorious moment in the history of the voyages, where "one fought against a hundred" and the spirit of Zheng He's men was "unbreakable."

> Straight-away, their dens and hideouts we ravaged,
> And made captive that entire country,
> Bringing back to our august capital,
> Their women, children, families and retainers, leaving not one,
> Cleaning out in a single sweep those noxious pests, as if winnowing chaff from grain . . .
> These insignificant worms, deserving to die ten thousand times over, trembling in fear . . .
> Did not even merit the punishment of Heaven.
> Thus the august emperor spared their lives,
> And they humbly kowtowed, making crude sounds and
> Praising the sage-like virtue of the imperial Ming ruler.

Singhalese histories tell quite a different story.

Alakeswara, they say, saw the return of the angry Chinese as a way of disposing of his adversary, Vijaya Bahu VI, and seizing the throne of Kotte himself. Alakeswara supposedly entered into negotiations with Zheng He and then lulled his adversary into receiving the gift-bearing Chinese envoys in his palace. Once in the palace, according to Singhalese accounts, the Chinese seized the king and several of his nobles and chiefs.

The emperor, however, released the "king" and promptly returned him to Ceylon. On this the Chinese and Singhalese sources agree. Perhaps Zhu Di uncovered the ruse and wanted to have no part in helping a pretender dethrone a legitimate king. According to Singhalese histories, when Vijaya Bahu VI returned to Ceylon, he was first welcomed by Alakeswara, who secretly murdered him in the night. Vijaya's wife and young son managed to escape Kotte and hide from Alakeswara for three years. During that time, Buddhist priests, who were loyal to the royal family, told Alakeswara that he could not be crowned king until he had rebuilt the capital. This Alakeswara proceeded to do. He added new buildings and baths to Kotte and widened the city's streets.

Finally, in the spring of 1415, a date was set for his coronation. At the very moment Alakeswara was to be crowned on a raised platform before a square filled with people, the sixteen-year-old son of Vijaya Bahu VI took the state sword that was to have annointed Alakeswara and killed him. The prince was hailed as the new king of Kotte, named Sri Parakrama Bahu VI. Other histories date the beginning of his reign to 1412 and say that it was Sri Parakrama Bahu VI—not Alakeswara—who rebuilt Kotte.

The story, whether fact or legend, makes a hero out of one of the island's great kings and portrays the Singhalese as fiercely proud and independent. In 1284, when Khubilai Khan's fleet visited Sri Lanka, the Singhalese believed that the Mongols had come to take away the sacred tooth of Buddha, and it is clear that they suspected Zheng He had the same purpose in mind. It may well have been more than supposition. There is at least one Chinese record that states Zheng He did, in fact, take the precious relic, which he placed in Jinghai Temple outside Nanjing. If true, the story, omitted in official histories of the voyages, would certainly explain the "rude" behavior of the Singhalese and why they "plotted to hurt Zheng He."

The anecdote, which appears in the *Ming bei ben ta Tang xi you ji* (the Ming edition of the "Travels to the Western Regions during the Tang") describes in some detail how delighted Zheng He's crew was to have the sacred tooth on board and how it seemed to protect them on their way home to China. "The tooth shone brightly. Everyone was amazed and turned their eyes from it. Then they commenced their journey. They encountered gigantic waves for hundreds of miles, but these did not disturb the ships for it was as if the fleet were moving across dry land. The fierce dragons beneath the sea and dangerous fish let the ships pass. The men were happy." On July 9, 1411, the tooth was taken into the capital, and "the emperor ordered a diamond and jeweled case to house the tooth for the well-being of all the people."

The truth of this important incident probably lies somewhere between the two partial accounts. Very likely both the Singhalese and the Chinese troops had their moments of glory in battle. Although the sacred tooth would have been a most coveted treasure at the Buddhist temple in Nanjing, it seems unlikely Zheng He would have taken it, given his obvious respect for the three religions of Ceylon, so eloquently expressed in the tablet. Rather, it may well have been that the Singhalese king was captured by Zheng He and took the sacred tooth with him to China to prevent it from falling into the hands of the usurper Alakeswara.

If Vijaya Bahu VI was captured and took the sacred tooth with him to China, it would certainly have helped convince the Yongle emperor that he was the legitimate ruler of Ceylon—and may have had something to do with his release thirteen months later. Likewise, the presence of the sacred tooth on board the treasure fleet would have created considerable excitement, which would have been remembered and recorded. Zhu Di may even have ordered the building of some special container or chamber for the tooth, as the *Ming bei ben ta Tang xi you ji* mentioned, during the year the relic was in China. But, by the time Vijaya's son was crowned in Kotte, the sacred tooth seems to have been safely back in Ceylon. Singhalese histories describe in considerable detail the new *dalada maligava* built by Sri Parakrama Bahu VI in Kotte and state specifically that, when the building and container were completed, the king personally placed the tooth relic inside:

> For the Tooth-relic of the Sage, the king caused to be built a three-storied palace delightful and beautiful to behold, and made a gold casket finely set with nine gems, and he encased it in another golden

> casket set with excellent gems, shining with vari-colored rays, which he encased in another golden casket. Moreover, when he had made a great and excellent covering casket, gilt with the best and most resplendent gold, that king, who longed for happiness during the continuation of existence and even at extinction (nirvana), placed the Tooth-relic within the four caskets.

Because of the capture of Vijaya Bahu VI, the Yongle emperor claimed sovereignty over Ceylon and demanded regular tribute. At first the young Singhalese king appeared to have had no wish to flout Chinese authority openly as Alakeswara had done and agreed to the arrangement. In 1459, however, after he had succeeded in reuniting the island under one authority and his power was at its height, he said his kingdom would acknowledge no master and sent the emissaries of the dragon throne back to China without tribute.

Zheng He returned from his third voyage on June 16, 1411 and in the months that followed, a steady stream of tribute-bearing ambassadors traveled to the Ming court from the countries the treasure fleet had visited. The Bengalese envoy arrived at the end of June, followed in July by the rulers of Calicut, Cochin, and Java, and finally by the newly appointed king of Malacca and his wife.

While in Nanjing, all foreign dignitaries were housed at the Hui Tong Hall on the west side of Chang'an Street in Nanjing. This extensive compound had four hundred servants to cook for the visitors and tend to their needs, and physicians remained on call in case any foreigners should become ill. Room assignments at the guest house were determined by the ranks of the visitors, and menus of wine, tea, meat, noodles, and other foods also varied according to status. All foreigners were given a piece of wood as an identification card, which was stamped with characters each time they entered or left the guest house. Envoys were strictly forbidden to go into the streets and mingle with ordinary people or to trade in street markets.

Elaborate procedures were set up by the Ministry of Rites to deal with the various kinds of tribute and trade items the foreign envoys brought with them. Horses were first carefully examined by veterinarians, who filed detailed reports. Then they were paraded before high-ranking officials, who assigned them to various imperial stables. Elephants were sent to special places to be tamed. Tigers, leopards, birds, and chickens, however, were kept at the guest house. Gold, silver, precious stones, pearls, and fabrics were examined in front of the envoys who had brought them, then handed over the following day to the Ministry of Revenue.

After presenting their tribute, foreign kings and envoys received personal gifts from the emperor. Then they were allowed to set up a market open to the public at the guest house for three to five days. Some favored countries, such as Korea, were granted unlimited trading time. A notice of the market was posted on the door of Hui Tong Hall. Government regulations stipulated that the trade be "fair," and if any Chinese merchants took fabrics to be dyed and did not return them to the foreigners, this would be considered a crime and the merchants would be shackled and placed in front of the guest house for one month. It was forbidden to sell foreigners certain Chinese goods, for example, official histories, because they contained information on the location of garrisons, canals and locks, and storage areas for grain, as well as other facts that might have compromised the security of the empire. Coins, metals, weapons of any kind, fine artisan's tools, medicinal herbs, and local products in limited supply were also forbidden. If anyone conspired with officials of the guest house to collect the forbidden goods, they would be shackled for one month, then exiled to the "border regions" of the empire. If foreigners violated the regulations and sneaked into houses of ordinary people to trade, they were spared the humiliation of arrest, but they would be punished by a paucity of gifts from the emperor.

Of all the tributes Zhu Di received that summer from the many envoys who paid their respects to the Ming court, one gift stood out among the rest—a curious device that had the remarkable power to make small written characters appear large. The Chinese called the mechanism *aidai,* approximating the sound of the Arab word *'uwaina,* meaning "eye." It was a primitive eyeglass, perhaps a single lens with a handle, that may well have been China's first encounter with spectacles. Parameswara of Malacca was said to have presented ten *aidai* to Zhu Di, valued at one thousand pieces of gold. Malaccan merchants undoubtedly obtained the lenses in trade with the West, where eyeglasses had been developed in Venice and elsewhere a few decades before. The early Ming marked the beginning of glass-making in China, and in fact some sources say that Zheng He returned to China with two skilled glassblowers, presumably from the Middle East.

Zhu Di's delight in this unusual gift is perhaps expressed in his generosity toward Parameswara, his family, and his ministers. They were showered with gifts: imperial robes with embroidered dragons and *qilin* (unicorns), jade and gold belts, horses with saddles, hundreds of ounces of gold and silver, twenty-six hundred strings of copper coins, and quantities of plain silk, silk gauze, and silk embroidered with gold flowers. Each of Parameswara's servants was given shoes and a new set of clothes. This far exceeded the usual display of imperial favor toward visiting heads of state.

During their several months' stay in Nanjing, the foreign envoys would have been feted with at least one imperial banquet, which frequently coincided with such important festivals as New Year's Day or the emperor's birthday. Smaller feasts were arranged when the ambassadors first arrived and when they departed China, usually from Guangzhou. At all banquets, special kinds of food were served in designated amounts to foreign visitors according to their rank, from servant to head of state. The highest officials were served five kinds of wine and fruit, soup with translucent bean noodles, roasts of horsemeat, beef and lamb, fried pancakes and steamed bread, and "flower tea" with little pastries arranged on a plate like a flower. Guards and servants of foreigners were given plain steamed bread. In addition, throughout Nanjing there were also sixteen *jiu lou* (wine houses) where foreign envoys could go during their stay to eat and drink and enjoy themselves with *guan ji* (official call girls). The girls, often purchased in markets for about the price of a pig, were trained in singing, dancing, theatrical performances, storytelling, and word games to please patrons. Like Japanese geishas, they also provided sexual pleasures. From time to time the Ministry of Rites arranged special entertainment for foreign envoys, such as polo matches, horse racing, and archery contests. At one such occasion, held by the emperor on a fine May day in 1413, court officials and dignitaries gathered in a large field outside Nanjing that was decorated with flags and banners. A shooting target—a small circle mounted on a willow stalk—had been set up at one end of the field, and archers tried to hit the mark from a hundred paces at a full gallop. It was reported that the emperor's grandson succeeded on the first try. Each round was heralded with flutes and drums, and after the contest the winners were rewarded with prizes and scholars recited impromptu poems before the crowd of officials and foreign guests.

• • •

Just how profitable the trade markets of Hui Tong Hall were during the summer of 1411—or indeed how rich the flow of tributary gifts—is not recorded in the Ming official histories. But it can be surmised that after three successful voyages of the treasure fleet, Zhu Di felt comfortable enough with the empire's finances to order the building of an extravagant porcelain pagoda to show gratitude to his putative mother, Empress Ma. This lavish display of filial piety, undoubtedly intended to underscore Zhu Di's claim to the throne, was located just outside the south gate of Nanjing. Begun in 1412, the octagonal pagoda took nearly twenty years to complete and was regarded by European visitors in the eighteenth and nineteenth centuries as one of the seven wonders of the world.

At nine stories, it stood over 240 feet high, and it was built of the finest white porcelain-glazed tiles with exquisitely carved porcelain figures and animals in various colored glazes around the windows and doors. Each story was fashioned with exactly the same number of tiles, and the tiles became smaller as the graceful structure narrowed to a point. The base of the gilt finial at the top of the temple was twelve feet in diameter and was decorated with 152 porcelain bells that chimed in the wind. The finial itself, covered in gold leaf, shone brilliantly in the sun. Around the temple were beautiful gardens and exotic trees that Zheng He had brought back from his voyages.

At times as many as a hundred thousand workers were employed in the construction of the Bao'en complex, which eventually consisted of more than twenty buildings and terraces in addition to the porcelain pagoda. The cost was reported to be over 2.5 million ounces of silver and was taken from surplus revenues of the treasure fleet. The voyages of the treasure fleet had clearly established China's superiority in the Indian Ocean trade, which it would maintain until the arrival of the Portuguese in the early sixteenth century.

Before the complex was completely destroyed in the Taiping Rebellion of 1856, Longfellow among other poets celebrated the delicate beauty of the pagoda, which had stood as a dazzling monument to maritime China and the success of Zheng He's mission:

> And yonder by Nanking, behold
> The Tower of porcelain, strange and old,

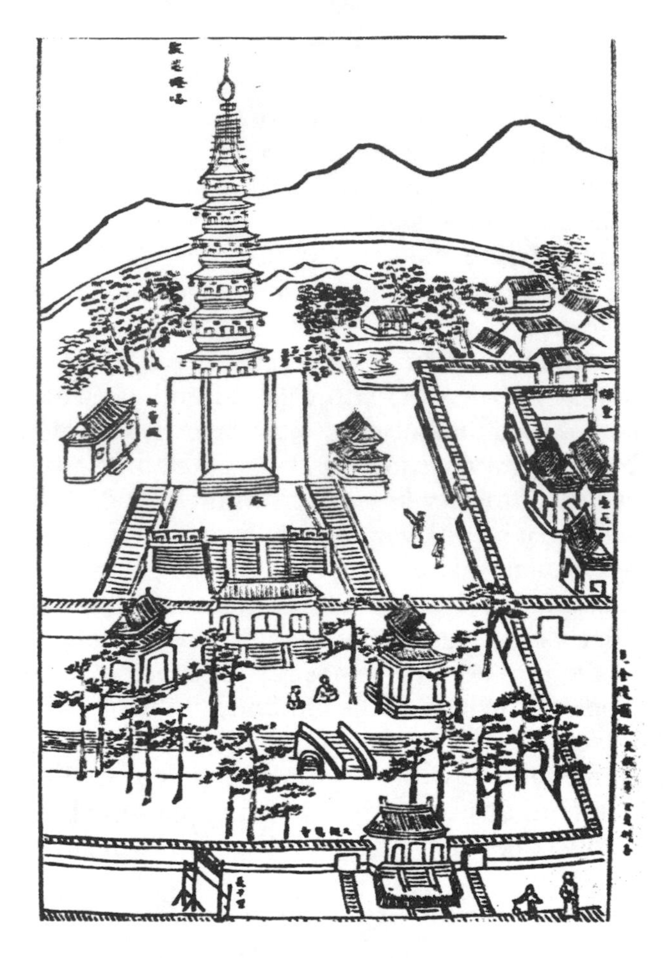

The Yongle emperor built Nanjing's magnificent Bao'en Temple complex with revenues from the treasure fleet's expeditions.

Uplifting to the astonished skies
Its ninefold painted balconies,
With balustrade of twining leaves,
And roofs of tile beneath whose eaves
Hang porcelain bells that all the time
Ring with a soft melodious chime,
While the whole fabric is ablaze
With varied tints all fused in one
Great mass of colour like a maze
Of flowers illumined by the sun.

7 Emissaries of the Dragon Throne

The Japanese were among the first to visit Zhu Di after he became emperor. Yoshimitsu, the third Ashikaga shogun, was a great lover of Chinese culture and anxious to commence commercial relations with China.

Bowing before the emperor, the Japanese envoy said he carried a letter from the shogun, who referred to himself as "your subject, the King of Japan." Later shoguns would bristle at the memory of this humiliating salutation. Delighted at this immediate and ingratiating acknowledgment of his accession to the dragon throne, Zhu Di promptly reopened government trading stations at Ningbo, Quanzhou, and Guangdong and sent a minister to Japan to set up a commercial agreement whereby Japanese trade delegations would be permitted to trade at Ningbo if they presented special government tallies. The agreement stipulated that two trading ships from Japan, which were to carry a total of no more than two hundred men and no weapons, could trade every ten years. Apparently with Zhu Di's acquiescence, the Japanese disregarded the last restriction, and trade missions arrived frequently from 1403 until the shogun's death in 1410.

Thus early in his reign, it was clear that Zhu Di, while giving lip service to his father's foreign policy directives, was charting a different course for China. Hounded by enemies both in and outside the empire, the Ming founder viewed unrestricted private trade as inherently destabilizing and threatening. He reasoned that the sole purpose of tribute trade was to keep his neighbors in check. Zhu Yuanzhang was also leery of sending armies outside the empire unless clearly provoked, and wrote in the *Zu xun lu* (Ancestral injunctions) "that future generations might abuse China's wealth and power and covet the military glories of the moment to send armies into the field without reason and cause a loss of life." Zhu

Di ignored this advice as well, invading Annam (northern Vietnam) in 1407 under the pretext of restoring a legitimate ruler to the throne. The war, which pitted Chinese imperial armies against Annamese guerrilla forces, dragged on for twenty years, foreshadowing the United States' own involvement there more than five hundred years later.

The Yongle emperor viewed the *Zu xun lu* merely as a guide to formulating his own foreign policy, not as decrees written in stone. Unofficially, his father's directives were overlooked as he believed changing circumstances warranted. Young and confident, Zhu Di was a prince who had been reared to reign, not a pauper soldier like his father, who was fearful of foreigners and outside influences. And from the moment Zhu Di seized the dragon throne, he played on a world stage as no emperor had done before. The voyages of the treasure ships were among nearly fifty emissarial missions dispatched by the Yongle emperor during his twenty-four-year reign. They were but one part of a grander scheme to extend China's influence and power to the world's "four corners."

At the same time that he sent Zheng He to the south seas, he also moved to stabilize relations with the troublesome Mongols on China's frontiers. For very different reasons, he reached out to improve relations with Tibet and Korea. For these missions Zhu Di also frequently chose eunuchs who like Zheng He had been captured as youths in frontier regions and had knowledge of foreign languages and customs. All of this was occurring simultaneously with the voyages of the treasure ships, in a dizzying display of diplomatic maneuvering that at times must have been bewildering even to the Ming court and that would have repercussions for centuries.

Zhu Di had little trouble establishing friendly relations with the Uriyangqad Mongols in the immediate area around Beijing. Uriyangqad horsemen had fought with him in the civil war and were essential to his victory. As a reward, the emperor withdrew the Chinese garrisons from north of the present-day Great Wall and left the Uriyangqad in charge of large portions of Inner Mongolia. Similarly, Zhu Di was quickly able to stabilize relations with the Jurchen in Manchuria by granting military titles to their powerful chieftains. The illusory honor meant that the chieftains were, in fact, subject to a degree of Chinese control. In 1406 horse markets were established on the border and there was some movement of Chinese settlers into southern Manchuria. At the markets, the Chinese exchanged silk and textiles for the sturdy Mongolian horses they so desired, as well as furs, gyrfalcons, and ginseng. Northern Manchuria, however, which was populated by the so-called wild Jurchen, tribal herdsmen, and other Siberian peoples, eluded Chinese influence. This area worried Zhu Di.

In 1411 the emperor sent a eunuch named Yishiha, who had been born in southern Manchuria, to try to approach the Jurchen chieftains in Nurkal, a remote section of northern Manchuria. Yishiha, who like Zheng He had been captured in skirmishes with the Chinese, castrated, and trained at the imperial court, departed Kirin with twenty-five ships and one thousand men. In Nurkal he succeeded in convincing the chiefs to send a mission of 178 men to offer tribute to Zhu Di. Delighted, the emperor rewarded the chiefs with titles and money and granted them trading privileges. Yishiha was subsequently sent on two more missions to northern Manchuria, in 1413 and 1432. He built a Buddhist monastery in honor of Guanyin, the Goddess of Mercy, in Yongning in the Amur region and erected a trilingual tablet celebrating his success in "pacifying" the Jurchens. The temple was damaged shortly after it was completed, and though it was repaired by Yishiha, it is doubtful that Buddhism or Chinese culture had much of an effect on these northern peoples. Chinese relations with the Jurchens gradually deteriorated after Yishiha's last mission, and the Jurchens joined with the western Mongols (Oirats) in Outer Mongolia in attacking China in the 1440s.

The Timurids, the Oirats, and the eastern Mongols, all Mongolian peoples on China's western frontier, were thorns in Zhu Di's side throughout his reign. His diplomatic efforts frequently provoked rather than quelled their belligerence. Though they had very real needs for Chinese goods, particularly Chinese medicines, they could not long stomach China's stifling protocol or demeaning insistence that they acknowledge the suzerainty of the dragon throne.

In official communications with the Timurids, Zhu Di repeated his father's mistake of calling himself "lord of the realms of the face of the earth." This so enraged the great Timurid leader Timur or Tamerlane—Turkish conqueror of Persia, India, and most of central Asia—that he detained the Ming envoys and vowed angrily to subdue the arrogant Chinese. Arriving in Samarkand, seat of the Timurid empire in 1403, Spanish envoy Ruy González de Clavijo was given the honor of sitting in a higher chair at court than the envoys of Zhu Di. Timur referred to the Chinese emperor disparagingly in Clavijo's presence as a "thief and a bad man" and his "enemy."

On January 8, 1405, Timur made good his threat to invade China and with an army of two hundred thousand proceeded to march across the frozen Jaxartes River in heavy snow. It was doubtful Zhu Di had any idea of the seriousness of this action, which could well have brought the Ming dynasty to a close when it had scarcely begun. The court apparently took no special precautions to avert the attack. Fortunately for China, the great Mongol commander was stricken with a fever in a place called Otrar and died on January 17, 1405, at the age of sixty-nine. His body was embalmed in musk, wrapped in linen, and taken back to Samarkand for burial. His successor, Shāhrukh Bahadur, had no designs on China, but simply wanted to keep his father's far-flung empire together. The Chinese emissaries who had been detained in Samarkand by Timur were released; Zhu Di, in response, sent a non-Chinese central Asian named Bo'a'erxintai to perform sacrifices at Timur's tomb. Good relations between Zhu Di and Shāhrukh were eventually established, perhaps with the help of envoys from both countries who softened their leaders' harsh words for each other with more pleasing translations. Shāhrukh's impertinent suggestion that Zhu Di convert to Islam in order to promote good relations with him may never have actually been communicated to the Ming court. It does not appear in official Ming annals.

Peace with the Oirats to the northwest and the eastern Mongols, who were closer to the Chinese borders, was, however, more difficult to achieve. Neither had made their peace with the Ming empire after the collapse of the Yuan dynasty, and they were frequently at odds with each other. In 1409 Zhu Di dispatched Guo Ji to try to reach a conciliation with the new Oirat chief, Arughtai, but the Chinese envoy was summarily executed. In response, Zhu Di personally led an army against Arughtai and succeeded in driving the Oirats back one hundred *li*. It would be the first of four campaigns against them; each time, like a shadow puppet, Arughtai would vanish into the steppe country and then reappear with fresh troops for another raid on the Chinese borders. Occasionally, Arughtai acknowledged China's demands for recognition of sovereignty and tribute payments, but peace was never more than a respite in the continued hostilities and futile military campaigns.

In 1413, however, during one of the periods of calm, Zhu Di sent envoy Chen Cheng on a hazardous fact-finding mission through the towns and capitals of central Asia. Chen's accounts of the journey north across the great Taklamakan Desert and extended stay in Shāhrukh's capital at Herat became important sources of information on the region in the early Ming.

The envoy, accompanied by the eunuch Li Ta and an official of the Ministry of Revenue named Li Xian, stopped in Hami, Karakhoto, and Turfan before heading into the Timurid territories and visiting the towns of Tashkent, Samarkand, and finally Herat. They passed through desert areas with little water and frozen lands of snow and ice where they were lost in blizzards. Skeletons of animals lined the route, testaments to the hostility of the region; and people, when they encountered them, were more often than not dressed strangely and described by the envoys as "ferocious."

In Herat, where the envoys stayed several months, they were entertained by Shāhrukh in his palace, which was decorated with plush carpets, silk screens, and exquisitely carved woodwork. They feasted on the sweet fruits from the sultan's orchards—peaches, pears, pomegranates, plums, and grapes—served on gold trays, and the envoys marveled at the enormous size of the local onions and cabbages and the delicately flavored pistachios. Exploring the city, the Chinese envoys found bazaars bustling day and night and commodities such as copper, iron, gold, silver, amber, coral, and diamonds in plentiful supply.

Chen wrote in his diary that people took great care of their fine horses, keeping them "warm in winter and cool in summer." He said there were no temples to the gods or ancestral shrines, but that Muslims bowed to the west in the direction of Mecca several times a day and that there were strange fanatics (dervishes) who abandoned their homes and possessions and wandered among the people instructing them in divine messages. The behavior of the women of Herat shocked him. He found them outspoken and unrestrained in their actions—they even rode horses astride like men. He made note of the city's bathhouses, whose masseurs catered to both men and women.

Zhu Di ordered a second mission to the Timurids in 1416 and a third in 1418. The language of his letters to Shāhrukh gradually changed. He began to call him "friend" and praise him as "enlightened, perceptive, knowing, mature, sensible and greater than all Muslims." He showered the Timurid ruler with gifts of silver, silks, brocades, falcons, and porcelains and expressed his desire that envoys and merchants should travel between the two countries without interruption. Shāhrukh responded generously, and during Zhu Di's reign some delegations from Samarkand and Herat, forty-four envoys from Hami, and another thirty-two ambassadors from other central Asian towns arrived at the Ming court with tribute gifts of horses, lions, and leopards for Zhu Di.

Profit was the main motive for Mongolian tribute missions to the Ming court, and professional traders always accompanied the diplomatic envoys. For this, the Timurids, the Uriyangqads, and the southern Jurchens were willing to kowtow to the Chinese emperor. While the chiefs coveted such luxuries as special flower-patterned and gold-embroidered silks, there were many ordinary things the Mongols lacked in their daily life. They depended on the Chinese for such essentials as metal tools, drugs, needles, and thread. In 1408 even the proud Arughtai humbled himself, sending an envoy named Hafiz to the Ming court to ask for medicines, which Zhu Di granted. A second request for medicinal herbs came in 1430, when Arughtai himself was ill. Mongol envoys sometimes specifically requested Chinese ginseng, wood aromatics, divination and "yin-yang" books, and cosmetics. Mongolian women used white powder and a vermilion powder, perhaps as a rouge,and also a yellow powder, which they rubbed on their foreheads. The Mongols also obtained from the Chinese a black ointment or greasepaint, which the wives of chiefs used as an eyeliner. They shaved their natural eyebrows, then painted a dramatic brow over each eye with the black liner. Requests for rice and grain were seldom granted because the court feared that such supplies would enable the Mongols to prepare for war.

When the Mongolian envoys entered Chinese territory, their horses and belongings were taken from them and placed in the hands of servants. All of the foreign envoys' needs were met by court-appointed escorts and post houses, where the Mongolian envoys stayed on their way to the capital. Post houses and a system of signal towers had been built from the edges of the empire to the capital to convey messages rapidly to the emperor. Fires blazing atop the towers, which were within sight of one another, spread word of important news to the capital in a day. Relay runners then sped from station to station with the message, covering in a few days a route of hundreds of miles that normally took several weeks.

For foreign envoys traveling within China, the post houses supplied carts, horses, and young boys to carry possessions. Every night, the envoys were given "a couch, a suit of silken sleeping dress,

Dragon boats racing on the palace lake.

Yuan dynasty handscroll by Wang Chen-peng (National Palace Museum, Taipei)

Court portrait of Zhu Di, the Yongle emperor. (National Palace Museum, Taipei)

Empress Xu, wife of Zhu Di. (National Palace Museum, Taipei)

Imperial riverboat procession, Ming dynasty. (National Palace Museum, Taipei)

Giraffe from Malindi on the east African coast, thought to be the mythical qilin, *is presented at the Yongle court in 1414. Court calligrapher Shen Du captured the moment and also composed the accompanying song, praising the virtues of the* qilin—

> *. . . Gentle is this animal, that in all antiquity has been sent but once.*
> *The manifestation to its divine spirit rises up to heaven's abode.*

(National Palace Museum, Taipei)

Portrait of a Daoist priest, Ming dynasty. (National Palace Museum, Taipei)

"Former Daoist Sages" (detail), Ming dynasty (ca. 1460). (Shanxi Provincial Museum, photograph by Don Hamilton)

"Former Masters of Professions and Arts" (detail), Ming dynasty (ca. 1460). (Shanxi Provincial Museum, photograph by Don Hamilton)

Giant carved statues, civil officials (right), and military officers, line the mile-long spirit path leading to the tomb of the Yongle emperor outside Beijing. After the emperor died in 1424, the voyages of the treasure fleet were stopped for six years. (Photograph by Louise Levathes)

As a rebel who usurped the throne, the Yongle emperor used size to reinforce his legitimacy. At the same time he was building the 400-foot-long treasure ships, among the largest wooden boats ever built, he also ordered an enormous stone tablet—135 feet high, 45 feet wide, and 12 feet thick—built for his father's tomb. Before the work was finished at a quarry outside Nanjing (below), the emperor was informed it was too heavy to be moved. It remains there today, a monument to the monumentality of the Yongle emperor. (Photograph by Louise Levathes)

There is no agreement as to exactly what the treasure ships of Zheng He looked like. But, the model (above), completed in 1985, represents a consensus of scholarly opinion in China and is on display at the Zheng He Research Institute in Nanjing, Jiangsu. (Courtesy of the Zheng He Research Institute, photograph by Louise Levathes)

The Xuande emperor took after his grandfather, Zhu Di, and was a great horseman. He also believed China should have more contact with foreign countries and initiated one final, grand voyage of the treasure fleet in 1430. (National Palace Museum, Taipei)

Always mindful of invasion from the sea, the Chinese built important ports, such as Kaifeng (above), on inland rivers, a safe distance from the coast. But with the disbanding of the Ming treasure fleet by the 16th century, Japanese pirates raided China's shores undeterred. (National Palace Museum, Taipei)

together with a servant to attend to their needs." They were also well fed with meals of mutton, fowl, bread, rice, pickled vegetables, wine, and beer. Post houses kept records of all arrivals and departures and what services had been rendered.

The daily rations allotted to one emissarial mission of seventy-seven people from Persia during the Yongle period consisted of 12 sheep, 4 ducks, 50 bottles of wine, about 200 pounds of rice and 140 pounds of fruit, 120 pounds of flour, 200 baked cakes, one tray of sugared cakes, vegetables, and spices. As the size of the Mongol missions grew toward the middle of the fifteenth century, food requirements clearly became a burden to the court. One Oirat mission in the 1440s consisted of twenty-four hundred men, who reportedly managed to consume five thousand sheep during their two-month stay in China.

When Mongols or other foreign emissaries arrived at the Ming court, they were interviewed by a member of the Ministry of Rites about the customs and geography of their country, and a map based on the information was drawn and presented to the emperor. If their costumes were particularly unusual, a drawing of their faces and clothes was also done.

From the outset of his reign, Zhu Di paid special attention to China's relationship with Tibet's various religious leaders. He made contact with many of them but seemed to have a closer association with the fifth karmapa, Bebshin Shegpa, who controlled the area of southeastern Tibet, to whom he offered support in suppressing rival Buddhist sects.

As a young prince, Zhu Di had heard of the extraordinary power of the karmapa, which means "master of karma" or "man of action." The first karmapa was honored as a living Buddha, an emanation of the compassionate bodhisattva Avalokiteshvara, who came into the world to alleviate the suffering of humanity. It was said that before his birth in 1384, the fifth karmapa was reciting prayers and the alphabet inside his mother's womb and that his mother dreamt of rainbows and showers of flowers and sweet fragrances.

In 1405 Zhu Di sent the eunuch Hou Xian and the monk Zhiguang to invite the karmapa, who was known in China as Halima, to come to Nanjing. The twenty-four-year-old monk accepted and traveled from his great religious center at Tshurphu, forty miles from Lhasa, via the Karma Gon and Lha Ten Gon monasteries, finally arriving at the Chinese capital on April 10, 1407. At the gates of Nanjing, where thousands of officials in formal attire and a large crowd of Buddhist monks had gathered to meet him, the karmapa was placed on an elephant and Zhu Di gave him the gold wheel of *dharma*, symbolizing the law of Buddha set into motion. The karmapa then presented the emperor with a white conch shell, symbol of the spoken word. At the reception and banquet that followed, Zhu Di honored the karmapa by placing him on a throne higher than his own and making him head of all Buddhist monks in China. The emperor invited the Tibetan lama to perform services for his father and mother at Linggu Temple. According to both Chinese and Tibetan accounts, the monk's stay in Nanjing was marked by a succession of "miraculous" occurrences, which may have been the result of the lama's skillful coordination of his services with extraordinary weather conditions.

Above the Buddhist temple containing sacred relics, it was reported, "a ray of light, like the full moon, shone out unblemished." Likewise, bands of gold rays appeared above the dwelling place of the karmapa himself. Several days later, the southwestern sky was suddenly filled with "iridescent clouds, shaped like begging-bowls" and the figures of deified *arhats* or saints, followed by a large retinue. People also believed they could actually see the saints in the streets. On two occasions "heavenly flowers" were said to have fallen from the sky, and on others several people thought they saw monks flying through the air. On the fourteenth day after the karmapa's arrival, a white crane was seen dancing in the sky, a rainbow seemed to encircle the sun, and various auspicious phantom shapes appeared in the clouds: lions, elephants, dragons, and bodhisattvas.

After these events the emperor gave the karmapa the title "Divine son of India below the sky and upon the earth, inventor of the alphabet, incarnated Buddha, maintainer of the kingdom's prosperity, source of rhetoric." He instructed the court painters to make a record of the miracles on a fifty-foot-long, silk-backed scroll, which the karmapa took back with him to Tshurphu. Before he left, however, the karmapa visited the Buddhist center at Mount Wutai in Shanxi and performed other ceremonies for the emperor's parents. The Yongle emperor also had a vision. He saw a mystic *vajra* hat made from the hairs of a hundred thousand *dakinis* or female deities hovering above the karmapa's head. He ordered that a square black hat with a diamond-studded emblem be made, and he gave it to the karmapa. It has been used by successive incarnations of karmapas, becoming the symbol of the sect, and is believed to have the power to bestow deliverance upon all those who see it.

During the karmapa's visit, Zhu Di had troops poised on the border to invade Tibet. He told the karmapa that there were too many Buddhist sects and offered to assist him in establishing one true sect by means of force. The karmapa explained that this was not his wish and it would not benefit mankind. Various methods of teaching, he insisted, were required to respond to people's spiritual needs. Against his ministers' advice, Zhu Di withdrew the troops, and the karmapa, who died not long after of smallpox at the age of thirty-two, was credited with saving his country from a Chinese invasion.

Of all the emissarial missions during the Yongle period, perhaps the most curious were the sojourns across the Yellow Sea to bring back hundreds of Korean virgins for the imperial harem. The envoys on such trips were almost exclusively eunuchs, whose primary responsibilities in the palace since ancient times had been as managers and guardians of the concubines and other matters of the imperial bedchamber.

Very little is actually known about the inner workings of the Ming court. Ming emperors were paranoid about personal information leaking outside the walls of the Forbidden City, and palace women too old to be of service to the emperor were confined in isolated compounds until they died. Later Qing Dynasty descriptions may reflect what was going on in the Ming court, but this is impossible to verfiy. In Qing times it was the responsibility of the *jing shi fang tai jian* (eunuch director in charge of the royal bedchamber) to record each time the emperor had intimate relations with the empress because the dates would be proof of the conception of a royal heir. Every night after dinner, the chief eunuch presented the emperor with a silver tray on which were arranged the nameplates of his favorite concubines. If the emperor was not in the mood for intimate relations, he would decline. If he was, he would select a nameplate and turn it facedown on the tray.

The chief eunuch supposedly would then hand the nameplate of the chosen concubine to another eunuch, whose sole responsibility it was to undress the concubine, wrap her in a feathered garment, and carry her on his back to the emperor's bedchamber. The eunuch would remain outside the bedchamber for a given length of time

Multiple partners were recommended particularly for the emperor, and part of the tribute trade with Korea involved "gifts" of hundreds of virgins during the Yongle reign.

and then shout, *"Shi shi hou le!"* (Now it's time!). This would be repeated if necessary three times before the eunuch finally entered the emperor's bedroom and collected the concubine. He would ask the emperor if he wanted the woman to bear his child, and if he said yes, the date would be recorded. If he replied in the negative, the eunuch would carry the concubine back to her quarters and administer contraceptive herbs, such as *ling hua* or "cold flower," which was suppose to induce menstrual bleeding.

In September 1402 Zhu Di dispatched Yu Shiji to inform Yi Pangwon, the ruler of Korea, of his accession to the dragon throne. Yi immediately sent an envoy to Zhu Di, requesting a new seal of investiture and acknowledging the suzerainty of the Middle Kingdom. Zhu Di granted honorary titles to the king and his heirs and initiated the exchange of several emissarial missions a year. Yi was anxious to receive Chinese herbal medicines for his ailing father, as well as silks, books, and musical instruments. China, in return, requested ginseng, local lacquerware, leopards, seals, and an unusually heavy tribute burden of 150 ounces of gold, 700 ounces of silver, and large numbers of horses and oxen. A thousand horses were sent to China in 1403, 10,000 oxen in 1404, 3,000 horses in 1407, and more boatloads of both in 1410.

In addition, Zhu Di demanded as tribute hundreds of the country's most beautiful maidens to serve at his pleasure in the imperial harem. Korean women were famous for their delicate features. The eunuch Huang Yan was sent to Korea in 1408 and selected three hundred girls, including one named Kwon, who would become one of Zhu Di's favorite mistresses. China demanded more virgins the following year, and the Koreans bristled. The memory of this humiliation, along with the use of Korean "comfort girls" by Japanese armies in this century, has still not faded from the Korean national conscience.

It was more than desire that prompted the emperor to order this steady influx of hundreds of young women into his bedchamber. As early as the Tang dynasty, elaborate treatises by Daoist physicians outlined sexual behavior for two very different purposes. For the conception of children, they believed that a man's "yang" essence and a woman's "yin" essence had to be brought together with "complete harmony." To this end, they advised that great care be taken in choosing an auspicious day and hour for sex and in preparing the bed and bedchamber, which had to be draped in yellow silk, the color of fertile earth. Couples were also instructed to insert the branch of a peach tree—peaches being the symbol of female genitalia and fertility—into the bed canopy or couch where they would lie. Sexual intercourse and the creation of children were embraced unself-consciously, guiltlessly, as part of the cosmic process, like life-giving rain saturating the earth.

Confucianism offered little advice in intimate relations other than to emphasize the overriding importance of filial responsibility and to express concern for the smooth running of polygamous households. Daoism, however, articulated men's and women's relationships with one another and with the natural world. According to its tenets, a man needed sexual contact "to nourish his vital essence" and to keep him "free from disease." This was thought to be par-

Daoist erotic treatises compared sex to a "battle" in which the man had to be careful to preserve his "yang" essence.

ticularly important for men over forty, who were supposedly susceptible to "countless diseases that descended upon [them] like a swarm of bees." To this end, it was vital that a man keep himself under complete control and preserve all of his "yang" essence, while at the same time engaging in extensive sexual play to stimulate a women to shed her "yin" essence. Since yin and yang were thought to be the two essential ingredients which brought forth all things, a man who retained both became spiritually complete and achieved "true yang." Every time a man experienced true yang, it was thought he added twelve years to his life. A man who had true yang with ninety-three women, Daoists believed, would become immortal.

In Chinese treatises this kind of sexual experience was likened to a battle, in which, in order to defeat the "enemy," the man had to spare his own force while using the strength of his opponent, that is, the woman. The same principle underlies Chinese military strategy and judo, the Japanese art of self-defense. It was advised that men first practice the control necessary for true yang on unappealing women, taking time to rest immediately afterward.

> I withdraw from the battlefield and dismiss my soldiers, I rest quietly to regain my strength. I convey the booty to the storeroom, thereby increasing my power to the height of strength.

"True yang" was best attempted with young women, because after a while a woman's yin essence would "become weak" and be of little use to a man. It was also said to be important that the sexual contact with any one woman not be prolonged, lest the yin essence absorbed by the man overpower his own yang essence and harm him. In effect, the Daoists cautioned against the power of intimacy and sanctioned multiple sexual partners. They specifically prescribed that the emperor have relations with nine concubines every night and sleep with the empress for two nights each month during the full moon.

Zhu Di was forty years old when he became emperor. After acceding to the throne, he would have no other children. He was also in poor health. He suffered from a variety of debilitating ailments, and his demands for shiploads of young women from Korea may have been frantic efforts to rejuvenate himself or at least to gain the appearance of vitality as he undertook the enormous tasks that lay before him.

8 The Auspicious Appearance of the Celestial Animals

On December 18, 1412, the Yongle emperor issued an order for the fourth expedition of the treasure ships. It was to be the largest fleet yet assembled—sixty-three vessels and a total crew of 28,560 men—and the most ambitious adventure. The first three voyages had accomplished their goals. The dragon throne had reopened trade with the countries of the south seas and managed to restore some harmony and peace to the area. At the 1416 dedication of the Jinghai Temple in Nanjing, the emperor had said the "seas had been conquered and there was quiet in the four corners." Now Zhu Di wanted to venture into the Persian Gulf and the purpose of the voyages shifted dramatically. The later expeditions of the treasure fleet became a very personal expression of the ambition and megalomania of the third Ming emperor and, as such, a unique expression in Chinese history.

Although Zhu Di's order for the fourth expedition was given in December 1412, Zheng He was not ready to leave Nanjing until almost a year later, and it was not until January 1414 that the treasure fleet finally departed the Fujian coast. The planned sojourn beyond India to the rich Arab port of Hormuz at the entrance to the Persian Gulf required additional preparation and planning.

For this voyage, Zheng He recruited the twenty-five-year-old Muslim translator Ma Huan, who would become the chief chronicler of the voyages. Although he humbly described himself as "a mountain woodcutter," the young man from Hangzhou Bay was well schooled in the Confucian classics and knew Arabic. His writing reveals a man who abhorred violence and killing and who was perhaps a bit gullible, quick to believe stories he had heard in foreign lands of ghosts and vampires and howling banshees. Yet he was a keen observer of social customs, providing in some cases the first eyewitness accounts of life among the diverse peoples of the Indian Ocean basin.

Zheng He made the long journey to Xi'an in north China to personally ask Hasan, the spiritual leader of the Qingjing mosque, to join the expedition as a translator and adviser. During a bad storm on the voyage, Hasan's prayers were said to have calmed the winds and seas, and upon his return Zheng He contributed generously to the Xi'an mosque, endowing a building that became known as Chong Lou, or "Building of Respect."

What sparked the emperor's sudden interest in going to the Persian Gulf is not certain, although the wealth of Hormuz was well known to the Chinese. The world's most magnificent pearls from the banks off Bahrain were strung by the skilled craftsmen of the port city, who drew on the rich resources of the surrounding countryside to offer foreign merchants gold, silver, copper, iron, cinnabar, and salt. It was also a center for trade in precious stones. After 1262 Hormuz was ruled by the Ilkhans of Persia and surpassed Suhar and Muscat as the area's most important commercial port. In the thirteenth century, Arab traveler Ibn Battūtah called it "a fine city with magnificent bazaars," and a Persian proverb stated, "If the world were a ring, Hormuz would be the jewel of that ring."

The prospect of trading with wealthy, cultured Hormuz clearly intrigued Zhu Di. After sitting on the dragon throne for twelve years, the emperor was approaching the peak of his power. At home he embarked on an ambitious plan to move the capital from Nanjing to his old fief at Beiping. All the resources of the empire were being mobilized for this enormous task, which involved the costly repair of the Grand Canal and the cutting and transport of huge quantities of timber from as far away as Sichuan and Annam. It may have been that Zhu Di wanted to tap the wealth of Hormuz and bring back exotic treasures to add to the glory of his new capital's palace, which was just beginning to be built. He gave officers of the treasure fleet coins to obtain goods. Why should the Son of Heaven not also reach for the ring of the world?

While Zheng He made his customary stops at Champa, Java, various Sumatran and Malay ports, the Maldives, Ceylon, and India before going on to Hormuz, a branch of the treasure fleet under the eunuch Yang Min sailed to the kingdom of Bengal, now mainly in Bangladesh. The trading in the south seas was uneventful, as far as one can judge, until Zheng He reached the city-state of Semudera on the northeast coast of the island of Sumatra. The Chinese name for Semudera was "Liuqiu," which means "sulfur ball," suggesting perhaps the city's importance as a supplier of precious sulfur for medicines. In any case, its unsettled internal affairs were sufficiently disturbing to the dragon throne that Zheng He was ordered to intervene militarily to restore order.

The trouble had started in 1407, when the king of Semudera was killed by a poison arrow in a battle with a neighboring state, which was called by the Chinese simply *hua mian wang guo*, meaning "the colored-face kingdom." The name may have referred to an upland Sumatran aboriginal people who tattooed their faces. The queen of Semudera was left with a son who was too young to avenge his father's death, and so she announced she would marry anyone who would stand up to their enemy. A fisherman came forward and led an attack on the colored-face kingdom, killing the ruler. The queen dutifully married him, and the people of Semudera called him *lao wang*, meaning "old king."

When the young prince grew up, however, he killed his stepfather and seized the crown of Semudera for himself. The younger brother of the fisherman king, named Sekander, fled into the mountains with a band of followers and led a rebellion against the prince. The prince sent envoys to the Ming court, asking to be recognized by the emperor as the rightful ruler and seeking his assistance against the usurper Sekander.

Zhu Di decided to overlook the murky legitimacy issue and gave his support to the prince. When Zheng He landed in Semudera, he proceeded to trade as usual with him, showering him with gifts. This enraged Sekander, who felt snubbed by the gesture and led ten thousand men against Zheng He. Zheng He now had a convenient explanation—self-defense—for attacking Sekander. His snub may well have been a deliberate way of luring Sekander into a fight without appearing to choose sides in the civil war. When Sekander withdrew to the neighboring town of Atjeh, Zheng He pursued and finally captured him and his family. To ensure there would be no further disturbances in Semudera, Sekander was taken back to China.

From Semudera the treasure fleet left the coast of Sumatra and sailed southwest across the Indian Ocean for ten days, reaching the Maldive Islands, where Ma Huan noted that there were no walled cities, only people "crowded together" against the islands' hills. The treasure fleet sailed cautiously through the treacherous waters among the eight principal islands. Coconut trees were abundant here, and sailors from every foreign port purchased ropes made of coconut fibers. The Maldive Islanders themselves used coconut twine to bind the planks of their boats together.

In the Maldives, Zheng He and his men also purchased ambergris, which was worth its weight in silver, and obtained tiny cowrie shells, used elsewhere as money. The delicate shells, which are folded like tiny clenched fists, were so numerous in the Maldives that the islanders simply piled them in high heaps on the shore.

Not lingering in Ceylon or Calicut, the treasure fleet set sail from the Indian coast for distant Hormuz. Fair winds shortened the journey to twenty-five days, during which the fleet covered sixty-one sea miles daily. (In 1432 the same voyage would take thirty-four days, and only forty-five miles were covered in a day's sail.) The excitement of the Chinese upon their arrival at Hormuz is evident in Ma Huan's record. He reported that the people were "very rich" and their dress "handsome, distinctive, elegant." There were no poor families in Hormuz, he added, because "if a family meets with misfortune resulting in poverty, everyone gives them clothes and food and capital, and relieves their distress."

The Chinese eagerly traded their porcelains and silks for Hormuz's sapphires, rubies, oriental topaz, pearls, coral beads, amber, woolens, and carpets. Some of these were given to the emissaries of the dragon throne as tribute gifts for the emperor, along with lions, leopards, and Arabian horses. Either here or in Calicut, Zheng He probably met merchants from the east African city-states of Mogadishu, Brawa, and Malindi whom he persuaded to return with him to China and pay tribute to the emperor—which they did.

Meanwhile, while Zheng He was in Hormuz, Yang Min returned to China with the new king of Bengal, Saifu'd-Din. The king had brought with him (at Yang Min's insistence, no doubt) an extraordinary present for the emperor. It was a gentle animal with a long neck and two fleshy horns—a giraffe—that had been given to the king by the ruler of Malindi in what is now Kenya. Yang Min, however, had never seen the creature before and mistook it for the mythical *qilin,* one of four sacred animals in China, along with the dragon, the phoenix, and the tortoise. The *qilin* was believed to make its appearance only in times of great peace and prosperity. It was said to have the body of a musk deer, the tail of an ox, the forehead of a wolf, the hooves of a horse, and a fleshy horn like a unicorn. Other descriptions noted that the male animal, called simply *lin*, sometimes had two or three horns. The *qilin* did not eat meat and avoided treading on any living thing, even grass, and thus became for the Chinese a symbol of goodness, appearing only in a land well governed or when a sage was born. Confucius's mother was thought to have become pregnant by a *qilin* when she stepped on the footprint of the animal while walking in the woods. Another such tale said that a *qilin* simply appeared before her and dropped a piece of jade from its mouth inscribed with the words "the son of the essence of water shall succeed to the withering Zhou and be a throneless king." Confucius's mother then was supposed to have tied a piece of embroidered ribbon around the *qilin*'s horn before the animal disappeared.

Yang Min knew that the appearance of such an auspicious symbol would please and flatter the Yongle emperor. Surely the *qilin* was a sign from heaven, a culmination of the emperor's sagacious virtue. What other explanation could there be? Court officials asked the emperor if they could be allowed to present him with a formal proclamation of congratulations. The emperor, however, turned down their request, saying, "Let the ministers from early [in the morning] until late exert themselves in assisting the government for the welfare of the world. If the world is at peace, even without *qilin*, there is nothing that hinders good government. Let the congratulations be omitted."

Behind the modest gesture, however, the emperor was undoubtedly very pleased. A Hanlin Academy calligrapher, Shen Du, was directed to paint the animal, and he also composed a laudatory hymn extolling the virtues of Zhu Di and his late father. The *qilin* was presented at the court on September 20, 1414, and, as Shen Du's song described, everyone gathered around "to gaze at it and their joy knew no end."

> In a corner of the western seas, in the stagnant waters of a great morass,
> Truly was produced a *qilin*, whose shape was as high as fifteen feet,
> With the body of a deer and the tail of an ox, and a fleshy, boneless horn,
> With luminous spots like a red cloud or purple mist.
> Its hoofs do not tread on [living] beings and in its wanderings it carefully selects its ground,
> It walks in stately fashion and in its every motion it observes a rhythm,

Its harmonious voice sounds like a bell or a musical tube.
Gentle is this animal, that in all antiquity has been seen but once,
The manifestation of its divine spirit rises up to heaven's abode.

The following summer, in 1415, Zheng He and the treasure fleet returned to Nanjing. On August 12 Sekander, the rebel leader in Semudera, was presented to the emperor, who ordered him executed. For one who was himself a usurper of the throne, Zhu Di showed no tolerance for civil disobedience in tribute countries, particularly where trade had been disrupted and his emissaries had encountered hostility. Unlike the Portuguese, who a hundred years later bulldozed their way into the South China seas by building a string of forts, the Chinese simply arranged to replace unfriendly foreign leaders in countries where they encountered difficulties with someone who was willing to trade on their terms.

At this moment Chinese influence abroad was at its peak, and all the important trading ports in the Indian Ocean basin and China seas—from Korea and Japan throughout the Malay Archipelago and India to the east African coast—were at least nominally under Chinese authority and acknowledged the suzerainty of the dragon throne. From this lofty pinnacle China could have consolidated its position and become the dominant power in shaping the modern world. While Europe was still emerging from the Dark Ages, China, with her navy of giant junks, was poised to become the colonial power of the sixteenth century and tap the riches of the globe. The appearance of the *qilin* indeed heralded an auspicious time, ripe with possibilities, but the emperor was already beginning to focus his and the empire's energies inward. That moment at the pinnacle would last barely more than five years.

The foreign envoys Zheng He brought back with him from his fourth voyage were formally received at court on November 16, 1416. Ambassadors from Malindi had arrived with another giraffe, undoubtedly at the encouragement of Zheng He. Again Lu Chen, president of the Ministry of Rites, had asked the emperor for permission to issue a formal memorial of congratulation for the appearance of this *qilin,* and again Zhu Di refused.

"If formerly, when the scholars and ministers presented the complete edition of the five classics and four books and asked permission to offer up a memorial of congratulation, we permitted it," said the emperor. "It was because this book benefits good government. But what gain or loss is there whether there is a *qilin* or not? Let the matter be shelved."

The Yongle emperor again gave the appropriate, self-effacing answer: Confucian texts were far more important to good government than the appearance of strange animals. Yet Zhu Di did formally receive the animal at the palace gate in Nanjing along with "celestial horses" (zebras) and "celestial stags" (probably oryx), also from Malindi. The crowd of officials and foreign envoys who gathered there prostrated themselves on the ground before the emperor.

"This event is due to the abundant virtue of the late emperor, my father, and also to the assistance rendered me by my ministers," said Zhu Di, looking out over the scene. "That is why distant people arrive in uninterrupted succession. From now on it behooves you even more than in the past to cling to virtue and to remonstrate with us about our shortcomings."

It was at this moment, when few would fail to be impressed by the repetition of heaven's favor, that Zhu Di for the first time requested formal court discussion of the planned move of the capital from Nanjing to Beiping. The emperor commissioned a series of propaganda paintings by court artist Wang Fu with accompanying poems to extol the virtues of Beiping, particularly its strategic importance as defender of Juyong pass and the northern frontier. Wang used the occasion to praise the achievements of the Yongle emperor (with his allusion to the North Star) and previous Ming emperors for expanding and unifying the empire:

> Mountain ridges in endless layers, trees luxuriantly dark.
> A radiance shimmers on dark green mountains, arrayed to face the sun.
> Standing tall in the blue clouds, they nearly reach the North Star.
> Covering a vast distance, they link the Great Wall and East Ocean.
> Their roads penetrate the remotest lands to bring foreign emissaries.
> Heaven created this deep pass to fortify the imperial capital.
> The empire is unified with standardized measurements and script.
> We might well make a rubbing from a cliff inscription to send to the emperor.

Court officials quickly obliged the emperor with the expected approval of what was, by then, a fait accompli. For in 1403, the year after he became emperor, Zhu Di had already ordered Beiping, "northern peace," renamed "Beijing," meaning "northern capital," and established a transitional government there with six ministries and a branch of the military. In the years following 1403, 120,000 households were relocated in Beijing and the new capital's military force was bolstered by the addition of nine border defense posts and three large army training camps.

In undertaking the move, Zhu Di was doing more than simply honoring his old fief. As his father well understood, a strong northern city with a large garrison was needed to fend off the constant threat of Mongol invasions. But building the new northern capital seems to have grown into an obsession with Zhu Di. Like the voyages of the treasure fleet, it became inexorably bound up with how the usurper emperor viewed himself. In its scale and grandeur, in its frantic pursuit of perfection, it reflected his insatiable need to prove his legitimacy. And, just as the treasure fleet dazzled foreign princes and awed (or forced) them into acknowledging the greatness of the third Ming emperor, so did the magnificence of the Forbidden City, when it was finally completed, humble all. It was on land what the treasure fleet was on sea: a symbol of Zhu Di's power and his indisputable right to possess that power. Both the treasure fleet and Beijing's Forbidden City would survive as the lasting legacy of his twenty-four-year reign.

By 1416 repairs on the Grand Canal had been completed. More than 130 miles of canal had been dredged and 38 locks built in just five years. The fledgling northern capital could now be well supplied from the south, and work on Beijing accelerated. Zhu Di ordered the construction of the palace complex of the Forbidden City and, the following year, moved to Beijing to supervise the project personally. The plan called for a compound of more than eight hundred rooms, including three main receiving halls and three palace residences, and over a hundred chambers for offices, archives, libraries, factories, artisans' studios, and storerooms. All major buildings were to be aligned on a strict north-south axis, creating a symmetry that reflected the stability and harmony of ideal Confucian rule. Its name, the Purple Forbidden City, was taken from the name of the constellation the Chinese call the Purple Luminous, which has the North Star—heavenly symbol of the emperor—at its center.

The court registry at the time recorded 62 trades and 232,089 skilled workers for imperial service. In addition, over a million laborers were engaged in general construction tasks in Beijing and hundreds of thousands more in lumbering and quarrying in various parts of the empire. Between 1417 and 1420, the peak construction years, it was estimated that one in fifty people in China, which then had a total population of about sixty million, worked on the Forbidden City.

Before finally settling in Beijing, Zhu Di had spent much of his reign on the road, shuttling between the two capitals. He always traveled with a guard of 10,000 cavalry and forty thousand foot soldiers and a minigovernment (called *xing zai*) of high officials and functionaries from each of the ministries. Anyone whose services might conceivably be needed was also brought along, from doctors to cooks to artisans who could replace broken seals. Since the emperor was the spiritual link between heaven and earth, a part of the cosmic order, it was necessary to take precautions not to disrupt the forces of nature when he was on the move. Prayers were said and sacrifices made to placate the spirits of the rivers and mountains he would pass. It was a taxing time for officials of the Ministry of Rites.

Back in Nanjing in the fall of 1416, Zhu Di issued an order to Zheng He on December 28 to escort home all envoys of the nineteen countries who had visited the court. The emperor gave Zheng He robes, silk gauzes, and brocades to present to the envoys as parting gifts, along with a seal of enfeoffment for the king of Cochin on India's west coast.

Just as China had recognized the independence of Malacca to keep the powerful Siamese and Javanese kingdoms in check, so it now honored Cochin, chief rival of Calicut on the Malabar coast. Zhu Di was said to have personally composed the text for the Cochin tablet, which expressed his philosophy of rule at the midpoint of his reign. The law of the emperor, he wrote, is linked to both heaven and earth and encompasses all people everywhere. Under heaven there is only one law, and all people have the same concerns. "How can the same feelings of sorrow, grief, joy, and pleasure and the same desires for peace, ease, satiety and warmth not be shared among all?" he asked. Like his father before him, he wished to see that "all distant countries and foreign domains each achieve its proper place under heaven."

Having accepted the teachings of China and been assimilated into the empire, Cochin reaped the benefits of peace with bountiful harvests and prosperity. The king of Cochin, continued Zhu Di, by submitting to rule by the Middle Kingdom, looked up to heaven and said,

> How fortunate we are that the teachings of the sages of China have benefited us. For several years now, we have had abundant harvests in our country and our people have had houses to live in, have had the bounty of the sea to eat their fill of, and enough fabrics for clothes. Our old are kind to the young, and our juniors respect their seniors; all lead happy lives in harmony, without oppression and contention for dominance. The mountains lack ferocious beasts, the streams are free of noxious fish, the seas yield rare and precious things, the forests produce good wood, and all things flourish in abundance, more than double what is the norm. Violent winds have not arisen, torrential rains have not fallen, pestilence has ceased, and there have been no disasters and calamities.

The Yongle emperor thus portrayed himself as a life-giving father to the city-state of Cochin and all the peoples of the earth. He echoed an early idea of the Son of Heaven as ruler of *tian xia,* that is, "all under the heavens." As far as the Chinese knew in the early centuries of the Christian era, there was little of consequence beyond the boundaries of their empire. If one owned everything, what was the point of going out and conquering it? The European concept of a militant, crusading colonialism beyond the necessity of creating a favorable climate for east-west trade demeans the Chinese ideal of an all-powerful, semidivine emperor and thus never occurred to Zhu Di. Prosperity was the reward for allegiance to the dragon throne; it would instill a greater loyalty in barbarian people than could be mustered with garrisons and foot soldiers. In any event, as the Hongwu emperor reasoned at the beginning of the Ming Dynasty, it was foolish to try to support garrisons halfway around the world, so neither Zhu Di nor his successors tried. It would take European colonial powers another four hundred years to reach the same conclusion.

Before leaving the coast of China on the fifth voyage, the treasure fleet made a stop in the port city of Quanzhou in Fujian province. Here the ship took on locally made porcelains and fine blue-and-white ware from the imperial kilns farther inland at Jingdezhen. Teas, silks, and cloth to be traded abroad were also stowed in the hulls of the treasure ships. The fleet stayed several months, during which time Zheng He, who boarded at the Lai Yuan Li guest house near the south gate of the city, was cordially entertained by local officials. The soldiers and sailors resided on the ships, anchored offshore.

Like Guangzhou, Quanzhou had been an important port for foreign ships for more than five hundred years and had a large Muslim population. Records show that during this stay, Zheng He worshiped at Quanzhou's main mosque on Tumen Street near the harbor and also at the tomb of two early Muslim prophets outside the city. Zheng He's conscientiousness in attending to Buddhist ritual and the proper ceremonies for the Daoist goddess of seamen did not overshadow his own Muslim beliefs. He had not abandoned the faith of his fathers and may even have played some role in combating the persecution of Quanzhou's Muslims in the early years of the Yongle reign.

The graves of the two Muslim prophets Zheng He visited are on top of a grassy hill, now the center of a large Muslim cemetery. They are marked by two stone slabs and a semicircle of covered stone pillars that date from the Tang dynasty. The "prophets" were probably early Arab traders who stayed in Quanzhou and married local women. A Ming tablet at the site, erected by a local official, commemorates the occasion:

> The imperial envoy and commander-in-chief, the grand Eunuch Zheng He, proceeding on official business to Hormuz and other countries in the Western Ocean, has on the 16th day of the 5th month of the 15th year of Yongle [May 31, 1417] here burnt incense, wishing [to procure] the Divine Sacred protection, in memory of which Judge Pu Heri has set up [this tablet].

The Ashab mosque, where Zheng He also burned incense and worshiped, was a patchwork of earlier structures. A stone terrace, from which the faithful watched the phases of the moon to judge when the holy days of Ramadan should begin, dated from the eighth century; the large worship hall, accommodating five hundred, and a graceful minaret had been built in the eleventh century. A tablet on the wall of a garden just outside the mosque, dated June 16, 1407, and signed by the Yongle emperor, described the followers of Islam as "sincere," "good," and loyal subjects "most deserving of commendation." The emperor ordered that all mosques be protected. Further, he decreed that "official, military and civilian [households] and other categories of people shall not maltreat, insult, cheat or bully [Muslims]; and whosoever dares to knowingly disobey Our command . . . shall be punished according to the crime."

According to local Islamic records, there was indeed considerable persecution of Muslims in the early Ming, and many left China or abandoned their faith. At the end of the Yuan, an estimated forty thousand Muslims lived in Quanzhou and supported seven mosques. Islamic authorities claim all seven were burned when the Ming came to power. Hostility toward Muslims may have had something to do with their role as tax collectors for the Mongols. The tablet suggests that there may have been some residual ill will against Muslims as late as 1407, and, since Zheng He was also in Quanzhou that year during his second voyage, it seems plausible that he may well have had something to do with the installation (if not instigation) of the imperial edict protecting the Muslim community there, though firm proof of this is lacking. The mosque in Fuzhou farther up the coast received a similar imperial edict protecting its building and worshipers.

At this time Zheng He did visit a small Muslim hamlet, Baiqi, on a peninsula just north of Quanzhou, where, it is believed, he recruited pilots and navigators for the voyage. An Arab trader named Yiben Deguang Gong was supposed to have fled from Quanzhou to this remote spot as the Yuan dynasty fell, and all of the villagers to this day are said to be his descendants. It is a windswept point with few trees and little protection from the elements. The buildings of the town are huddled close together, all built of stone with decorative displays of colored tiles, more like an Arab than a Chinese village. A small community hall, dating from the Song, stands near the harbor, where small fishing junks, still built mostly with hand tools, are moored. The boatmen of Baiqi say that Zheng He played *xiangqi* (Chinese chess) with the villagers in the hall when he came in 1417, and some remember stories their forefathers told them about the time on the fifth voyage when supposedly one of Zheng He's ships got stuck in shallow waters off Java and men from Baiqi had to pole furiously to release it. After the boat was free, they say, one pole remained stuck in the sand to mark the treacherous spot.

On this expedition Zheng He made stops at Champa and Java; Palembang, Semudera, and Atjeh on Sumatra; Pahang and Malacca on the Malay Peninsula; the Maldives, Ceylon, and Cochin and Calicut on the Indian coast. Venturing beyond Hormuz, the fleet then sailed for the first time to Aden on the southern coast of Arabia at the entrance to the Red Sea. Historically, Aden was the main port en route from the Mediterranean to India and the Far East. At this time it was ruled by the Rasulid dynasty (1229–1454), whose capital was at Ta'izz. The Rasulids ruled all of southwest Arabia as far north as Mecca. Ma Huan reported that Aden had seven or eight thousand "well-drilled horsemen and foot soldiers" (by other counts it was twenty thousand) and that such an army was intimidating to Aden's neighbors. So rich was Aden that the Muslim women decked themselves in jewels—four pairs of gold earrings inlaid with gems, strands of pearls and gemstones, bracelets, armbands, and rings on their fingers and toes.

Zheng He was well received by the sultan of Aden, who was perhaps seeking an ally against the aggressive Mameluke sultans of Egypt, with whom he vied for control of the holy cities of Mecca and Medina. "At the king's [sultan's] palace, they rendered a ceremonial salutation with great reverence and humility," wrote Ma Huan. The sultan then issued an order that only those with "precious things" were permitted to trade with the emissaries of the dragon throne. The Chinese bartered gold, silver, porcelains, sandalwood, and pepper for Aden's opalescent stones and rare gems, large pearls, pieces of coral over two feet high, amber, and rose water. Lions, zebras, leopards, ostriches, white pigeons, and a giraffe were given in tribute by the sultan for the Yongle emperor. In addition, the sultan gave Zheng He two gold belts inlaid with jewels, a gold hat with pearls and precious stones, two horns, and a special memorial to the dragon throne engraved in gold leaf.

Departing Aden, the fleet set sail for the first time for the African coast, to return the ambassadors from Mogadishu, Brawa (in what is now Somalia), and Malindi (in Kenya) to their homes. Scattered along the thousand miles of coast from Somalia to Tanzania were numerous towns that shared a common Swahili (from the Arab "sahil," meaning coast) language and culture and considered themselves "civilized" (*uungwana*) as opposed to the "uncultured" (*ushenzi*) people of the hinterland. Swahili culture emerged after the Islamic dispersal in the ninth century, when Arabs settled Mombasa, Malindi, Kilwa, and elsewhere and intermarried with the local population. Successive waves of immigrants from the shores of the Indian Ocean—Indians, Persians, Indonesians—and periodic infusions of inland African peoples contributed to the polyglot culture of the coastal cities.

In the early fifteenth century, when the treasure fleet sailed to Mogadishu and Mombasa, Swahili towns were ruled by independent Arab sheiks. Dhows traded local agricultural produce up and down the coast and probably sailed as far as Arabia, where the traders were able to obtain Chinese porcelains, silks and damasks, carpets, pearls, perfumes, and glass beads. The Swahili towns had pristine, three-story houses of coral rag and lime mortar with lush gardens of citrus trees and vegetables. Islam took a firm hold here but seems to have pursued a rather independent course, as evidenced by the Swahili mosques with their Indonesian motifs and strange pillar tombs. Yet the coastal people the Chinese met were by all accounts extremely pious. A tomb inscription from the mosque in Jumba La Mtwana, just north of Mombasa, quotes this passage from the Koran:

> Every soul shall taste death. You will simply be paid your wages in full on the Day of Resurrection. He who is removed from the fire and made to enter heaven, he it is who has won the victory. The earthly life is only delusion.

Though the Swahilis coveted Chinese goods, particularly porcelains, which they plastered into the walls of their mosques and tombs, it is not certain that they welcomed the treasure ships with open arms. Compared with the Arab dhows, they must have been overwhelming—and frightening—to the Swahilis, who tended to be leery of foreigners, who frequently invaded their shores.

Fei Xin reported that the inhabitants of Mogadishu were "quarrelsome." Luo Maodeng's 1597 novel about the voyages of Zheng He, which is believed to have some historic reliability, states specifically that Zheng He used gunpowder explosives against a walled town called La-sa, thought to be near Mogadishu in Somalia, and that the ruler of Mogadishu was wary of welcoming the Chinese. "The Ming empire and our country are thousands of miles apart, and today without reason it has sent soldiers against us," the king was supposed to have said. "Obviously, they want to take us over." According to the author, the Mogadishu chief considered fighting Zheng He but in the end surrendered to the superior forces of the treasure fleet.

When Zheng He returned to China on July 15, 1419, the emperor richly rewarded all of the fleet's officers. The foreign ambassadors who came to pay tribute to the emperor were received at court on August 8 and caused a sensation. The African envoys paraded their curious animals, and court officials "craning their necks looked on with pleasure, and stamping their feet when they were scared and startled, thinking that these were things that were rarely heard of in the world and that China had never seen their likeness." The second *qilin* from Aden was received with the same fanfare as the first, including a commemorative song by Jin Youzi:

> There is no darkness but is brightened; there is no distance but is illuminated. From where the water father and the clouds assemble, bowing their heads all bear gifts. Thus, many auspicious signs are collected, arriving one after another in pairs. How did this come about? Only through the perfect virtue of the emperor.

These ambassadors remained in China for almost two years, until the spring of 1421, when Zhu Di finally issued the order that they should be taken home. Of all Zheng He's voyages, the mysterious, short sixth voyage begins to take on the color of exploration, driven more by curiosity than by profit. Africa was China's El Dorado—the land of rare and precious things, mysterious and unfathomable. Chinese accounts describe the dryness of the east African coast and the hardship of the native people and mention little trade on this visit or the one before. Mogadishu was "intolerably hot," Fei Xin wrote, and "since there is no cultivated soil, [the people] live on fishing. Because of the torrid weather only a few plants can grow . . . [and] if anyone wandered over this country he would have only met with sad glances. An entire land having nothing but sand."

On the sixth voyage, it appears, the fleet divided at Semudera on Sumatra. One of Zheng He's deputies, the eunuch Zhou Man, led the main portion of the fleet on to Aden and Africa. Zheng He himself and a smaller contingent of boats seem to have returned to China. Historical records indicate that Zheng He was back in the capital in November 1421, whereas the rest of the fleet did not return until a year later. Zheng He's hasty return may have had something to do with joining in the festivities honoring the completion of the Forbidden City, formally designated as the capital in 1420.

The imposing palace compound with its shimmering golden-colored glazed tile roofs was a progression of open spaces and columned halls, beginning with the U-shaped Wumen Gate. The vermilion gate rose fifty feet above the ground and supported three long pavilions with double-eaved roofs. Here imperial orders were given and captives received. Passing through the gate, one entered a large courtyard covering more than seven acres, where the emperor, seated at Fengtianmen, Gate of Receiving Heaven's [Mandated Protection], issued proclamations of war and peace and celebrated the New Year and his birthday. Later in the sixteenth century, an artificial stream wound its way through the paved square, which was spanned by five exquisitely carved marble bridges symbolizing the five virtues. Only the emperor was permitted to cross the middle bridge or walk on the middle path through the Forbidden City.

On New Year's Day, which fell on February 2, 1421, the Fengtianmen courtyard was filled with thousands of foreign envoys, officials, and military officers, gathered to congratulate the emperor on the completion of the Forbidden City. In unison the officials bowed and kowtowed to the emperor nine times. Then a representative of each of the nine ranks of both civil and military officials presented a tribute to the emperor, wishing him long life and a reign of "ten thousand years." A scroll celebrating the occasion was lowered to people below Wumen Gate and copied for wide distribution. Chimes sounded when the emperor rose and moved inside the Huagai, or Splendid Parasol Hall, and then on to his living quarters. The north side of the Forbidden City consisted of living areas for him, the empress, and his scores of concubines as well as the imperial gardens and a Daoist temple for the personal use of the imperial family. Beyond the moat and high walls of the palace was a man-made mountain, the highest point in Beijing, from which the emperor, if he wished, could survey his residence.

The Yongle emperor not only supervised the details of the new palace but took an interest in the arts, particularly porcelain and lacquerware. The emperor favored a creamy white procelain that later became known as *tian bai,* or "sweet white." Minute bubbles in the glaze scattered the light, giving the procelain an unusual softness. In 1406 he refused a tribute gift of jade bowls from a foreign envoy, saying, "The Chinese porcelain that I use every day is pure and translucent, and it pleases me greatly. There is no need to use the jade bowls. Besides, we have the same articles in the imperial storeroom and I have not wanted to use them." During his reign the blue-and-white porcelains developed a richness of color due in part to the use of an imported cobalt ore—high in iron and low in manganese—that is called "sunima" or "sulama" and thought to have come from Kashan, Persia. (Chinese ore containing cobalt were just the opposite, high in manganese and low in iron.) Zheng He helped secure this prized imported cobalt and thus played some role in creating the improvements in the distinctive blue-and-white porcelains for which the Ming dynasty would become well known. At this time, Sanskrit script and sea creature motifs—fish, sea monsters, waves—also came into porcelain design for the first time. It is thought that the new imperial city's Feihong Bridge, with its magnificent fish carvings, was made from white stone brought back by Zheng He and inspired by his journeys. Proudly, the Yongle emperor allowed "Yongle" to be stamped on imperial porcelains, and thereafter procelain would be defined not by place of origin but by reign name.

Zhu Di also appreciated fine lacquerware. When Japanese envoys presented him with pieces of lacquerware by Chinese masters Zhang Cheng and Yang Mao, both from Jiaxing in Zhejiang, the emperor immediately sent eunuchs looking for them. Both, unfortunately, had died, but Zhu Di ordered Zhang's son Degang to join the imperial workshop, and he and Bao Liang, another Jiaxing master, are credited with the development of some of the finest lacquerware in China's history. Intricate floral designs were created with detail so fine it could barely be seen with the naked eye. Close examination of a box lid covered with a dense field of poppies, for example, would disclose a unique pattern in the center of every flower.

A parade of auspicious *qilins* had one by one appeared before the gates of the newly completed Forbidden City. The emperor's virtue was recognized throughout the world, and in the spring of 1421 an era of boundless prosperity seemed at hand. There would be no end to the cycle of voyages and tribute-bearing foreign envoys to the Ming court. The universe was in order. Or was it?

Without warning, devastating fires swept through the Forbidden City. Pampered *qilins* on the grounds of the imperial zoo looked up at the billows of black smoke in bewilderment.

9 Fires in the Forbidden City

When the universe is in harmony, the land is fertile and harvests bountiful. The sea brings forth abundant fish and the forests fine woods. Prosperity and happiness come to every family. There is no sickness, fighting, storm, disaster, or evil of any kind. And the virtue of the emperor, the Son of Heaven, is perfect.

But when there is discord in the heavens, floods and famine ravage the earth. There is plague and pestilence, and a storm of sorrow broods over all mankind. It is then that the virtue of the Son of Heaven is questioned, when he must examine his ways. The fault is with him, arbiter between Heaven and Earth, between the world of the spirits and the world of man.

As the Master, Confucius, said, "He who offends against Heaven has none to whom he can pray."

The months after the dedication of the Forbidden City should have been a time of great joy for the emperor. Instead, trouble festered like an infected wound.

First, there was the death of Zhu Di's favorite concubine, Madame Wang from Suzhou. At his father's urging in 1376, Zhu Di had married the daughter of one of his father's most trusted generals, Xu Da, to strengthen the alliance between the two families. He was sixteen and the future empress was fourteen, but by all accounts it was a love match that produced three sons and four daughters. Empress Xu, an educated woman who strengthened the power of the Confucian court advisers—an act that would have important consequences in her son's reign—died in 1407. After her death, Zhu Di made no other woman empress but remained closest to Madame Wang, who became guardian of the imperial family. She was frequently the mediator between the aging emperor, now often ill and irascible, and the palace staff, who greatly feared him. After Madame Wang's death, it was said, Zhu Di's ill humor turned to cruelty and scores of palace attendants were summarily executed for causing the emperor the slightest displeasure.

In the spring of 1421, two concubines were discovered having intimate relations with a eunuch. This was not an unusual occurrence, but for some reason, perhaps because the two women were also having relations with each other, they committed suicide. The emperor was furious when he learned of their deaths because he had been fond of one of the women. He immediately ordered an inquiry. Palace servants slandered the dead women, saying they had been plotting to kill the emperor. Before the investigation was concluded, 2,800 concubines and eunuchs had been implicated in the alleged treason, and it was reported that the emperor himself executed many of them. How many were killed is not clear, but some of the palace women bitterly cursed the emperor to his face before dying at his hand.

"You are losing your yang force and that is why your concubines had a relationship with a young eunuch!" they cried. "We are innocent!"

That same spring, the sixty-year-old emperor had a bad accident while on a hunting trip with the Timurid ambassadors outside the capital. He was thrown from a horse that had been a tribute gift from the Timurid king, Mirza Shāhrukh, and injured. Zhu Di was angry that the envoys had dared to give him such an unruly horse and ordered his officials to shackle them and send them to an army garrison on the northeastern frontier. The officials counseled patience. Fortunately, the emperor was in a better humor the next day, when he received the trembling ambassadors in his tent. They prostrated themselves on the ground before him, not daring to speak. Finally the emperor, still sore from his bad fall, invited them to ride with him and brought up the subject of the tribute horse.

"If one wishes good relations between two countries and selects a horse or some other precious object and gives it to a prince or emperor, one must select the best one," he said. He wore a red riding mantle brocaded with gold to which was stitched a black satin pouch containing his long beard. "Yesterday we rode the horse you gave us. It was already too old. In the end it threw us to the ground. My hand was injured and turned black and blue. After applying a great deal of gold to it, the pain has now begun to lessen somewhat."

"This horse was formerly the steed of Timur," said the chief envoy, Shadi Khwaja. "[His son] King Shāhrukh presented it to Your Majesty to show the greatest respect for you. The king said your country must have this horse as a treasure among horses." Zhu Di was suddenly pleased at the thought that this difficult horse had been the horse of his enemy Timur sixteen years ago. Instead of punishing the envoys, he rewarded them generously. A Persian account of the incident recorded by the historian Hāfiz-i-Abrū in his 1423 chronicle, *Zubdatu't Tawarikh,* differs, claiming that it was in fact a Chinese official who persuaded the emperor to be lenient.

"The ambassadors . . . are in no way to blame," the official was supposed to have counseled, "for if their sovereign had sent good horses or bad as presents, these persons had no choice in the matter. . . . Moreover, even if Your Majesty has the envoys cut in pieces it shall make no difference to their sovereign. On the other hand, an evil report concerning the emperor would spread here. The whole world would say that the emperor of China had acted contrary to all convention by imprisoning the envoys after so many years of absence from home and punishing them."

On May 9, 1421, not long after the hunting accident, Heaven presented Zhu Di with another sign of its displeasure, a sign he could not ignore.

In the midst of a spring storm, lightning struck the three great ceremonial halls of the newly completed Forbidden City—Fengtian, Huagai, and Jinshen. Fire spread quickly up the tall vermilion columns, devouring the exquisitely carved, painted ceilings and support beams. The heavy, gold-colored tiled roofs that rose nearly a hundred feet caved in, while voluminous silk canopies and curtains and the emperor's carved wooden thrones were quickly reduced to ashes. Court official Yang Rong and several palace guards bravely entered the burning buildings and managed to salvage a few documents, which they piled outside the Donghua Gate.

The blaze looked as if "a hundred thousand torches" had been lit, according to a Persian envoy who witnessed the disaster. The envoy's account, also included in Hāfiz-i-Abrū's history, reported that the fire quickly spread to the apartments of concubines and palace offices including the treasury, destroying "250 quarters" altogether and killing "a large number of men and women." The fire raged out of control all night and until the afternoon of the following day.

Barely had the embers cooled when whispers flew through the

Forbidden City that the disaster had been foretold. Hu, master of the water clock, had predicted it. He had even named the day and the hour. He had told the emperor, who, enraged by the thought of such an evil portent, had him imprisoned and sentenced him to be executed at the exact hour he had said the disaster would occur, if nothing happened. When the time arrived, according to the palace legend, poor Hu swallowed poison and died, less than an hour before the lightning struck the halls.

Zhu Di was shaken by the disaster and immediately went to the palace temple to pray. "The God of Heaven is angry with me, and therefore, has burnt my palace," he reportedly said. "Although I have done no evil act; I have neither offended my father, nor mother; nor have I acted tyrannically."

The emperor sought advice from his officials, inviting them to speak frankly about his shortcomings. Confucius had said, "If a ruler's words be good, is it not also good that no one oppose them? But if they are not good, and no one opposes them, may there not be expected from this one sentence the ruin of his country?"

In a display of sincere emotion, Zhu Di issued the following imperial edict:

> My heart is full of trepidation. I do not know how to handle it. It seems that there has been some laxness in the rituals of honoring Heaven and serving the spirits. Perhaps there has been some transgression of the ancestral law or some perversion of government affairs? Perhaps mean men hold rank while good men flee and hide themselves, and the good and the evil are not distinguished? Perhaps punishments and jailing have been excessive and unjustly applied to the innocent, and the straight and the crooked not discriminated? . . . Is this what brought about [the fires]? Harshness to the people below; and, above, going against Heaven. I cannot find the reason in my confusion. . . . If our actions have in fact been improper, you should lay these out one by one, hiding nothing, so that we may try to reform ourselves and regain the favor of Heaven.

Zhu Di ordered a halt to the making of copper coins and the buying of raw copper, silk, and horses in the northwest. To ease "the burden of the people" and "eliminate those things not essential to the running of government," he remitted all grain taxes in areas that had suffered calamities in the past year and temporarily suspended future voyages of the treasure fleet as well as preparations for all foreign travel.

Although Zhu Di omitted mention of the new capital in the edict, officials took the occasion to express their concern about the move to Beijing, which they felt had been too costly and too hard on the population. Surpluses in the imperial treasury had by now disappeared, due not only to the emperor's expansionist foreign policy but also to severe famines in Shandong and Hunan and epidemics in Fujian, which claimed 253,000 lives. In some areas people were forced to eat wild plants to survive and many died of starvation. There were so few able-bodied men that people were left unburied in the fields and roads where they had died.

Adding to the fiscal problems of the empire was the costly rebellion in Annam, sparked by excessive government demands for timber for the Forbidden City. Though rebel bands led by Le Loi were defeated by imperial forces in 1419 and 1420, the Annamese continued to fight a guerrilla war in the countryside, draining Ming armies and resources.

After the edict, criticism of the emperor's policies flowed freely, but the time for frank words was to be short-lived. Hanlin Academician Li Shimian, who was from an old Jiangxi family, told the emperor that Beijing was simply not a suitable place to receive foreign envoys.

"Slanderers!" the emperor shouted one day at court, silencing his officials. One by one he banished or imprisoned those who were critical of the relocation of the capital. A young counselor named Xiao Yi, whom the emperor found particularly abrasive, was sentenced to death. Xia Yuanji, the minister of revenue, disturbed by the emperor's behavior, stepped forward to take responsibility for the fires.

"Those who responded to your edict are blameless," he said. "It is only we in high offices who have not been able to assist [you] with the grand plan. The fault is ours."

Gradually the crisis passed, but all discussion of the fires and the burden of building the new capital ceased. No effort was made to rebuild the burned halls until the middle of the century.

Less than a year after the palace fires, oblivious to warnings about the empire's financial problems, Zhu Di announced his intention to launch a large military campaign against the Tartars, who were raiding China's western border. Zhu Di had mobilized forces against the Mongols twice before: in 1410, to push the Tartars back, and in 1414, to fight the Oirats in northern Mongolia. Now the Tartar leader Arughtai had refused to pay tribute to the Ming court. It was like waving a red flag in Zhu Di's face.

In December 1421 Zhu Di ordered the provinces of Shanxi, Shandong, and Henan to deliver grain for the troops to Xuanfu at the edge of the northern frontier by the end of the second lunar month of 1422. In earlier campaigns the northern provinces had been able to supply the army's needs; now food had to come mainly from the south. More than 340,000 horses and mules, 177,500 carts, and 235,000 men were required to transport more than one million bushels of grain—just to cover the basic food requirements of the troops during this maneuver.

Zhu Di's loyal minister of revenue, Xia Yuanji, who always carried figures on population, households, tax surpluses, and shortages so he could respond quickly to the emperor's requests, had managed to find the funds to finance the six expeditions of Zheng He, the Annamese invasion, the building of the new capital, and the earlier Mongol campaigns. But he balked at this last imperial order. It was simply too great a burden. There were barely enough men to station at the garrisons on the frontier. He was promptly arrested by the emperor, along with the minister of justice, Wu Zhong, who also expressed his objection. Fang Bin, the minister of war, was also opposed to the campaign, and killed himself rather than face the angry emperor.

Undeterred, Zhu Di moved forward with his plans. Six of his closest ministers were dead or in jail because of his stubbornness, but he would listen to no one. On April 12, 1422, the large Ming army left Beijing, led by the emperor despite his rheumatic condition. Marching slowly, with their supply trains in the rear, the army took almost two months to reach Kaiping, where Zhu Di sent twenty thousand men to attack the Uriyangqad Mongols.

Seeing how futile the expedition was, a eunuch named Mu Jing urged Zhu Di to return to Beijing. The emperor scoffed at him and insulted him, calling him *fan man* (rebellious and savage). The eunuch persisted. "I do not know which of us is being *fan man,*" he said. Indignant, the emperor called for his execution on the spot, but the eunuch showed no fear whatsoever. This courage moved Zhu Di.

"If all the people around me were like this, wouldn't it be beneficial?" he said. He spared the eunuch's life.

Though the Uriyangqad Mongols had fought on Zhu Di's side

during his rise to power, they had turned on him and were now assisting Arughtai. The Ming forces handily defeated the Uriyangqads, but Arughtai fled to Outer Mongolia. Zhu Di decided not to pursue him there and finally returned to Beijing.

But the following summer, in 1423, the emperor was back on the dusty road to Mongolia in pursuit of Arughtai. This time his army did not even see the enemy, though Zhu Di learned that the Tartars had been defeated by the Oirats and eastern Mongols. In the summer of 1424, the aging emperor, now obviously very ill, once again insisted on a search for his old enemy, which also proved futile.

Zhu Di had not been in good health for some time. Even as a young man he had suffered from intestinal parasites, and after the 1414 Mongolian campaign he was afflicted with a malady called *feng shi* ("damp wind"), a rheumatic disorder. Some histories say that the emperor was also partially paralyzed and took Daoist elixirs laced with arsenic as a stimulant. In his later years, therefore, he may have been slowly dying of arsenic poisoning. Yet other sources claim that Zhu Di scoffed at folk cures, saying that illnesses could be avoided if one was "at peace with oneself and curbed desires." "The Qin and Han emperors were cheated by this," he was supposed to have told well-meaning Daoists who offered him their potions in 1417. "Shall I now be, too?"

On August 12, 1424, after two months of marching toward Beijing, Zhu Di "succumbed to illness" in a place called Yumuchuan. He was sixty-four. On his deathbed, he said, "Yuanji loved me," perhaps recognizing that his finance minister had been right in opposing the folly of these last campaigns.

On the hot plains north of Inner Mongolia, tin cooking utensils were melted down to make a coffin to carry the emperor's body back to Beijing. Senior officers and eunuchs kept the emperor's death secret until the procession actually arrived at the capital. There the body was transferred to a thick casket made of *nanmu* and placed in the Forbidden City for one hundred days. During this period of mourning, the playing of music and all religious ceremonies ceased. Weddings were forbidden. Temples were required to ring their bells thirty thousand times. The site for the tomb of the emperor had been selected years before, in 1411, at the base of the Tianshou Mountains twenty miles northwest of Beijing. Empress Xu was buried there. Like Zhu Yuanzhang's tomb outside Nanjing, the burial mound was located between a mountain and a river to prevent the soul from wandering. Eventually, thirteen Ming emperors would be buried there, and the gentle plain and low foothills would be compared to the Valley of the Kings in Egypt.

When the day of Zhu Di's funeral arrived, the body of the dead emperor was carried out through the Meridian Gate. At that point the new emperor stayed behind, within the walls of the Forbidden City. The rest of the procession of ten thousand military and civil officials, led by Zhu Di's honor guard, walked slowly in a zigzag pattern out of the west gate of the city and then north to the tombs to foil evil spirits, who were believed to travel in straight lines. The slow march took two days. At the grave site sixteen of Zhu Di's concubines, who had been killed by hanging or forced to take their own lives, were buried with him in the *zuan gong,* or underground palace, a complex of four chambers eighty feet beneath the surface. In the days of the ancient dynasties, animals would have been killed and entombed with the emperor as well, but in the fifteenth century skinned, boiled animals were presented to the ancestor gods as food and then buried. In the coffin the emperor's clothes, ornaments, utensils, and favorite things from daily life were carefully arranged around his body. Above the underground chambers was a magnificent sacrificial hall and altar with three connecting courtyards, where ceremonials were performed twice a year thereafter in his honor. And for eternity, the tomb of the Yongle emperor was guarded by a mile-long row of stone officials, warriors, and animals, each carved from a single large block of granite. Solemn-faced statues of imperial counselors, dressed in long robes with the square-shaped hats of their office, held *hu,* or rank tablets, waiting for the next instruction from the emperor.

Zheng He was not in China when the emperor, his master and friend, died. Although voyages abroad had been banned by his own decree, the emperor had sent Zheng He and a small entourage to Palembang on Sumatra to settle the dispute over the succession to the throne. The trip was never counted among the seven great expeditions of the eunuch commander. Zheng He traveled no farther than Palembang, but by the time he returned Zhu Di's studious eldest son, forty-six-year-old Zhu Gaozhi, had already ascended the dragon throne.

Father and son could not have been more different. Zhu Gaozhi was a fat, listless boy who had none of his father's vigor. He had no interest in soldiers or fighting. Once, when he was a boy and his grandfather was still alive, Gaozhi had been asked to review the troops at dawn with the other princes. But after a little while the boy returned to the palace alone, saying he was cold and would actually rather have his breakfast.

While Zhu Di was off fighting the Mongols or building the new capital at Beijing, Gaozhi stayed in Nanjing to learn the business of government and came under the influence of his well-read mother, Empress Xu. The empress had supervised the writing of the *Gu jin lie nü zhuan*, a collection of biographies of exemplary women; she herself edited a popular edition of Confucian and Buddhist sayings and stories entitled *Quan shu* (Exhortations). She gave personal audiences to members of the Hanlin Academy, the elite organization of Confucians, and their wives, increasing the academy's power and prestige at court. The emperor, meanwhile, became close to his strong, athletic second son, Zhu Gaoxu, who accompanied him on his campaigns. At one point, Zhu Di considered appointing Gaoxu heir, but he did not, perhaps because Gaozhi proved himself adept at statecraft.

Upon becoming emperor, Gaozhi immediately released all officials who had been imprisoned for offending his father, including Xia Yuanji and Yang Pu. He surrounded himself with a group of traditional Confucians, including Qian Yi, his tutor, who stressed the importance of benevolent rule, and Yang Rong, another tutor, who believed in curbing the power of the eunuchs and withdrawing from Annam. The view of all was that moderation and attention to the "root of the state," that is, agriculture, should be the basis of government policy. Expensive military campaigns and the enormous cost of the new capital were, in their eyes, harmful to the root of the state and should be cut back. From a pragmatic standpoint, the officials were protecting the interests of the wealthy landowners of the Taihu area, who paid a disproportionate amount of the empire's land tax.

Xia Yuanji resumed his position as finance minister and further urged conservative fiscal measures to curb the rampant inflation. He counseled the new emperor against the mining of gold and silver; the purchase of gems, incense, spices, and other luxuries; and the continuation of the voyages of the treasure fleet.

On September 7, 1424, the day he formally ascended the throne, the emperor issued his first edict, which clearly reflected the philosophy of his tutors and advisers:

> All voyages of the treasure ships are to be stopped. All ships moored at Taicang [near the mouth of the Yangzi River] are ordered back to

> Nanjing and all goods on the ships are to be turned over to the Department of Internal Affairs and stored. If there were any foreign envoys wishing to return home, they will be provided with a small escort. Those officials who are currently abroad on business are ordered back to the capital immediately . . . and all those who had been called to go on future voyages are ordered back to their homes.

Moreover, "the building and repair of all treasure ships is to be stopped immediately. The collecting of *tielimu* [a special hardwood] is to be done as it was in the time of the Hongwu emperor. [Additional harvesting] should be stopped. All official procurement for going abroad (with the exception of items already delivered at official depots) and the making of copper coins, buying of musk, raw copper, [and] raw silk must also be stopped . . . [and] all those involved in purchasing should return to the capital."

The operative Confucian principle at work was that land is the basis of the empire's prosperity. The security of the empire lay within the Great Wall, not on the sea. Also, had not Confucius said the welfare of the people was more important than the profit or advantage of the state? Where there was famine, the state should send grain. And was it not wrong to ask the people for gold, silver, and precious things?

Zhu Gaozhi was genuinely concerned about alleviating undue tax burdens on the population, and when challenged once by a reluctant official, he responded, "Relieving people's poverty ought to be handled as though one were rescuing them from fire or saving them from drowning. One cannot hesitate."

Because the emperor had spent most of his life in Nanjing, he initiated plans to return the capital to Nanjing and had Beijing designated an "auxiliary" capital, although this was more in name than in fact. (Eventually, the qualification was dropped in 1441 and Beijing formally became the Ming capital again.) The emperor also relieved Zheng He of his duties as commander of the treasure fleet and put him in charge of the military command in Nanjing. It was an important post and set the precedent for eunuch military commanders in other provinces. As his counselors favored curbing the power of eunuchs, it is unclear why the emperor gave Zheng He this key position.

Zheng He, of course, had lived in Nanjing for many years, supervising the building of the treasure ships. He built a large house with a garden on the south side of the city near the main mosque.

Nanjing's Muslim population was estimated at one hundred thousand at this time. Zheng He's house was supposed to have had seventy-two rooms and a door so large that the sound of it closing resonated throughout the house. He also owned land around the shipyard and outside the walls of the city, which he gave to his adopted nephew, Zheng Haozhao. The boy could not inherit Zheng He's rank, but with the land, he and his descendants had a means of providing for themselves. Zheng He's immediate task upon returning from Palembang was to supervise the completion of the Bao'en Temple complex and to make repairs to the palace where the new emperor wanted to live.

All was thus set in motion to reverse the great initiatives of Zhu Di's reign, when, after just nine months on the throne, the emperor died, leaving his eldest son as heir. The suddenness of Zhu Gaozhi's death led to some speculation that he had been poisoned. But a palace eunuch named Lei reported that it was some imbalance in his "yin-yang" system, perhaps heart failure. In fact, the emperor had been ill and on the day he died, May 29, 1425, had said that he wanted to be buried simply.

"I have reigned a very short time," he said. "I have not been able to bring any benefits to my people. I cannot bear the idea that they should be burdened with heavy work. My tomb should be constructed with great economy."

His mausoleum in the Tianshou Mountains, much simpler than his father's, was completed in three months.

The untimely death of Zhu Gaozhi left two strong elements in the Ming court vying for power. The eunuchs, so trusted by Zhu Di, held important positions both inside and outside the palace and had a vested interest in reinstating trade and the voyages of the treasure ships. Then there were the Confucian scholar-officials, recently appointed by Zhu Gaozhi, who wished to restore fiscal stability to the empire by conservative and traditional methods that clearly did not include excessive taxation of the population and risky sea ventures.

To whom would the new emperor listen?

10 The Last Voyage

On May 13, 1413, the day foreign envoys were to be received at court, Zhu Di was talking to his fourteen-year-old grandson, Zhu Zhanji. The emperor, who was very fond of *dui shi*, or "matching verse," asked the boy to think of a verse that corresponded in structure to the first line of the couplet he had just composed to mark the ambassadors' visit: "Jade and fabrics from every corner meet like wind and clouds."

The boy thought for a moment and then replied, "Mountains and rivers come together and the sun and moon shine brightly."

The prince's verse implied the unity of the land under one glorious rule, and, when people heard it, they said it showed Zhanji shared his grandfather's ambition and would be like the great Yongle emperor when he ascended the dragon throne one day.

From an early age, Zhu Zhanji accompanied his grandfather on his northern excursions to inspect Beijing and fight the Mongols. The two became close. Zhanji acquired his grandfather's great love of riding and hunting and shared his fondness for the open steppe country at the fringes of the empire. When Zhanji became emperor in 1426 at the age of twenty-six, he quickly reversed his father's directive, reinstating the capital in the north at Beijing. Zhanji also continued the tradition started by his grandfather of giving eunuchs important military posts and formally set up a palace school to instruct them. He shared Zhu Di's keen interest in porcelain, and he himself was a painter of some talent. But let it not be said that Zhanji, who would go down in history as the "Xuande" emperor (meaning "Propagating Virtue"), had none of his father's scholarly, Confucian bent.

Once, passing a field where a farmer was working, Zhanji stopped his imperial entourage and took the plow from the farmer's hand. He made several turns around the field before becoming exhausted.

"After only three turns at the plow, we are already unequal to the labor," he said. "What if one does this constantly? Men always say there is no toil like farming—and they are right."

Like his father, the young emperor subscribed to the Confucian ideal of benevolent rule, and in fact he surrounded himself with the same scholars who had advised his father: Minister of War Yang Shiqi, Minister of Revenue Huang Huai, Minister of Rites Jin Youzi, and the cautious, conservative senior official Xia Yuanji. Most had been his tutors, and, when Zhanji became emperor, he had the habit of stopping by their offices unannounced with a bottle of wine to discuss poetry, philosophy, or history. On their advice Zhanji eventually allowed the menacing Annamese rebel Le Loi to "administer the affairs of Annam," effectively ending China's draining twenty-year struggle with its southern neighbor. Unlike Zhu Di, Zhanji's philosophy was to keep China free from foreign wars, and even his engagements with the Mongols were minor. After a series of droughts and locust infestations, the emperor took strong steps to relieve the provinces, particularly in the southeast, of their annual grain taxes, and he shifted the burden of transporting grain northward to a branch of the military.

The young emperor's benevolence and generosity went perhaps further than his own advisers would have liked when at first he treated his rebellious uncle Zhu Gaoxu leniently. Gaoxu tried to seize the throne in the same way Zhu Di had done twenty-three years before. But rather than execute him after the unsuccessful coup, Zhanji simply detained him in special quarters in the Forbidden City. Only after the discontented uncle tripped Zhanji on one of his visits there did the emperor, finally angered at this insolence, ordered him put to death. A horrible death it was. Gaoxu was covered with a copper vat, which was then melted over him.

Zhu Zhanji was thus a combination of his father and grandfather. Some would say the balance he achieved between the blind expansionist policies of Zhu Di and the rigid Confucianism of Zhu Gaozhi was the finest hour of the Ming dynasty, a time of peace, prosperity, and good government. The reign of the Xuande emperor also produced one last, glorious expedition of the treasure fleet.

By 1430 Zhanji was concerned about the noticeable decline in China's tribute trade and what he perceived to be the loss of influence in the international community, due in part, certainly, to the loss of Annam. He vowed publicly to restore the dynasty's prestige abroad and to once again make "ten thousand countries our guests." Not long after the death of court adviser Xia Yuanji, the most vocal opponent of overseas expeditions, the emperor issued an order for the seventh voyage of the treasure fleet. The June 29, 1430, edict stated:

> The new reign of Xuande has commenced, and everything shall begin anew. [But] distant lands beyond the seas have not yet been informed. I send eunuchs Zheng He and Wang Jinghong with this imperial order to instruct these countries to follow the way of Heaven with reverence and to watch over their people so that all might enjoy the good fortune of lasting peace.

Part of the mission was also to try to restore peaceful relations between Siam and the Malay kingdom of Malacca. Zheng He was given an imperial edict to present to the Siamese king, urging him to stop harassing Malacca. In the order the emperor scolded the Siamese ruler for detaining the Malaccan king on his way to the Ming court.

"Is this the way to protect your wealth and happiness?" Zhanji wrote. "You, king, should follow my order and treat your neighbor well and instruct your officials not to invade and humiliate others without provocation. If you do this, we will regard you as one who respects Heaven and brings peace to people and makes friends with your neighbors. This is in accord with the benevolent principles I hold in my heart."

Preparations for the voyage took longer than usual, because it had been more than six years since the last expedition of the treasure ships. This was also to be the largest expedition, with more than 300 ships and 27,500 men. The ships had names such as "Pure Harmony," "Lasting Tranquility," and "Kind Repose," reflecting their peacekeeping mission.

It seems as if Zheng He, now in his sixties, knew this would be his last voyage. He took pains to document the achievements of his previous expeditions by erecting two stone tablets. One, dated March 14, 1431, was placed at an anchorage near the mouth of the Yangzi River; the other, dated "the second winter month" of the sixth year of Xuande (December 5, 1431 to January 3, 1432), in what is now Changle at the mouth of the Min River on the Fujian coast. Ostensibly, these tablets were erected to thank Tianfei, the

Celestial Consort of seamen, for her protection on previous voyages. In addition, however, the tablets carefully documented the achievements of each voyage, no doubt as Zheng He surely wished them to be remembered. But familiar as he was by now with the court's strong opposition to the voyages, he may have been unsure how the official chroniclers would record the expeditions.

In the Changle tablet, Zheng He proudly stated his belief that the expeditions of the treasure fleet "in unifying seas and continents" had far surpassed the maritime achievements of previous dynasties. Moreover, "the countries beyond the horizon from the ends of the earth have all become subjects . . . bearing precious objects and presents" to the Ming court. And now, as a result of the voyages, "the distances and routes" between these distant lands "may be calculated," implying that the voyages had made a substantial contribution to the accumulation of geographic knowledge in China. In conferring presents on these distant peoples, Zheng He made it clear that he believed the expeditions also had an impact in spreading Chinese culture abroad, that is, in making "manifest the transforming power of imperial virtue."

The treasure fleet departed Nanjing on January 19, 1431, and, after collecting its precious cargo and augmenting its crews in Jiangsu and Fujian, finally left the south China coast almost a year later, on January 12, 1432. Qui Nhon in southern Vietnam was the first stop. Then the fleet went on to Surabaja on the north coast of Java, Palembang in Sumatra, Malacca on the Malay Peninsula, Semudera on Sumatra's northern tip, and Ceylon, finally arriving at Calicut on the west coast of India on December 10, 1432.

This was Zheng He's seventh trip to India, but for all his experience there, the Chinese at this time mistakenly believed that the country was the origin not only of Buddhism but of the world's other great religions, Christianity and Islam. To them India encompassed all of the Middle East. According to material preserved in the *Ming tong jian*, India was thought to be divided into five parts: central, east, west, south, and north. Central India was "the country of Buddha" and "six hundred years after Buddha," according to the account, "Jesus of Western India appeared. His was the religion of the Lord of Heaven [Christianity]. Yet another six centuries after Jesus was born, Mohammed of Western India appeared. His was the religion of Tianfang or the Heavenly Quarter [Arabia]." As early as the Tang dynasty, the Chinese had knowledge of both Christianity and Islam, and Nestorian Christians had visited the court of Khubilai Khan.

But it was not until Matteo Ricci published his accounts of Christian dogma in the late sixteenth century that the Chinese had detailed knowledge of the religion. The *Ming tong jian* passage goes on to say that only when Zheng He reached Calicut did he realize for the first time that Tianfang, the land of the Arabs, was much farther to the southwest. He still, however, according to this source, considered Tianfang to be part of India.

From Calicut the great fleet divided into smaller fleets, with the eunuch Hong Bao undertaking the important mission to Hormuz and other Arab city-states and ports down the east African coast as far south as Malindi in Kenya. At Aden on the Arabian peninsula, two treasure ships attempted to unload their cargo but were unsuccessful because of the political instability there. The captains of these ships then wrote to the emir of Mecca and the controller of Jidda and were granted permission to come to Jidda. The sultan of Egypt, who controlled these ports, ordered the local rulers to show the Chinese honor, as was his custom with Indian Ocean traders. In Jidda and Dhufar, the center of the frankincense trade, the Chinese exchanged their silks and porcelains for aloe, which was used as a purgative and tonic; myrrh, the ancient Egyptian preservative the Chinese believed invigorated the circulation; benzoin, the aromatic gum resin used to treat respiratory ailments; storax, an anti-inflammatory drug; and an herbal medicine the Chinese called *mubietzi,* a paste of momordica seeds used to treat ulcers and wounds. Chinese interest in Arab drugs and therapies was particularly keen following the publication in China of an Arab medical text, *Hui yao fang* (Pharmaceutical prescriptions of the Muslims).

In *Ying yai sheng lan* (The overall survey of the ocean's shores), Ma Huan wrote that if one traveled west from Mecca for a day one would arrive at Medina. In fact, Medina is three hundred miles north of Mecca and takes some ten days by caravan. He described a well in Medina with holy water that sailors used to calm rough waves at sea. The well, the "Water of Zamzan," actually lies close to the Kaaba or House of God in Mecca. Ma Huan was more accurate in depicting Mecca's main mosque, which he said had four minarets (Arab traveler Ibn Battūtah mentioned five) and a wall surrounding it "with 466 openings" and pillars "all made of white jadestone." But he added incomprehensibly that "two black lions" guard the door of the Kaaba. Lion sculptures would have been anathema in Islam, which forbids human or animal depiction of any kind.

It is presumed from their names that both Zheng He's father and grandfather made pilgrimages to Mecca. If Zheng He himself had worshiped at the holy site, it is hard to imagine how this important fact would have gone unreported. Rather, it seems likely that Zheng He's failing health kept him in Calicut, unable or unwilling to confront the hazards of a long caravan ride across the desert. Given the inaccurate and secondhand nature of Ma Huan's account of the holy cities, one is tempted to speculate that Ma Huan remained close by the side of his ailing commander. What is clearer is that sometime on the voyage home, after the entire fleet was reunited in Calicut and had begun the journey east across the Indian Ocean, Zheng He died at sixty-two. A life at sea ended at sea. This is what his family believes.

According to Muslim tradition, his body would have been washed and wrapped in white cloth. Burial at sea was simple. Positioning his body with his head pointed toward Mecca, the Muslims on board would have chanted and prayed: "Allah is great, Allah is great, Allah is great . . . " before finally delivering Zheng He's body to the sea. His shoes and a braid of his hair, at his request, were thought to have been brought back to Nanjing and buried near Buddhist caves outside the city. A Muslim grave marks the spot today and a grave keeper guards the site, but farmers in a neighboring village whisper that there is really nothing under the stone marker. "Curious people have explored Zheng He's grave and found nothing," said one farmer. "No coffin. No box. Nothing." Descendants of Zheng He's adopted nephew who live in Nanjing also believe nothing is there, but on special memorial occasions, they come to the grave site and honor his memory. Shortly after Zheng He's death in Semarang in north Java, a *ghaib* service (from the Arab *gayb*, or absent) was performed. It is a funeral for the dead where the body is missing. Prayers drifted out over the still Java Sea: "Allah is great, Allah is great . . ."

In July 1433 the treasure fleet sailed into the mouth of the Yangzi River. On July 27 in Beijing, the emperor bestowed vestments of honor and paper money on the officers and men of the treasure fleet. He was pleased with the results of the voyage. On September 14 the ambassadors of Sumatra, Ceylon, Calicut and Cochin, Hormuz, Dhufar, Aden, and the other Arab states paid tribute at Fengtian Palace with horses, elephants, and a giraffe, which was again believed to be the auspicious *qilin*. An official from the Ministry of Rites suggested to the emperor that since the *qilin* was such a valuable gift there should be an official celebration at court. But, as his grandfather had done before him, the emperor rejected the request, believing it unwise to read too much into this expression of heaven's favor.

"I do not care for foreign things," he said. "I accept them because they come from far away and show the sincerity of distant peoples, but we should not celebrate this."

That autumn four more *qilins* arrived in China from the south seas. The king of Malacca came, with a retinue of more than two hundred people. It was bitterly cold. The emperor gave the Malaccans heavy clothes and shoes and advised them to stay in Nanjing until spring. Zhu Zhanji was not being overly cautious. In the spring, the younger brother of the King of Sumatra, unaccustomed to China's severe winters, died in Beijing after having spent the winter there. The emperor ordered him buried with due ceremony and respect, and dispatched the eunuch Wang Jinghong to Sumatra to personally express his sympathy to the king for the loss of his brother. Off the coast of Java, however, Wang lost his life in a shipwreck.

It seemed as if Zhu Zhanji had accomplished his purpose in re-establishing the tribute trade with the Indian Ocean basin and making "ten thousand countries our guests." In the years immediately following the seventh voyage of the treasure fleet, a dozen countries came to pay tribute to the emperor, and, when he died unexpectedly in early 1435 after a short illness, Chinese sea power seemed as secure as ever. Nanjing's Longjiang shipyard continued to function, and plans for the treasure ships existed until the 1470s. But with the death of the Xuande emperor the tide had indeed turned on China's dominance in the Indian Ocean, and Zheng He's seventh voyage was to be the last great expedition of the treasure fleet.

At first the changes were hardly perceptible. Emissaries continued their missions to China's shores. But in 1436, when Nanjing officials repeatedly appealed to the court for more craftsmen, their request was summarily denied. Concerned about the burden on the people, Zhu Zhanji's successor halted construction in shipyards and urged frugal economic practices. In 1437, after paying tribute, the king of the Ryūkyū Islands (south of Japan) asked the emperor for new court costumes, which had been given to his envoys since the beginning of the dynasty. The ones he had, he said, had "become old." And who knew when he would be able to return to China? The seas were now "dangerous and difficult." The emperor, however, declined to grant the king's request. The following year, the Siamese mission to the court was robbed of its cargo of pearls, gold, and jade by two dishonest officials in Guangdong. Through no fault of his own, the Siamese ambassador arrived in court without tribute. Such behavior from local officials would have been impossible to imagine in the Yongle reign. That same year, the emperor sent a message to the king of Java saying that the "envoy" he had sent was wild and drunk and had caused the deaths of several people, including himself. "You should be more careful," the emperor commanded, "in choosing envoys in the future."

Little by little, the imperial tribute system was beginning to break down. Foreign countries no longer showered the emperor with tribute gifts, and the emperor was hesitant to give any gifts at all. The true identity of the "ambassadors" was more dubious than ever; some were clearly thieves and smugglers. Provincial officials and local merchants, anxious for a piece of the enormous profits of foreign trade, were also boldly snatching tribute headed for Beijing, and the emperor seemed unable (or unwilling) to stop it. In 1444 a large trading expedition from Guangdong went to Java, where thirty-three of the smugglers remained behind, presumably to facilitate future transactions. Only a handful of the "vagabonds" were caught and punished.

Local markets sprang up along the China coast, offering the foreign goods to which the general population had now become accustomed. The government was clearly losing its monopoly on foreign trade and feared that links between the coastal provinces and foreign powers could further undermine its authority. Finally, the imperial navy was no longer able to provide safe passage for official trade missions on the high seas.

At its height in the early fifteenth century, the great Ming navy consisted of 3,500 vessels: 2,700 of them were warships at the dozens of coastal patrol stations up and down the coast, 400 were warships based at Xinjiangkou near Nanjing, and 400 were armed transport vessels for grain. In Zhejiang province alone, the fleet consisted of over 700 junks. But by 1440 the number of Zhejiang ships had been reduced to less than half that. By the middle of the fifteenth century, the provincial fleets were at a fraction of their former strength. By 1500 it was a capital offense to build boats of more than two masts, and in 1525 an imperial edict authorized coastal authorities to destroy all oceangoing ships and to arrest the merchants who sailed them. By 1551, at the height of *wako* piracy on the southeast China coast, it was a crime to go to sea in a multimasted ship, even for purposes of trade. In less than a hundred years, the greatest navy the world had ever known had ordered itself into extinction. Why?

Part of the answer has to do with court politics and the heightened tension between the eunuchs and the Confucian advisers to the emperor in the mid–fifteenth century. Seafaring and overseas trade were the traditional domain of the eunuchs, and in striking down those enterprises the Confucians were eliminating a primary source of their rivals' power and income.

During the reign of Zhu Zhanji, the power of both the Confucians and the eunuchs had been strengthened, laying the groundwork for this conflict. The emperor elevated the position of the grand secretaries, held by members of the Confucian Hanlin Academy, from a mere advisory body to a kind of working executive committee, which now submitted memorandums for approval on the operation of the six key ministries. More often than not, Zhu Zhanji simply adopted their recommendations. And, by insisting eunuchs be educated at a palace school to handle documents, Zhu Zhanji enabled them to take over all communication between ministries and therefore to decide which matters would be brought to his attention. If the emperor rejected the recommendations of the grand secretaries, eunuchs could take action on his behalf. Zhu Zhanji, however, kept the eunuchs in firm check. In 1427 and 1431 eunuchs were found guilty of graft and corruption; without the slightest hesitation, the emperor had them and their associates executed. Concerned that the eunuchs might tamper with official documents, he insisted that imperial edicts were valid only when confirmed by a supervising secretary.

With the force of his personality and a watchful eye, Zhu Zhanji kept the two powers at bay. But when he died suddenly in 1435 at the age of thirty-six, his young son, just seven, was ill equipped to deal with them. During the early years of the reign of the boy emperor Zhu Qizhen, eunuchs took control of the secret police and strengthened their supervisory roles in the army and as fiscal agents. They surreptitiously conducted their own commerce and inflated taxes, accumulating huge fortunes. And they tortured, executed, or banished anyone who opposed them. The young emperor himself was the unwitting pawn of his tutor, the infamous eunuch Wang Zhen, who parlayed his position as head of the eunuch agencies in the imperial city into de facto ruler of the empire. He was responsible for one of the most humiliating moments in Chinese history, setting China on a course that lead eventually to the downfall of the dynasty. It was a course that was at odds with the expansive, risk-taking philosophy of the Yongle emperor and everything the voyages of the treasure ships stood for.

Wang's greed knew no bounds. His warehouses were full of goods extorted from the daily operations of the government. He had even stolen Mongolian horses given in tribute to the emperor. By placing his friends and family in important military and administrative posts, he effectively stopped all opposition to his actions. When Hanlin adviser Liu Qiu raised questions about military involvement on the Yunnan-Burma border, Wang had him imprisoned and killed. Few dared cross the arrogant eunuch dictator again.

In 1449 Wang led a half-million Chinese troops to subdue Mongols on the northwestern frontier. Near Tumu on the Mongolian border, Wang held up the emperor's entourage to wait for more than a thousand wagons carrying his personal baggage. When, sensing danger, the minister of war urged Wang to move on, Wang cursed him.

"You fool of a bookworm!" he shouted. "What do you know about military affairs? Say another word and you will be beheaded on the spot."

Mongol horsemen, numbering no more than twenty thousand, soon closed in as the minister had feared, surrounding and cutting off the forward Chinese units with the emperor. Most of those attending the emperor were cut down by the fast-moving horsemen. But twenty-two-year-old Zhu Qizhen dismounted and sat on the field in a shower of arrows until, in disbelief at their good fortune, the Mongols took the emperor prisoner. Wang himself was killed in the battle—some say by angry Chinese officers. Had the Mongols seized the initiative, they could have easily marched on to Beijing. But they hesitated long enough for a Chinese resistance to be organized and for the emperor's younger brother to be installed as emperor.

An extraordinary scene ensued. In the new emperor's first court audience, the Confucians demanded the breakup of Wang's powerful eunuch network. They insisted that Wang personally be denounced for this historic disaster and his property confiscated. If these demands were not met, the officials threatened, they would kill themselves in protest.

Before the emperor had a chance to respond, one of the eunuchs' lackeys, Ma Shun, head of the imperial guard, said the officials were "out of order." Able to contain their rage no longer, the officials grabbed Ma. They ripped off his shoes, scratched out his eyes, and within minutes killed him with their bare hands. Two other eunuchs in the hall met a similar fate.

Frozen in fear, the emperor watched. He immediately agreed to the officials' demands. It seemed as if the eunuchs' hold on the court had been broken and the Confucian officials had won the day. But a year later the Mongols returned his older brother, and six years later, in a daring coup d'état, Zhu Qizhen reclaimed the throne. The minister of war, who had led the resistance, was executed as a traitor, and Zhu Qizhen ordered a shrine built for his beloved tutor, the tyrant Wang Zhen.

More important for the future of Chinese seafaring, eunuchs continued to be involved in foreign trade. Private merchants, aided and abetted by the eunuchs, flourished at the expense of official tribute trade missions until the end of the fifteenth century. This prompted a series of government restrictions limiting boat size and civilian participation in overseas trade. If court officials could not control the eunuchs' trade activities, at least they could impede them. The tragedy of such measures, however, was that as the shipyards for large oceangoing junks were shut down, the Chinese advances in naval technology were eventually lost. By the sixteenth century, few shipwrights knew how to build the large treasure ships. The development of guns and cannon also slowed, allowing the European powers to surpass the Chinese in firepower. The Chinese began to lose their technological edge over the West, never to regain it.

A series of economic factors also made it difficult for the government, regardless of this political infighting, to maintain shipyards for oceangoing vessels and a large coastal navy. With the opening of the Grand Canal in 1415, there was no longer a need for oceangoing junks to carry southern grain supplies northward to feed the capital. The focus of shipbuilding shifted to river barges. In addition, in the mid–fifteenth century, there was a severe inflation and paper money fell to less than one percent of its face value. The Ming dynasty's favorable exchange rate with foreign countries evaporated, due in part to the loss of prestige following the emperor's capture and the hoarding of goods for private trade. As Chinese scholar Lo Jung-pang observed, "Tribute trade worked for the court as long as it kept its monopoly on trade and forced foreign countries to accept

The decline of the Ming navy was due in part to the reopening of the Grand Canal in 1415. Emphasis gradually shifted from building ocean-going junks to flat-bottomed river barges (above), which carried grain to the new northern capital at Beijing.

low prices and payment in paper currency." Now the Ming government was forced to pay market value for the goods it needed, such as horses, timber, and medicines. Foreign countries scoffed at paper money and demanded goods in kind or large quantities of copper coins. The imperial coffers ran very low.

In the fifteenth century, China's tax base shrank by almost half. In 1398, 8.5 million *qing* (120 million acres) of land had supported the empire's taxes; a hundred years later the tax base had shrunk to 4.2 million *qing* (59 million acres) of land. Not only had the flooding of the Yellow River in 1448 left millions homeless and thousands of acres unproductive, but the wealthy managed to avoid paying taxes altogether and there was rampant corruption.

The third factor in the decline of the Ming navy was the increased threat of the Mongols after the emperor's capture. The government's limited military resources had to be drawn away from the coasts to guard the traditional trouble spots north of the Great Wall on the frontier. The union of the eastern and western Mongols under Altan Khan posed the biggest threat in a century. The draining cycle of raids and counterraids began, culminating in the successful invasion of the Manchus and the downfall of the Ming dynasty in 1644.

And as the military took up its fearful and defensive posture, the civilian population retreated from adventurous avenues of thought. Confucians stressed memorization of the classics for the arduous civil service exams and discouraged creativity or an interest in anything foreign. The Hanlin advisers developed the point of view in the mid–fifteenth century that China would "conquer" by the superiority of its civilization; the state should not be engaged in foreign commerce or foreign wars.

In advocating China's withdrawal from Annam in 1428, Hanlin adviser Yang Shiqi had said, "China should not stoop to fight with wolves and pigs." Two years earlier, Fan Ji had advised the emperor to give up sending expeditions to foreign countries, saying, "give the people of the Middle Kingdom a respite so that they can devote themselves to husbandry and schooling." He added, "The people from afar will voluntarily submit and distant lands will come into our fold, and our dynasty will last for ten thousand years."

Such thinking was in sharp contrast to that of Liao Yongzhong, an adviser to the Hongwu emperor, who had said in 1373 at the beginning of the Ming, "The construction of seagoing ships to halt invaders and protect our people is a great virtue."

In 1477 there was one last attempt to revive Chinese seafaring. A powerful eunuch named Wang Zhi, head of the imperial secret police, called for the logs of Zheng He to stimulate interest in naval expeditions. The vice president of the Ministry of War, Liu Daxia, confiscated Zheng He's documents from the archives and, according to some histories, either hid or burned them. He damned the records as "deceitful exaggerations of bizarre things far removed from the testimony of people's eyes and ears" and said that the products the treasure ships brought home—"betel, bamboo staves, grape-wine, pomegranates and ostrich eggs and such like odd things"—contributed nothing to the country. Liu reported to his superior, the head of the Ministry of War, that the logs of Zheng He's expeditions had been "lost."

"How is it possible for official documents in the archives to be lost?" said the minister incredulously.

"The expeditions of San Bao to the West Ocean wasted tens of myriads of money and grain," responded Liu, "and moreover the people who met their deaths (on these expeditions) may be counted in the myriads. Although he returned with wonderful, precious things, what benefit was it to the state? This was merely an action of bad government of which ministers should severely disapprove. Even if the old archives were still preserved they should be destroyed in order to suppress (a repetition of these things) at the root."

The minister rose from his chair, understanding now what had happened. "Your hidden virtue, sir, is not small," he said. "Surely this seat will soon be yours!"

The loss of the logs of Zheng He and his voyages was another tragic result of China's internal conflicts at this time. For the Confucians, foreign trade and contact with the outside world were linked to eunuchs and all that was wasteful and extravagant in the empire. A desire for contact with the outside world meant that China itself needed something from abroad and was therefore not strong and self-sufficient. The mere expression of need was unworthy of the dragon throne.

Ironically, China withdrew from the seas just at the moment when European powers were venturing farther and farther from the safe haven of the Mediterranean, trying to find a sea route to the Far East. Two centuries before, Marco Polo had ignited Europe's imagination with tales of his travels to Cathay and the Spice Islands and the unfathomable riches there. Portugal sought a passage to China in the 1440s by inching its way down the west coast of Africa. Bartolomeu Dias rounded the Cape of Good Hope in 1488; Vasco da Gama finally reached Calicut in India in 1498. In 1492 Christopher Columbus, of course, traveling with a heavily annotated copy of Marco Polo's travels, ran into the unexpected impediment of another continent on his way to Cathay. Until he died he insisted the islands he had reached were in fact islands off the Asian coast. Not until 1521 did Ferdinand Magellan finally fulfill Columbus's dream of reaching the China seas by sailing west.

China's voluntary surrender of her interests in southeast Asia did not go unnoticed in Europe. Missionary Juan González de Mendoza saw it as a good thing, of which expanding European powers should take note. In 1585 he wrote in his history of China:

> [The Chinese] have found by experience [that] to go forth of their owne kingdome to conquer others, is the spoile and loss of much people, and expences of great treasures, besides the trauaile and care

> which continually they have to sustaine that which is got, with feare to be lost againe; so that in the meane time whilest they were occupied in strange conquests, their enemies the Tartarians and other kings borderers vnto them, did trouble and inuade them, doing great damage and harme. . . . [So] they found it requisit for their quietnes and profite . . . to leaue al [that] they had got and gained out of their own kingdome, but specially such countries as were farre off. And from that day forwards not to make wars in any place.

Mendoza's warning of the futility of colonialism certainly went unheeded in his own time. Empire building would consume Europe for another three hundred years.

From the beginning of the sixteenth century, the Chinese suffered devastating raids by Japanese pirates. Sometimes the *wako* (from the pejorative Chinese term, *wokou*, meaning "dwarf pirates," and referring to the Japanese), assisted by collaborators on shore, took over entire Chinese villages, robbing and terrorizing the inhabitants. Local merchants and civilians made some effort to protect themselves, but for the most part, the *wako* came and went as they pleased. The former lord of the China seas was now at the mercy of looters and bandits.

11 The Sultan's Bride

There is a story every schoolchild in Malacca learns. It is a tale about a beautiful Chinese princess named Hang Libo, whom Zheng He was supposed to have escorted to Malacca to become the bride of Sultan Mansūr Shah. So that the princess would not be lonely in her new home, her father sent five hundred maidens with her, who eventually also married and settled at the base of a hill near Malacca's harbor that became known as Bukit China, or China Hill. The princess converted to Islam and bore the sultan a son named Mimat, and the descendants of the noble maidens were said to be the nucleus of Malacca's large Chinese community.

According to official Ming histories, however, no true imperial princess was ever given in marriage to a Malaccan sultan, and there are just two graves in Bukit China's large Chinese cemetery, as far as anyone can determine, that date from the Ming period. Hang Libo might have been simply a lady of the Chinese court, or she could have been the daughter of one of the so-called Chinese captains of Malacca who were appointed by the Portuguese authorities in the sixteenth century to manage the affairs of the Chinese community. Portuguese records do note the marriage of the second sultan of Malacca to the daughter of "the king of China's captain."

The Chinese in Malacca are fond of the story of Princess Hang Libo and proud of its intimation that their families have some distant connection with Chinese royalty or nobility. More likely, however, is the possibility, proposed by Fei Xin, that they might be descended from Zheng He's sailors who stayed in Malacca and married local women. Despite the Yongle emperor's strict prohibition against desertion, some of Zheng He's sailors were tempted by life in other lands and jumped ship. One of the far-reaching consequences of the voyages of the treasure ships, as the story of Hang Libo suggests, was the dispersal of the Chinese throughout southeast Asia.

Until the fifteenth century there were a few scattered Chinese communities in Asia. Northern Vietnam, which was a Chinese colony for twenty years, and Siam each had some resident Chinese. On periodic visits to Tumasik, old Singapore, in the mid–fourteenth century, Chinese traders reported seeing an indeterminate number of Chinese merchants there, living "intermingled" with the Malay population. There may also have been a population of Chinese in the northern neck of the Malay Peninsula. As early as the tenth century, Chinese refugees, mainly from Guangdong and Fujian provinces, settled Java. And, as we have seen, in the early fifteenth century, Zheng He found large settlements of Chinese in Gresik, Tuban, and Majapahit on Java's north coast as well as the large nest of Chinese pirates in Palembang in northwest Sumatra. Most Chinese left, it is assumed, under some duress—flood, famine, or threat of persecution—and unwillingly abandoned the important filial obligation to tend the graves of their ancestors.

The emigration that began during the voyages of Zheng He seemed to be of a different nature. Here and there, emissaries of the dragon throne suddenly disappeared, lured from their imperial mission by factors we can only surmise. The contacts they made in foreign lands no doubt presented the temptation of illegal trade and profits beyond their wildest dreams. The exodus began as a trickle, but like an unplugged leak in a dam it flowed steadily throughout the fifteenth century.

In 1403, on an official mission to Cambodia, three subordinate envoys fled and could not be found. The worried king of Cambodia enlisted three of his own people as replacements for the missing men. When the party returned to China and appeared before the Yongle emperor, he discovered the ruse and said to the Cambodians, "The Chinese fled of their own accord. This has nothing to do with you, and you do not have to take their places. Moreover, you do not know our language and customs." He sent them back to their own country with gifts of money and clothing. It is not known what became of the missing Chinese in Cambodia. Others emigrated illegally to neighboring Siam. In 1409 the emperor told a visiting Siamese envoy that he was concerned about his "wandering" countrymen, in particular, a man named He Baiquan and his followers, and wanted them returned to China for punishment.

Although emigration was banned in the early Ming, the Yongle emperor somewhat contradictorily sent thirty-six families to Japan as "a gift" to the shogun to facilitate trade between the two countries. One assumes that they were allowed to trade only on behalf of the emperor with profits earmarked for the imperial treasury, but these families had already tasted the forbidden fruit of foreign goods. What happened after the voyages of Zheng He and the gradual decline in official tribute trade? Some sailors and officers of Zheng He's fleet, clearly hungry for more, took to the sea on their own. They left China secretly with their families, settling throughout the south seas in the hope of making a better life for themselves.

By the end of the sixteenth century, there were tens of thousands of Chinese in such places as Luzon in the Philippines. So many settled there, in fact, that the local Spanish authorities were afraid they would be overthrown by the resident Chinese and tried to chase them off the island. The Chinese who did not leave were "insulted," according to the *Ming shi*, suggesting they may have been mistreated.

After the mid–fifteenth century the exodus of Chinese coupled with an official ban on private trading gave rise to piracy and an illegal trade in the China seas to an extent previously unknown. The Japanese *wako* who began to harass the Chinese coast with increasing frequency and ferocity were, in fact, international bands of bootleggers that included marauding Chinese merchants as well as some Malaysians and Portuguese. By the mid–sixteenth century, more than twenty Chinese coastal cities or garrisons were taken over by these pirates. The area around the mouth of the Yangzi, the traditional center of international trade, was particularly hard hit.

In the spring of 1556, for example, Xu Hai, a Buddhist monk from Hangzhou turned bandit, joined forces with another Chinese renegade, Wang Zhi, known as "king of the *wako*," whose base of operations was the Goto Archipelago off Japan. Xu used religious chants and divination to win the loyalty of his crew, who called him "general commissioned by heaven to pacify the oceans." With several thousand men, the two pirate gangs struck ports both north and south of the Yangzi River, threatening the flow of supplies at the terminus of the Grand Canal and even the treasures of the imperial Ming tombs outside Nanjing. With government armies focused on the serious Mongol threat in the north, Xu and Wang easily overpowered the local naval forces and plundered market towns around the port of Hangzhou for months on end, massacring peasants and filling a thousand boats with booty. During the long siege of the walled city of Tongxiang, however, the pirates began fighting among themselves over the spoils, which included a beautiful woman named Mistress Chu. Eventually government forces surrounded Xu, who drowned himself in a stream, and in 1557 took Wang Zhi into custody.

After that the raiders were not well organized, and ten years later the problem of piracy was brought under control. The ban on maritime trade was lifted, and the southeast coast was officially opened for trade. In the 1550s China began to trade with Portugal through Macao and in the 1570s with Spain at Manila, its base in the Philippines. Commercial relations with other European colonial powers followed.

China's coastal farmers and fishermen, however, who had been robbed of their livelihood as well as, at times, their wives or daughters, never forgot the *wako.* Young girls in the Hui'an peninsula north of Fuzhou in Fujian to this day tie blue scarfs tightly around their heads, hiding their faces. The scarfs are decorated with barrettes and ribbons, and it has become the local fashion, the style of Hui'an. But the stories, passed down for generations in villages, of a time when young women fled from the lecherous glances of the bandits who came from across the sea in ships with red sails, have not died.

The legacy of Zheng He was thus the diaspora of the Chinese in southeast Asia and, unwittingly, piracy and unleashed greed for the riches of the world markets. But there were still other consequences of the voyages, for in the hulls of the treasure ships were the calendars, books, musical instruments, weights, and measures that in some small measure spread Chinese culture to every port the fleet touched.

The first Ming emperor, Zhu Yuanzhang, gave calendars to tribute countries because he was anxious to have China's immediate neighbors accept the empire's customs. The calendars were compendia of Ming rituals and indicated the best times for every activity in life—not only such seasonal activities as planting, hunting, and raising cattle but also bathing and grooming, seeing a doctor or acupuncturist, getting married, moving, building a house, placing bets, or scheduling a funeral. There was a special calendar for rulers, the *huang li,* or imperial calendar, which included information on praying for good fortune (the duty of all kings), the giving of awards and titles, the training of soldiers, and the recuitment of talented people for government service. Zhu Yuanzhang reinstated the old Chinese system of civil service examinations that had been somewhat corrupted under the Mongol reign and sent his officials to Korea and Vietnam to reintroduce the system there as well.

There were different dress requirements for each of the major festivals throughout the year and for each of the nine ranks of civil and military officials. Ordinary men were forbidden to wear silk and anything of colored cloth, particularly yellow, which was reserve for the emperor. The *min li,* or civil calendar, noted the most auspicious times for trading, starting a business, collecting money, and even the best day "to be close to the people." In a world populated by spirits in every tree, stone, and stream, nothing in Ming life was left to chance.

In 1369, just after acceding to the dragon throne, Zhu Yuanzhang sent an imperial calendar and three thousand civil calendars to south Vietnam. That year other calendars were sent to Japan and Java. The Yongle emperor, in dozens of emissarial missions throughout his reign, sent calendars to more than thirty countries and fledgling city-states. How assiduously these countries followed the Ming calendar is unknown. Chinese books, exported during this period by the thousands, perhaps had more impact. In 1404 Zhu Di ordered the Ministry of Rites to print ten thousand copies of *Lie nü zhuan* (Biographies of heroic women), which were then sent to all the tribute countries. The famous work, first compiled by a noted Confucian scholar of the first century B.C., contains portraits of women who gave beneficial advice to their husbands or taught their children well; it was intended to inspire women as well as to remind men of the advantages of virtuous companions. Foreign texts also came into China during this period of cultural exchange, particularly Buddhist scriptures, transplanting southern sects of Buddhism into the Ming empire.

"Poetry and writing are the means by which the human heart is purified," said an Annamese envoy to the Ming court in 1457. "Since ancient times our country has always relied on Chinese books and such things to ensure the longevity of our control of the land. Now we beg you to follow the ancient custom of giving us what we lack in return for our products and aromatics."

Requests from foreign countries for Chinese systems of measurement, including brass rulers, containers for volumes, and balances and scales, as well as various Chinese musical instruments, were generally granted by the Ming emperors. Zhu Yuanzhang even invited the Chams to send a few of their people to his court to learn to play Chinese instruments. Any exchange of Chinese weapons, however, was strictly forbidden. This important bit of technology China kept for itself. The Ming emperors undoubtedly feared that these weapons might someday be used against them, but officially other reasons were given. Zhu Yuanzhang once explained to the Chams that, because they were at war with the Annamese, the court could not supply them with weapons because it would appear as if China were encouraging conflict, not helping to achieve peace.

By the end of the sixteenth century, when the Ming dynasty had begun to lose its luster and was vulnerable to the advances of foreign powers, Zheng He and the voyages of the treasure ships had already become nostalgic memories of better days gone by. Zheng He himself evolved from historic figure to fictional cult hero. At a time when China was no longer so confident of its powers, he became the embodiment of the virtuous commander who always wins the day.

In a scene from the Ming play about Zheng He called *Feng tian ming san bao xia Xiyang* (Obeying the emperor's orders, the three-jeweled [eunuch] goes out to the western oceans), written by an anonymous author in 1615, the treasure fleet is suddenly ambushed in Indonesian waters. The kings who have trapped the fleet demand porcelains and silk for safe passage through their domain.

"You just want porcelain—that is not difficult," says Zheng He. He gestures toward the crew to bring him some porcelain bowls. "Give several to each of these boats."

Porcelains are handed to the kings, who eye them in wonderment.

"What are these treasures of yours made of?" asks the king of Sulu.

"You do not know?" says Zheng He. "If you would like I can give you more. In our land, they grow everywhere on the mountains and in the fields. They are the product of trees. If you do not believe me, I can show you a porcelain tree."

"Yes, yes," say the kings.

The curious kings then board Zheng He's ship to get a closer look at the miraculous tree.

"Wonderful thing—this must be the root," says one.

"Give me several seeds," says another. "I will grow them myself."

As the kings study the trees, Zheng He signals three of his crew, who grab the kings and take them prisoner.

The scene was designed to showcase the cleverness of Zheng He as well as the gullibility of foreigners. The play was sometimes performed at court as a puppet play with two-foot-tall carved wooden puppets on sticks representing Zheng He and the barbarian kings and a long, narrow tub of water serving as the treacherous "ocean." Live shrimp and crabs in the water, suggesting monsters of the deep, further enhanced the set. Puppeteers behind silk screens moved the puppets over the tub, and the crabs in their unconscious zealousness undoubtedly provided some unscripted drama. The playwright perhaps hoped to stir his seventeenth-century audience into trying to restore China's supremacy on the sea.

Similar motives may have been behind Luo Maodeng's popular Ming novel about Zheng He, written in 1597. Here, Zheng He becomes a Danteesque figure whose travels now include a fantastic voyage to the underworld. Luo's hell, with its various tortures and punishments for the damned, reflected China's moral codes in the same way Dante's inferno explicated medieval European values. And for the first time we have the hint, albeit clothed in fiction, that the Chinese may have had some misgivings about Zheng He's military activities and the loss of life on the expeditions.

According to Luo, when the fleet was in the Middle East visiting Mecca—what the Chinese called Tianfang, or the Celestial Quarter—Zheng He wondered what countries lay farther west. Though he was warned that nothing lay beyond the western sea, he boldly continued. The fleet sailed west for several months until the sun and stars vanished and it was impossible to navigate. For another month the ships progressed slowly in a thick fog until land was sighted, a forbidding coast covered in snow. The admiral sent one of his officers, Wang Min, to explore the country.

Wang discovered a strange walled city in which the people had heads of oxen or horses and snakelike mouths with forked tongues and bulging eyes. It was not, however, until he met his wife—who had died ten years before—that he realized to his horror he was in the underworld. He was then given a tour by one of the gods, who had taken Wang's wife as his own. Wang saw a tower leading to Heaven, to which virtuous souls were beckoned with banners and music, and eight elegant halls, filled with blossoms and perfume, where they would enjoy celestial bliss until such time as a wise ruler came in China, when they would be reborn.

He also visited the two mountains where the damned were punished. Those who had been cold and indifferent to the suffering of others in life were burned in a blazing fire, then chilled in a cold oven; those who had been two-faced and had hurt people with "secret arrows" were sliced to pieces with lances and knives. In addition, there were separate hells, reflecting a mixture of Confucian and Buddhist ethics, for those who had neglected their obligations to their parents and siblings, for the disloyal, untruthful, unscrupulous, or dishonorable, or for any who had been lax in performing proper rituals. The ten unforgivable sins, for which condemned souls were persecuted in perpetuity, were murder, theft, adultery, lying, deception, coarse language, foul language, anger, covetousness, and perversion.

Luo then described how Wang's underworld guide was suddenly called away to listen to the complaints of thousands of foreigners and innocent people who said they had been killed unjustly by Zheng He's soldiers; they demanded the eunuch commander's death in retribution. The spirits of three to five thousand Javanese foot soldiers and their officers told a grisly tale of how they had been beheaded, skinned, then boiled and eaten by Chinese at Zheng He's command. The thirteen officers had been slashed a thousand times with sharp knives.

"What crimes did we commit to deserve such a punishment?" demanded the angry, weeping Javanese.

Other victims of Zheng He's exploits had been killed as religious sacrifices or simply as "a demonstration" to terrorize local populations, and fifty spirits claimed to have been beheaded "with a single stroke of a sharp sword" while they were sleeping.

At that moment, five of Zheng He's generals stormed the palace of the king of the underworld and arrogantly demanded tribute to take back to the Ming emperor. Brushing aside this insult, the king of the underworld gave a cryptic warning to the generals, which the priests aboard the treasure ships later interpreted. Unless Zheng He made amends for the unnecessary deaths he had caused, the fleet would be in grave danger. Zheng He immediately ordered the priests to conduct the appropriate ceremonies to appease the king of the underworld and ensure the safety of the mission.

Despite some misgivings about how many men may have died at his hand during the voyages of the treasure fleet, in the seventeenth and eighteenth centuries Zheng He ultimately emerges as a kind of patron saint for the expatriate Chinese, an Asian Saint Christopher who is worshiped in temples throughout southeast Asia. One of the largest temples to Zheng He is San Bao Gong outside of Semarang on the north shore of Java, near the place where the treasure fleet was said to have moored. The place was called Bergota, but after the Chinese began to settle there it became known as Sanbaolong.

According to local legends, on the fifth voyage Zheng He's principal deputy, Wang Jinghong, became ill and was taken ashore here to rest in a cave. Zheng He personally attended to him, preparing herbal medicines. After ten days, when Wang Jinghong had somewhat recovered, Zheng He and the fleet departed and continued on their way. Wang Jinghong, however, was said to have remained in Java for some time with a contingent of ten men and a small boat. They began to cultivate fields to feed themselves and also traded gold along the Java coast. Wang Jinghong preached the Islamic faith to the local people, who soon revered him, calling him "imam" and "pilot of the Honorable San Bao."

According to the Javanese, Wang Jinghong remained in Java until he died at the age of seventy-eight and was buried there according to Islamic rites. From then on, it is said, people began to worship Zheng He as well as to pay their respects to Wang Jinghong's grave on the first and fifteenth days of each month. A temple was built to Zheng He in the cave where Wang Jinghong and his men lived. Although the original temple was destroyed in 1704 when the cave collapsed, a new one was built in Chinese style, with a dragon gate guarded by two stone lions and several inner sanctuaries. In one sanctuary, an anchor from one of the treasure ships is venerated as a sacred object with incense that is burned day and night. In the temple there is also a statue of Zheng He, dressed in his official robes, before which offerings of fruit are frequently placed by the devoted. Just outside the cave is a spring that never runs dry, which is said to have been dug by Zheng He. People come from all over the island to drink the water, which is thought to be able to cure serious illnesses and keep the faithful young forever.

A tablet by the temple, erected in 1879, reads:

> The place where the honorable San Bao became a god is a beautiful site with exquisite mountains and clear water and abundant greenery. At the foot of the mountain, there is a stone gate in front of a natural cave where the spirit of San Bao appears and that is why it is called San Bao Cave. We, Chinese, lived in this uncivilized place always praying for his protection, especially those [of us] who were about to venture out on the sea for commerce. His protection of common people is known to all. So every month on the first and fifteenth day many people come to the cave with sincerity to worship. Many people come shoulder to shoulder and many carts with neighing horses. It is a sight to behold.

On the thirtieth day of the sixth lunar month, a large festival is held at San Bao Gong, honoring the day on which it is believed Zheng He first arrived in Java. Tens of thousands of Chinese from throughout Indonesia, the Philippines, Malaysia, and Thailand gather the night before, many sleeping on straw mats in the streets. On the day of the festival, a copy of Zheng He's statue in the Dajue Temple four miles away is carried to San Bao Gong to "meet" the original statue so that the duplicate will receive its sacred power. When the Dajue statue reaches the cave, it is turned to face the east and the devoted burn incense and pray. Then, waving banners and wooden swords, beating drums, and dancing, the large throng carts the statue back to Dajue Temple. Along the way, people push and shove one another, competing to carry the statue because it is supposed to bring luck and good fortune to the bearers. Even old men fight their way into the crowd just to touch the statue. If they succeed, they then touch themselves with the hand that touched the statue and ask Zheng He to grant them a long life.

In another part of Java, a large "footprint" several feet across is said to mark the place where Zheng He once walked and is a metaphor for the larger-than-life image the eunuch admiral commands among the Chinese community there.

In Malacca, a temple to Zheng He was erected in 1795 at the base of Bukit China as a shelter for Chinese who had come to worship at the graves of their ancestors. A walled courtyard leads through a columned hall to a sanctuary where incense burns day and night in front of a small gilt statue of Zheng He enclosed in a case. To the right is a shrine to the Celestial Consort, goddess of seamen, and to the left a memorial to the temple's founder. Chan Suat Lian, daughter of the caretaker of the temple, sat one morning in a corner selling incense to those who came to worship.

"To us, Zheng He was a great man," she said. "Long ago, he told our people to build our homes on stilts, and so we did. And he said we should wear hats in the streets, and so we did. Whether this is true or not I don't know, but he gave meaning to the lives of our ancestors as he does to us now."

Throughout the day people came and went in the temple. They lit sticks of incense and held them in their hands, bowing before the statue of Zheng He and praying to him about their daily concerns. They prayed to a man long dead who had now become a legend and saint and who, they hoped, was listening to their joys and sorrows. A young man wondered whether he should marry; a woman prayed for the health of a sick grandchild; a girl whispered out loud for help on her exams. The present reached out to the past. And as the sweet white smoke of the burning incense filled the sanctuary, the statue of Zheng He was barely visible, but the perception of him to those who came was clear.

Epilogue: A People Called Baijini

Aboriginal songs of northern Arnhem Land in Australia record the arrival before the Indonesians and Europeans of a people called "Baijini," who have been linked to the Chinese. They came in sailing ships, arriving with the northwest monsoons in October and November and departing for home on the southeast winds six months later. They came to fish for trepang, a sea slug, and also to collect the tortoiseshell, pearls, and sandalwood found farther inland. Anchors found along the coast have been attributed to the Baijini. They have one or two arms at sharp angles to the main shaft, a characteristic of Chinese adze anchors dating from the late Han dynasty. The Baijini were remembered as having light, golden-colored skin, and the aborigines said the women were very beautiful and wore robes or pantaloons of many colors, even when they worked. The Baijini built houses of stone and bark, as opposed to the Macassans from the Indonesian island of Sulawesi, who built wooden houses on stilts with thatched roofs. They brought looms with them to make cloth, but, as the aboriginal songs say, they did not share the secret of cloth making with the people of Arnhem Land. The women mixed dyes in large pots and produced yarns of beautiful colors.

The Baijini also planted fields of rice. A song of the Yirritja people of Yirrkala on the Gulf of Carpentaria tells of the cooking of this special "clean food":

> Cooking rice on the fire; pouring it into a pot from a bag.
> Pouring rice from a bag: rice, rice for food . . .
> Rice with its husk, pouring it there into earthen pots;
> Into pots of ant-hill earth . . .
> White, clean food, clean rice . . .
> Removing its husk and pouring it into pots: making it clean.

> Rice sticking in lumps, white scum on the boiling water.
> Rice with its stems and husks . . .
> Food poured from that bag and into the termite-mound pot . . .
> Pouring water, washing, cleaning the rice, removing the stems.

Places in northeastern Arnhem Land and the islands offshore from Blue Mud Bay to Elcho Island resonate with stories of the Baijini. At Banalbai near Yirrkala, the Baijini were supposedly frightened by a spirit they called "Thunder Man," who is suggestive of the thunder gods worshiped by the Yi people since the Han dynasty. Campsites remain in the area where they are said to have stayed, and, both on an island at the mouth of Port Bradshaw and on the adjacent mainland, large quantities of Chinese shards from all periods have been found, the earliest dating from the Han.

One day, another aboriginal song tells us, the Baijini saw smoke out on the sea in the direction of the island of Sulawesi, and they abandoned their rice fields in Arnhem Land, never to return.

Were the Baijini the Chinese or a very fair-skinned Indonesian people who came before the Macassan fishermen of Sulawesi? The aborigines are quite decided that Baijini were not Macassans because they are remembered specifically for the golden color of their skin.

Early Chinese histories indicate that the Chinese had knowledge of the stars of the Southern Hemisphere and recorded eclipses in the islands of the Philippines and places thirty degrees below the equator as early as the fourth century A.D. This suggests that the Chinese, whose kingdom was then centered around the Yellow River basin, may indeed have had some direct knowledge of the Australian continent. Early sources also describe places at the ends of the earth where the sun sometimes never set and where there were long periods of total darkness. These lands may have just been rhetorical conventions to illustrate the harmony of the Middle Kingdom, where day and night were balanced and periods of heat alternate with periods of cold. Or the descriptions may indeed have indicated that the Chinese at this early period had some knowledge of the extreme conditions at the polar regions.

> At the south corner of the far West there is a country . . . Gumang. . . . The light of the sun and moon does not shine there, so there is no distinction between day and night. Its people do not eat or wear clothes and sleep most of the time, waking once in fifty days . . .

> In the north corner of the far East there is a country called . . . Fulou. Its climate is always hot, for excessive amounts of sun and moon light shine there . . . [the people] are always awake and never sleep.

It is generally believed the Chinese carried on a vigorous porcelain trade with Borneo from the eighth century A.D. onward, when they may also have been making regular trips to the north coast of Australia to fish for trepangs, which were smoked and used as a base for a soup. The *Sui shu* (History of the Sui dynasty) of 636 A.D. includes oral accounts of various lands sixty to one hundred days south of the mainland of Asia by sail. One of them sounds like a disjointed portrait of Australia. It describes a bird called the *sheli,* "which understands human speech"—perhaps a reference to Australia's indigenous parrots—and people who are adept at throwing *lun dao,* or "circular knives," with deadly accuracy. The account goes on to describe the weapon as having a hole in the middle and ragged edges like a saw—which is, in fact, a very accurate description of what a boomerang looks like whirling through the air.

Another early compilation, the *Shan hai jing* (Stories of mountains and seas), though full of fiction and fantastic tales, does mention a wilderness area across the south seas called "the Great Beyond," where there are dark, hopping animals called *shuti,* which appear to have two heads. Carrying their young in a pouch, kangaroos might well have seemed to have two heads to people who had never seen them before, and the drawing of the *shuti* in *Shan hai jing* accurately portrays the slender face of the kangaroo with its doelike eyes, small ears, and long talons on both feet and forepaws. The *Shan hai jing* also mentions a strange land called "the country of the small people," inhabited by "small black men"—perhaps the Pygmies of neighboring New Guinea.

By the time Marco Polo visited China in the thirteenth century, Chinese mariners had frequented "two Javas"—one small, the other large—with boundaries that were not entirely known. This large Java then appeared on French maps of the sixteenth century as "Java la Grande" with the approximate size and shape of Australia. Search for Java la Grande prompted further exploration of the south seas, culminating in Cook's extensive surveys of the Australian coast in the eighteenth century. It seems unlikely, with all the traveling the Chinese had done in the area, that they should not have reached Australia centuries before the Europeans. Traveling with Zheng He,

Fei Xin reported that the treasure fleet reached Timor, which is just four hundred miles north of Darwin.

In 1879 a statuette of the Daoist god Shou Lao, the spirit of longevity, was discovered in the roots of a two-hundred-year-old banyan tree near Darwin during the building of a road. The southern Chinese frequently carved niches in banyans and used them as small shrines, which may have been the case here. The statuette, which is in the Ming style, was undoubtedly left in the tree, and over time, as the tree sank into the earth, must have become entwined with the roots, where it was eventually found. Banyans are not native to northern Australia, so their presence alone speaks of some Asian contact.

The navigation charts of Zheng He indicate a place called "Habu'er" that has been identified as Kerqueland Island in the Antarctic Ocean, suggesting that the treasure fleet may well have ventured into the southern hemisphere. But still, this evidence is inconclusive. Chinese votive statues were also popular with Malay fishermen, who could have been in possession of the statuette. We may never know for sure whether Zheng He or any other Ming seafarer brought the Shou Lao statuette to Australia.

Half a world away from Australia, on remote islands off the coast of Kenya, there are fishermen with fairer skin than other Swahilis. They are known as "Bajuni."

The islands are the place where ships first make landfall sailing with the southwest monsoon across the Indian Ocean. When whales were plentiful in the oceans, precious ambergris washed up on their shores, and on the mainland nearby there were large concentrations of elephants. The islands of the Lamu Archipelago, also known as the Bajun Islands, have good supplies of fresh water, and their offshore reefs teem with marine life. When fifteenth-century Portuguese explorers arrived on the island of Pate, which is accessible only at high tide, they found a cottage industry in luxurious silk cloth.

Traveling up the east African coast in 1569, the Jesuit Father Monclaro noted that Pate had "very rich silk cloths, from which the Portuguese derive great profit in other Moorish cities where they are not to be had, because they are only manufactured on Pate, and are sent to the others from that place." In the town of Siyu on Pate, craftsmen had a special way of carving the doors, using delicately incised designs with a fine lacquerlike stain that was unique on the African coast. The music on Pate and throughout adjacent islands was infused with an Asian quality. Drums were played with the fingertips, as they are in the East, instead of with the palm of the hand, as is more customary in Africa.

An Italian anthropologist, studying the Bajuni islanders on Pate in 1935, noted that even then these people had "a physical type absolutely different from other people in the region. The skin is rather light, in some slightly olive and in the men you can spot flowing beards and the women part their hair in the middle and then braid it into two side braids." The Bajunis were also slight of build and generally fine-featured. One of the leading clans on the island, the Famao, claim to be descended from a variety of foreign peoples—Arabs, Persians, and Portuguese. One Famao subclan, which is called Washanga, believes that its ancestors were shipwrecked Chinese sailors.

The story passed down from generation to generation among the Washanga people is that a Chinese sailing ship was wrecked off the coast of Pate near the town of Siyu. Having no way to return home, the Chinese sailors settled near Siyu, at a place called Mui Wanga Bakari, and converted to Islam. Though they married local women, there was still some tension between them and the Siyu people, whom they fought from time to time.

Washanga elders remember that some of their people were supposed to have lived on houses built on stilts out in the water for protection against raiders. And a story has survived about a young Washanga girl, a virgin, who was afraid of being raped during one of these times of conflict. She prayed to Allah, the story goes, and the ground opened and she sank into it. A well marks the spot today, and the Washanga still go there to pray.

There is another story the Washanga remember well. One day, they say, when their ancestors returned from fishing, they found everyone in their village slaughtered except the old men and the children. They were "walishanga," which means "astonished." After that, their village became known as "Shanga" and they were called "Washanga," which means "of Shanga." The people who remained alive in Shanga, however, soon abandoned their village and fled to the mainland.

They lived there until the ruler of Pate sent a messenger to them, urging them to return to the island, which they did. The Washanga wanted to settle in Siyu, but again the local people were fearful. According to one story, the Siyu people told the Washanga that they could stay if they killed the large snake that lived in their mosque. The Washanga put a cow into the mosque, and the snake ate the cow. But because the cow's horns were so big, the snake eventually died and the Washanga were permitted to stay in Siyu. According to another legend, however, the people of Siyu were worried that the Washanga, who were very rich, would control them. They said that the Washanga could stay if they built a wall around the town. It was a costly enterprise that the Siyu people thought would dissipate the Washanga's fortune and thus protect them. The Washanga agreed to build the wall and stayed in Siyu, where they were known as expert craftsmen, skilled in carving and fine woodworking.

The two dozen or so members of the Washanga tribe who live on Pate and some of the surrounding Bajun islands today all believe they are descended from Chinese. Some are proud of this heritage; some are not and will say they belong to another clan. The proud ones remember with particular fondness a story their parents passed on to them about the time long ago when the king of Malindi gave the emperor of China a gift of a male giraffe and a female giraffe. They like to point out that although one giraffe died on the way to China, the other lived. The Chinese emperor was very pleased with the unusual beast, which became a symbol of the friendship between the Chinese and the Swahili. It is remarkable that on this remote corner of the African coast, people who speak no Chinese should know the details of a story that is written in classical Chinese and read only by a handful of scholars.

The possibility that there may have been Chinese settlers on the east African coast, whether by accident or design, is supported in the geographical writings of medieval Arab travelers. In the tenth century, al-Masūdī noticed a strange people neighboring the black "Zanj" people whom he called "Yājūj" and "Mājūj" and linked to the wild tribes on the fringe of the Chinese empire. Had al-Masūdī seen Mongolian-looking people in Africa? Two centuries later, al-Idrīsī reported that, because of internal troubles in India, the Chinese had transferred their Indian Ocean trade base to Zanzibar and other islands off the African coast, where they entered into familiar relations with the inhabitants of the islands.

> This island [Zanzibar] has many buildings linked together and many villages in which cattle were also kept. Rice is cultivated. [The people] conduct much commerce and have a great variety of annual imports. And it was said that when there were rebellions in China and injustice and excesses prevailed in India, the Chinese transferred their commerce to Zanzibar and the dependent islands nearby. They entered into relations with the inhabitants and felt very comfortable with them because of their fairness, the pleasantness of their conduct, and the ease with which they transacted business. And so it is for that reason that the island prospered and travelers to it were many.

The Arab word *'ishra,* which al-Idrīsī used to describe the relationship between the Chinese and the Swahili, implies friendship over an extended period of time and close, sometimes intimate, association. The description certainly opens the possibility that the Chinese did in fact intermarry with the local population and were one of the foreign populations, along with Arabs, Persians, Indians, and later the Portuguese, who contributed to the mélange of coastal peoples on the Swahili coast. Clearly, there were tribes of very fair-skinned Africans that were noticed by early European travelers. In 1705 the Dutch merchant François Valentyn observed "women and children who were unusually white, and could well be compared with many European children." He said the light-skinned children had their bodies smeared with mud and dirt in order to, for whatever reason, darken their appearance.

The town of Shanga today lies in ruins on the eastern edge of Pate Island. Archeologists estimate that Shanga was abandoned sometime in the late fourteenth century. Many of the buildings of the town, made of white coral, appear to have been burned. Few are still standing. A white wall emerges out of the tangled bush here, another there, with small windows and wall niches that once held possessions. Near the remains of the large mosque in the center of the village is a strange stone tomb with wing-shaped cornices and a curious phallus-shaped pillar decorated with a green celadon Chinese bowl. "Pillar tombs" are common on Swahili sites up and down the coast and are not well understood, except that they represent some outside influence on Islam.

Large quantities of Chinese pottery have been found at Shanga, dating from its period of settlement between the eighth and fourteenth centuries. Excavations have also uncovered a bronze lion statuette in the style of Hindu Indian votive pieces, an unusual find on the African coast. The small lion has a ferocious stance—eyes protruding, front paw raised, mouth open to reveal a long, pointed tongue—and bears some resemblance to the fierce lion guardians of Chinese temples. The statuette has an alloy content very similar to that of Song dynasty coins and could have been made from melted Chinese currency. But like the Shou Lao statuette found on the north coast of Australia, it is impossible to say exactly where the statue was made and who brought it to Shanga.

Many pieces in this curious puzzle are missing. But while archeological evidence is currently lacking, folklore traditions in both regions are compelling and suggest that there was sporadic Asian contact and that Chinese may have settled the African and Australian coasts.

Language studies, were they to be done, might prove to be very helpful. The names Baijini and Bajuni are similar. They are both foreign words in their respective linguistic traditions, and no one is sure of the origins of either term. Unlike most Kiswahili words, Baijini has the same form for both the singular and the plural, as Chinese nouns do. Baijini and Bajuni may both have come from "baju"—the word Chinese living in Indonesia and Malaysia use for "long robe," which comes from the Mandarin Chinese word *pao*, for a long garment. The single most distinguishing characteristic about Chinese dress from earliest times was the long silk robe worn by men and women alike. If Zheng He and his men or earlier Chinese seafarers landed and stayed in Australia and Africa, their dazzling long robes would have made a distinct impression on the local populations. And the name, given in answer to inquiries about these curious garments, may well have become the name by which the people themselves were called and later remembered.

Working in north Arnhem Land in the late 1940s, the late anthropologist Ronald M. Berndt discovered that the old Baijini name for the design of their special cloth was *darabu*. Darabu designs, he said, made up of colored triangles, later became the basis of certain aboriginal clan designs. While conducting research in Lamu, I found that the Washanga people have a special word in their textile vocabulary that has the same sound as *darabu* used by the aborigines of North Arnhem Land. But the word *darabu* in the local Kiswahili dialect of the Bajuni refers to a loom. The Chinese word for cloth is *bu* and may possibly be the common root of these two related words.

Further investigations may confirm that the Baijini and the Bajuni were, in fact, descended from the same people. And, if their ancestors were not Chinese, then they certainly appear to have been, at some point in time, within the Chinese sphere of influence to have learned the closely guarded secret of silk and cloth making.

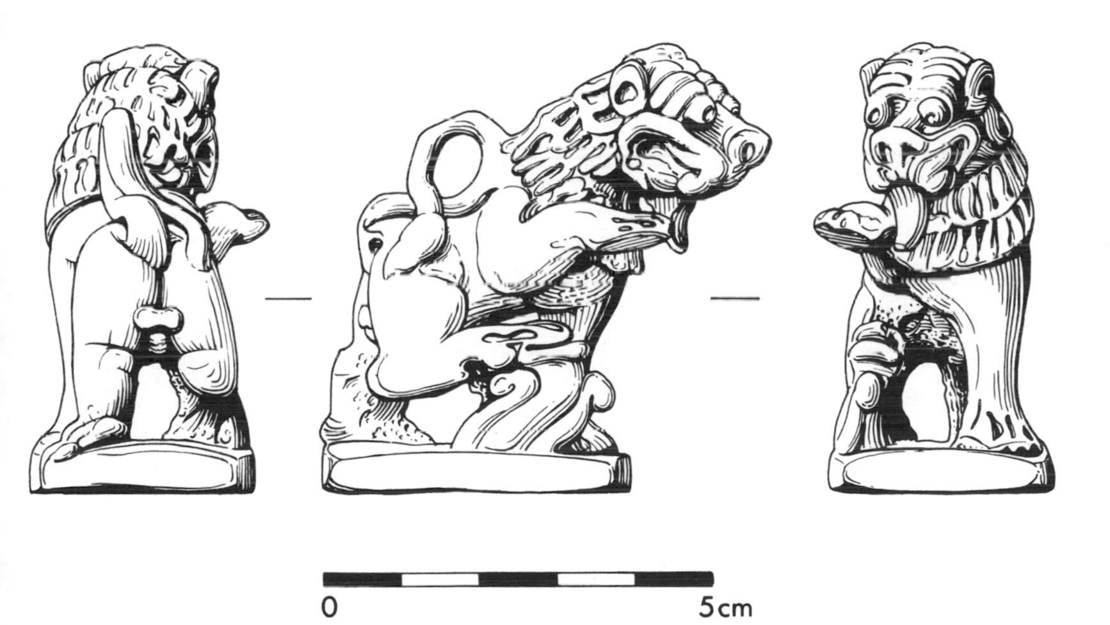

Bronze lion statuette from Shanga off the Kenya coast supports claims of early African links to India or Asia. (Mark Horton/Debbie Fulford)

Notes

PRINCIPAL CHINESE SOURCES

EYEWITNESS ACCOUNTS OF ZHENG HE'S VOYAGES:

Fei Xin, *Xing cha sheng lan* (Marvelous visions from the star raft) [1436], Shanghai, Commercial Press, 1938. Partial translation included in Gabriele Foccardi, *The Chinese travelers of the Ming period*, Wiesbaden, Harrassowitz, 1986. Fei was one of Zheng He's officers.

Gong Zhen, *Xiyang fan guo zhi* (Record of foreign countries in the Western Oceans) [1434], Beijing, Zhonghua shuju, 1961. Gong was an officer on the last voyage of the treasure fleet (1431–33).

Ma Huan, *Ying yai sheng lan* (The overall survey of the ocean shores), [begun in 1416; completed about 1435; first published in 1451], trans. with notes by J. V. G. Mills, Cambridge, England, Cambridge University Press, for the Hakluyt Society, 1970. Ma Huan was a Muslim translator who accompanied Zheng He on the later voyages.

OFFICIAL GOVERNMENT PUBLICATIONS:

Da Ming hui dian (Collected statutes of the Ming dynasty) [1503 and 1587], Taibei, Dongnan shubao, 1963. Compilation of laws and administrative regulations of the Ming empire, beginning with the Hongwu period. First edition has 180 chapters; later edition, with additional regulations from later reigns, 228 chapters.

Ming shi (Official history of the Ming dynasty) [begun in 1646; completed in 1736; first published in 1739], ed. Zhang Tingyu et al., Beijing, Zhonghua shuju, 1974. Some 220 of the 332 chapters of the history are devoted to important biographies of the period.

Ming shi ji shi ben mo (Narrative of events in Ming history from beginning to end) [1658], Beijing, Zhonghua shuju, 1977. A chronological presentation of events by topic.

Ming shi lu (Veritable records of the Ming dynasty) [1368–1644]. An official account of each emperor's reign was written shortly after the emperor's death. Subdivisions of the enormous work use the emperors' posthumous temple names, including *Taizu shi lu* [1418]; *Taizong shi lu* [1430], with a history of the Jianwen emperor [1398–1402] and the Yongle emperor [1402–24]; *Jenzong shi lu* [1430]; *Xuanzong shi lu* [1438]; and *Yingzong shi lu* [1467], Taibei, Zhongyang yanjiu yuan, 1962–64.

Others:

Anonymous, *Shun feng xiang song* (Fair winds for escort) [ca. 1430], in Xiang Da, annot., *Liang zhong hai dao zhen jing* (Two classics on navigation by compass), Beijing, Zhonghua shuju, 1961. A pilot's handbook.

Chen Cheng, *Xiyu xing cheng ji* (Diary of traveling in the Western Regions) [1414], ed. Zhang Yuanji, Taibei, Shangwu yinshu guan, 1975. Record of an emissarial mission by the author and Li Hsien, an assistant secretary of the Ministry of Revenue, from Kansu through central Asia to Samarkand and Herat. This work and the *Xiyu fan guo zhi* (Record of the countries in the Western Regions), by the same authors, are the most important sources of information on central Asia during the early Ming. Partially translated by Morris Rossabi, "Two Ming Envoys to Inner Asia," *T'oung Pao*, 62:3(1976), 1–34; and also by Rossabi, "A translation of Ch'en Ch'eng's *Hsi-yü fan kuo chih*," *Ming Studies*, 17(Fall 1983), 49–59.

Kong Lingren et al., *Zheng He*, Xian, Sanqin, 1991. A recent biography of Zheng He prepared by scholars associated with the Zheng He Research Institute in Nanjing.

Li Zhaoxiang, *Longjiang chuan chang zhi* (Records of the shipyards on the Dragon River) [1533], Taibei, Cheng chung, 1985. Monograph of the history and organization of the Longjiang shipyard, established during the Hongwu reign outside Nanjing. An important source on ships and shipbuilding during the Ming.

Luo Maodeng, *San bao taijian Xiyang ji tongsu yanyi* (Journey of the three-jeweled eunuch to the Western Oceans) [1597]. Shanghai, Guji, 1985. A historical novel believed to be based in part on the *Ming shi* and *Xiyang fan guo zhi*. The true historic value of the novel, however, has not been determined and I use it cautiously.

Mao Yuanyi, *Wu bei zhi* (Records of military preparations) [1621; printed about 1628]. Comprehensive work on the history of military tactics and armaments with maps and special emphasis on the Ming dynasty. Contains what are believed to be very faithful reproductions of the fifteenth-century sailing charts of Zheng He. Discussed in W. Z. Mulder, "The Wu Pei Chih charts," *T'oung Pao* 37(1942), 1–14.

Shang Chuan, *Yongle huang di* (The Yongle emperor), Beijing, Zhonghua shuju, 1989. The first comprehensive biography of the Yongle emperor drawing heavily on original source material by a Ming historian at the Chinese Academy of Social Sciences.

Zheng Hesheng, *Zheng He*, Sichuan, Victory, 1945. A comprehensive biography of Zheng He.

Zheng Hesheng and Zheng Yijun, *Zheng He xia Xiyang ziliao huibian* (Collection of research materials on Zheng He's voyage to the Western Oceans), Jinan, Qilu, 1980–89. The three-volume work contains a wealth of original source material on Zheng He and early Ming foreign relations. Zheng Yijun is a scholar at the Maritime Transportation Institute in Qingdao, Shandong.

Zhou Zhongyu, ed., *Zheng He jiapu kaoshi* (Investigation into the family history of Zheng He), Kunming, Chongwen, 1937. Contains the texts of important tablets relating to Zheng He and his family.

SELECTED ENGLISH AND FRENCH SECONDARY SOURCES

Crawford, Robert. "Eunuch power in the Ming dynasty," *T'oung Pao*, 49(1961–62), 117–48.

Dreyer, Edward L. *Early Ming China: A Political History 1355–1435*, Stanford, Stanford University, 1982.

Duyvendak, J. J. L. (1) *China's Discovery of Africa*, London, Probsthain, 1949. (Lectures given at London University, January 1947.)

———. (2) "The true dates of the Chinese maritime expeditions in the early fifteenth century," *T'oung Pao*, 34(1939), 341–412.

———. (3) "Desultory notes on the *Hsi Yang Chi*" [Luo Maodeng's novel of 1597 based on the voyages of Zheng He], *T'oung Pao*, 42(1953), 1–35.

Farmer, Edward L. *Early Ming Government: The Evolution of Dual Capitals*, Cambridge, Mass., Harvard University, 1976.

Goodrich, L. Carrington, and Chaoying Fang, eds. *Dictionary of Ming Biography*, New York and London, Columbia University, 1976.

Kierman, Frank A. and John K. Fairbank, eds. *Chinese Ways in Warfare*, Cambridge, Mass., Harvard University, 1974.

Lo Jung-pang. (1) "The emergence of China as a sea power in the late Sung and early Yuan periods," *Far Eastern Quarterly*, 14(1955), 489–503.

———. (2) "The decline of the early Ming navy," *Oriens Extremus*, 5:2(1958), 149–68.

———. (3) "China's paddle-wheel boats; the mechanised craft used in the opium war and their historical background," *Qinghua (T'sing-Hua) Journal of Chinese Studies* (New Series, Taiwan), 5(1958), 189–211.

———. (4) "The controversy over grain conveyance during the reign of

Khubilai Khan (1260–1294)," *Far Eastern Quarterly,* 13(1953), 263–85.

Mitamura, Taisuke. *Chinese Eunuchs,* trans. Charles A. Pomeroy, Rutland and Tokyo, Tuttle, 1970. Based in part on an earlier study by G. Carter Stent, "Chinese Eunuchs," *Journal of the North-China Branch of the Royal Asiatic Society,* New Series, 11(1877): 143–84.

Mote, Frederick W., and Denis Twitchett, eds. *The Cambridge History of China,* Vol. 7, *The Ming Dynasty [1368–1644], Part I,* Cambridge, England, Cambridge University Press, 1988.

Mulder, W. Z. "The *Wu Pei Chih* Charts," *T'oung Pao,* 37(1944), 1–14.

Needham, Joseph. *Science and Civilization in China,* Cambridge, England, Cambridge University Press. Vol. III, sec. 20, "Astronomy," and sec. 22, "Geography and Cartography," 1959; vol. IV:2, sec. 27, "Mechanical Engineering," 1965; vol. IV:3, sec. 29, "Nautics," 1971; vol. V:7, "Military Technology," 1986.

Pelliot, Paul (1) "Les grands voyages maritimes chinois début du 15e siècle," *T'oung Pao,* 30(1933), 237–452.

———. (2) "Notes additionelles sur Tcheng Houo et sur ses voyages," *T'oung Pao,* 31(1935), 274–314.

———. (3) "Encore à propos des voyages de Tcheng Houo," *T'oung Pao,* 32(1936), 210–22.

1. The Yi Peoples

23. "Yi" 夷 is used in later Chinese sources as a pejorative term describing non-Chinese "barbarian" people. Here, an earlier, more restrictive meaning of the word is intended. Yi designates a cultural complex, probably with Austro-Asiatic (Mon-Khmer) linguistic affiliations, stretching up the China coast through the ancient kingdoms of Yue and Wu (now the provinces of Zhejiang and Jiangsu) to the Shandong Peninsula. The Yi of Shandong province and the northeast coast were sometimes referred to as "Dong Yi," or Eastern Yi, the Yi of the southeast as "Nan Yi" (Southern Yi) or "Yue" or "Pai Yue." The Yi and Yue are sometimes considered separate peoples, but there is increasing linguistic and archeological evidence linking the two and possibly connecting both with the early Man people of the Yangzi River valley and eastern Sichuan, whose language appears to have been distantly related to the Mon-Khmer tongues of the early coastal people. E. G. Pulleyblank and Chang Kwang-chih discuss the relationships among all these peoples in "The Chinese and their neighbors in prehistoric and early historic times," in *The Origins of Chinese Civilization,* ed. David N. Keightley, Berkeley, University of California,

1983, 423–42, 459–60, 498. The picture of Neolithic China at the present time, however, is at best shadowy and incomplete.

23. Migrations from southeast Asia to Australia: A. G. Thorne, "Mungo and Kow Swamp: Morphological Variation in Pleistocene Australians," *Mankind,* 8:2(1971), 85–89; R. L. Kirk and A. G. Thorne, eds., *The Origins of the Australians,* Canberra, Australian Institute of Aboriginal Studies, 1976; Alan Thorne and Robert Raymond, *Man on the Rim: Peopling of the Pacific,* Sydney, Angus and Robertson, 1989.
24. Genetics study linking southeast Asians and Australians: Joanna Mountain et al., "Evolution of modern humans: evidence from nuclear DNA polymorphisms," in *Philosophical Transactions of the Royal Society of London,* 337(1992), 159–65. Evidence of early man in northern Australia: R. G. Roberts et al., "Thermoluminescence dating of a 50,000-year-old human occupation site in northern Australia," *Nature,* 345(1990), 153–56.
24. Possible change in the course of the Yangzi: G. R. G. Worcester, *The Junks and Sampans of the Yangtze,* Annapolis, Naval Institute, 1971, 4; Lyman P. Van Slyke, *Yangtze: Nature, History, and the River,* Reading, Penn., Addison-Wesley, 1988, 8–9, 17–18; Ren Mei'e et al., "Yunnan xibeibu Jinshajiang hegu dimao yu heliu xiduo wenti" (The land form of the Jinsha River valley in northwestern Yunnan and the problem of river capture), in *Acta Geographica Sinica,* 25:2, 1959, 135–55.
24. Migration of mountain people to the coast and the rise in sea levels: William Meacham, "Origin and development of Yueh coastal neolithic: A microcosm of cultural change on the mainland of East Asia," in Keightley, *The Origins of Chinese Civilization,* 151–56.
25. Timing of the dispersal of Austronesian people: Edwin Doran, Jr., *Wanka Austronesian canoe origins,* College Station, Texas A & M, 1981, 49–53.
25. Bronze drum drawings: Mino Badner, "Some evidence of Dong-son-derived influence in the art of the Admiralty Islands," in *Early Chinese Art and Its Possible Influence in the Pacific Basin,* ed. Noel Barnard and Douglas Fraser, New York, Intercultural Arts, 1972, Vol. 3, 597–629.
25. Discussion of Oceanic words for boat: Ling Shun-sheng, "Formosan sea-going raft and its origin in ancient China," in *Min-tsu hsüeh yen-chiu so chi-k'an* (Bulletin of the Institute of Ethnology), Taibei, Academia Sinica, No. 1 (1956), 40–45.
25. The upland people of Madagascar have light skin and straight hair and many of the physical features of Malays and Indonesians. Malagasy is very closely related to Kawi, the ancient language of Java and southern Sumatra. Mervyn Brown, *Madagascar Rediscovered,* Hamden, Conn., Archon Books, 1979, 10–13; James Hornell, "In-

donesian influence on East African culture," *Journal of the Royal Anthropological Institute,* 64(1934), 305–22.

25. Pacific sailing raft: Ling Shun-sheng, "Formosan sea-going raft," 25–65; Clinton R. Edwards, "Sailing rafts of Sechura: History and problems of origin," *Southwestern Journal of Anthropology,* 16(1960), 368–91; Edwin Doran, Jr., "The sailing raft as a great tradition," in *Man Across the Sea,* Austin, University of Texas, 1971.
26. Asian bark cloth manufacture as well as blowgun technology were thought to have been transmitted from Indonesia to the New World sometime in the first millennium B.C. Paul Tolstoy, "Cultural parallels between southeast Asia and Mesoamerica in the manufacture of bark cloth," *Transactions of the New York Academy of Science,* 25:2 (April 1963), 646–62; Stephen C. Jett, "The Development and Distribution of the Blowgun," *Annals, Association of American Geographers,* 60:4(December 1970), 662–88.
27. Art historian Paul Shao argues that population disruptions were characteristic of Chinese history and may well have prompted flights across the sea, as evidenced in the exile of millions of Nationalist Chinese to Taiwan in the 1940s. Paul Shao, *The Origin of Ancient American Cultures,* Ames, Iowa State University, 1983, 335–37.
27. South China coastal legend: Michele Pirazzoli-T'Serstevens, "The bronze drums of Shi-zhai shan, their social and ritual significance," in *Early South East Asia,* ed. R. B. Smith and W. Watson, New York, Oxford University, 1979, 133.
28. Similarities between Shang and Chavin figurines: Garry Tee, "Evidence of the Chinese origin of the jaguar motif in Chavin art," *Asian Perspectives,* 21:1(1978), 27–29.
28. Shang and Olmec jades: Jerry Towle, "Jade: an indicator of trans-Pacific contact?" in *Yearbook of the Association of Pacific Coast Geographers,* 35, Corvallis, Oregon State University, 1973, 165–72.
28. Summary of the arguments for pre-Columbian Asian contact in the New World: Joseph Needham and Lu Gwei-djen, *Trans-Pacific Echoes and Resonances: Listening Once Again,* Singapore, World Scientific, 1984. Bibliography of pre-Columbian research: John L. Sorenson and Martin H. Raish, *Pre-Columbian Contact with the Americas Across the Oceans: An Annotated Bibliography,* 2 vols., Provo, Research, 1990.
29. Search for the islands of the immortals: Sima Qian, *Shi ji* (Records of the historian) [90 B.C., first printed ca. 1000 A.D]. Partial translation in Burton Watson, *Records of the Grand Historian of China,* New York, Columbia University, 1961, vol. 2, 26–27. Also, Needham, IV:3, 551–53; V:2, 121–23.
30. Han ships: Needham, IV:3, 444–48.
31. Earth like the yolk of an egg: Needham, III, 217.

31. Possible Asian influence on the Maya: Needham, *Trans-Pacific Echoes,* 16, 32–33.

2. Confucians and Curiosities

33. "He replied that . . .": Confucius's actual words were, "If a superior man dwelt among them, what rudeness would there be?" James Legge, *The Chinese Classics,* Hong Kong, Hong Kong University, 1970, I, 107, from *Analects,* IX:13.
33. "While his parents . . .": Legge, *Chinese Classics, Analects,* IV:19, 171.
33. "The mind of . . .": Legge, *Chinese Classics, Analects,* IV:16, 170.
35. Tang exotics: Edward H. Schafer, *The Golden Peaches of Samarkand,* Berkeley, University of California, 1963; "Iranian merchants in T'ang dynasty tales," *Semitic and Oriental Studies Presented to William Popper,* University of California Publications in Semitic Philology, XI, 1951, 403–22.
36. "That which you now seek . . .": Sima Guang, *Zi zhi tong jian* (Comprehensive mirror for aid in governance) [1067–84], Beijing, Zhonghua shuju, 1956, chap. 211.
36. "indulgent treatment . . .": Legge, *Chinese Classics, Doctrine of the Mean,* XX:12, 409.
37. "there is an island . . .": Duyvendak (1), 22, translation of Zhou Qufei, *Ling wai dai da* ([Written] in place of replies about [the southwestern regions] beyond the mountain passes) [1178].
37. "The country of Bobali . . .": G. S. P. Freeman-Grenville, *The East African Coast: Select Documents from the First to the Earlier Nineteenth Century,* London, Rex Colling, 1975, 8, translation of Duan Chengshi, *Yuyang za zu* (Miscellany of Yuyang mountain) [863].
38. "if they do not die . . .": Duyvendak (1), 24, translation of Zhu Yu, *Pingzhou ke tan* (From chats in Pingzhou) [1119].
39. Guangzhou massacre: George F. Hourani, *Arab Seafaring,* Princeton, Princeton University, 1951, 76–78.
40. "I have seen oceans . . .": *Sindbad the Sailor,* trans. C. Ross Smith, New York, Doubleday, 1972, 2.
40. Voyage to Fusang guo: Paul Shao, *Asiatic Influence in Precolumbian Art,* Ames, Iowa State University, 1976, 5–7, translation of *Liang shu* (Official history of the Liang dynasty), seventh century A.D.
40. Buddhist robes: Shao, *Asiatic Influence,* 34.
40. Statue hand gesture: Shao, *Asiatic Influence,* 163.
40. Buddhist-Hindu influences on the Mayan: David H. Kelley, "Nine lords of the night," in *Studies in the Archaeology of Mexico and Guatemala,* 16, Berkeley, University of California Department of Anthropology, October 1972; "Calendar animals and deities," *Southwestern*

Journal of Anthropology, 16, Albuquerque, University of New Mexico, 1960.

41. "Profits from maritime commerce . . .": Needham, IV:3, 488.
41. "Goods and wealth are needed . . ." Wing-tsit Chan, trans. *Neo-Confucian Terms Explained* (The *Pei-hsi tzu-i* by Ch'en Ch'un [1159–1223]), New York, Columbia University, 1986, 136.
42. "Our defenses today are . . .": Lo Jung-pang (2), 502, translation of Zhen Ke, *Dongnan fang shou li bian* (Advantages of defending the southeast) [1131], *Xue hai lei bian* (Categorical compilation of the sea of learning) [1619 ed.], 3:28–29.
43. Song navy: *Song shi* (Official history of the Song dynasty) [ca. 1345], 186:8–9; Wu Qian, "Xu guo gong zou yi" (Memorials submitted to the throne by the duke of Xu guo) [1231–60], in *Shi wan zhuan lou congshu* (Collectanea of the hall of one hundred thousand volumes) [pub. 1876–92], 3:5.
43. Mo Ji's expeditions: Zhou Mi, *Qi dong ye yu* (Words of a retired scholar from the east of Qi) [late thirteenth century], in *Xue jin tao yuan* (Searching for the source at the ford of learning collectanea) [1805 edn.], 18:3.
44. "The ships which sail the southern sea . . .": Zheng (1), I, 196, excerpt from Zhou Qufei, *Ling wai dai da*.
47. Battle of the paddle wheelers, 1135 and 1161: Lo Jung-pang (3), 196–98; Needham, IV:2, 420–21, and V:7, 166, translation of Yang Wanli, *Hai qiu fu* (Rhapsodic ode on the paddle-wheel ships).
48. "The rest of the men were weary . . .": Lo Jung-pang, "Maritime commerce and its relations to the Sung navy," *Journal of the Economic and Social History of the Orient*, 12(1969), 92.
49. Low standing of Confucians in Yuan: Chen Yuan, *Western and Central Asians in China under the Mongols*, trans. Ch'ien Hsing-hai and L. Carrington Goodrich, Los Angeles, University of California, Monumenta Serica, 1966, 290–91.
49. Ibn Battūtah's description of Yuan ships: Needham, IV:3, 469–70.
55. Yuan grain transport: Lo Jung-pang (4).

3. The Prisoner and the Prince

57. When the practice of castrating young boys as eunuchs started, no one is quite sure. Heroditus believed the Persians were the first to have eunuchs because they thought eunuchs were more dependable than men. Eunuchs existed in pre-Christian Rome, as well as after the church was founded, when young choirboys were castrated to keep their voices high. In the early centuries B.C., Egyptians and Assyrians had eunuchs and the Greeks sold eunuchs as slaves. Mi-

tamura, 21–28 and Stent, 147. In China, the early Zhou dynasty rulers (about 1100 B.C.) listed castration as one of five forms of punishment that included branding the forehead, cutting off the nose, severing a limb, and death. It was called "palace punishment" because those who were castrated were forced to serve members of the royal household.

57. In 1461 a court eunuch named Yuan Rang supervised the castration of 1,565 boys in Sichuan, of whom 329 died of "sickness." He castrated additional boys to make up for those who had died. Zheng (2), 34.
58. Story of the capture of Zheng He from unpublished Zheng He family records, obtained from nineteenth-generation descendants of Zheng He's adopted nephew, Nanjing, April 1990.
58. Zhu Yuanzhang's belief in spirits: Romeyn Taylor, "Ming Taizu and the gods of the walls and moats," *Ming Studies*, 3 (Spring 1977), 31–49.
59. "I am as much the mother . . .": *Dictionary of Ming Biography*, 1024.
59. Zhu Di's Mongol birth: Henry Serruys, "A manuscript version of the legend of the Mongol ancestry of the Yung-lo emperor," *Occasional Papers No. 8*, Bloomington, The Mongolia Society, 1972. Despite the persistence of this legend in Mongolian traditions, it is likely to be untrue because Zhu Di was born on May 2, 1360, and Zhu Yuanzhang did not enter Beijing until 1368.
59. Premature birth of Zhu Di: Kong, 86–87.
60. Despite the later Qing renovation, the layout and scale of the miniature Ming palace can still be recognized at Chaotian Gong (now the City Museum) in Nanjing. Interview with City Museum Director Wang Xing, Nanjing, June 1990.
60. Palace wall inscriptions: *Dictionary of Ming Biography*, 1227.
61. Princes' matching verses: Shang, 36.
61. Fu Youde's death: *Dictionary of Ming Biography*, 470. This is one version of his death. The *Ming shi* records only that he was "ordered to commit suicide."
61. "I'm getting rid of the thorns . . .": Shang, 33.
62. "The title of this gentleman was Hajji. . . .": Zhou, 1–2.
63. The sex organs of a eunuch were called his *bao*, or "treasure." Eunuchs kept their organs with them throughout their life in order to be buried with them, when, they believed, their manhood would be restored. Without their *bao*, Yanwang, the king of the underworld, would, it was said, turn them into female asses. *Bao* also had to be shown at court upon being advanced in rank. Mitamura, 32–34.
63. "They should not be given responsibility . . .": *Ming shi*, chap. 74.
63. "Eunuchs should not intervene in . . .": Yin Shou-heng, *Ming shi qie*

(A private history of the Ming dynasty) [ca. 1634], Taibei, Huashi, 1978, chap. 25; *Ming shi,* chap. 74. Recent scholarship, however, suggests the eunuch sign was a later invention.

64. Eunuch bureaucracy: Crawford, 122–23.
64. "seven feet tall . . .": Zhou, 10, quoting *Gu jin shi jian* (Things past and present known or seen) [mid–fifteenth century].
66. Zhu Di's capture of Naghachu: Chang, 24–25, citing *Taizu shi lu,* chap. 200. Also, Dimitri Pokotilov, *History of the Eastern Mongols During the Ming Dynasty,* trans. Rudolf Lowenthal, Philadelphia, Porcupine, 1976, 15.
66. Zhu Yuanzhang's burial: Interview with Wei Yuqing, historian at the Ming tombs outside Beijing, June 1990. Some sources put the number of concubines interred with Zhu Yuanzhang at 38; others at more than 100.
68. "The treasonous officials . . .": *Ming shi ji shi ben mo,* chap. 16.
68. "born with a weak . . .": Shang, 19.
69. "Has my Lord not heard . . .": *Ming shi ji shi ben mo,* chap. 16.
69. Zhu Di's revolt: David B. Chan, *The Usurpation of the Prince of Yen, 1398–1402,* San Francisco, Chinese Materials Center, 1976. Also, Dreyer, 157–72.
70. Defense of walled cities: Frank A. Kierman and John K. Fairbank, *Chinese Ways in Warfare,* Cambridge, Mass., Harvard University, 1974, 177, citing Xu Xuefan, *Wu bei ji yao* (Compilation of the essentials of military skills) [1826].
71. Tale of escape of Zhu Yunwen: Shang, 131–32.
72. Naming of Zheng He: Interview with Zhou Shaochuan, Ming historian, Chinese Academy of Social Sciences, June 1990.
73. Theory of the Suzhou burial site for Zhu Yunwen: Xu Zuosheng, "Ming Hui Di chuwang Qionglong shan xin zheng" (New evidence that the Ming emperor Hui fled to Mount Qionglong), *Shixue Yuekan* (Journal of History Studies), 6(1986), 24–29.
73. "Regarding the Jianwen emperor's escape . . .": Zheng (2), II:2, 1152, citing Xia Xie, *Ming tong jian* (Comprehensive mirror of Ming history) [1873], chap. 14.

4. The Treasure Fleet

75. Shipbuilding figures: *Taizong shi lu,* chaps. 19, 21, 23, 26, 35, 38, 39, 46, 52, 54; summarized in Xi Longfei and He Guowei, "Shilun Zheng He baochuan de chuanxing yu jianzao didian" (A preliminary discussion of the ship type of Zheng He's treasure ship and places where the ships were built), in *Zheng He yu Fujian* (Zheng He and Fujian), Fujian, Fujian jiaoyu, 1986, 106.
76. Workshops at Longjiang, *Zheng He shiji wenwu xuan* (Selected cultural

artifacts and sites relating to Zheng He), Beijing, Renmin jiaotong, 1984, 17–18.

77. Demonstration models: Needham, IV:3, 409, translation from *Jin shu* (Official history of the Jin dynasty) [635 A.D.], chap. 79.
77. Proposed repair of dragon boats in drydock: Shen Kuo, *Mengxi bi tan, bu bi tan* (Supplement to notes taken in Mengxi) [written 1086–93], annotated by Hu Daojing, Hong Kong, Zhonghua shuju, 1975, 313.
78. Caulking: Li Guoqing, "Archaeological evidence of the use of 'chu nam' on the 13th-century Quanzhou ship, Fujian Province, China," *The International Journal of Nautical Archaeology and Underwater Exploration*, 18:4(1989), 277–83.
78. Building materials: Needham, IV:3, 413–14, translation from Song Yingxing, *Tian gong kai wu* (Exploitation of the works of nature) [1637].
78. *Shachuan: Shuyun jishu cidian* (Dictionary of transportation technology), Beijing, Renmin jiaotong, 1980, 24.
79. *Fuchuan:* Chen Qi and Chen Yangdong, "Chinese fuchuan," *Proceedings* of the International Sailing Ship Conference, Shanghai (December 4–8, 1991), the Shanghai Society of Naval Architecture and Marine Engineering, 298–308.
80. Complicated accounting characters were used in some histories, such as the *San Bao zheng yi ji* (Record of San Bao's pacification of the barbarians). Discussion in Chen Yanhang's "Zheng He bao chuan wei fuchuan xin kao" (A new study on Zheng He's treasure ships being fuchuan), in *Zheng He yu Fujian*, 92.
80. On Fujian *chi:* Chen Yenhang et al., "Zheng He bao chuan fuyuan yanjiu" (Research on the reconstruction of Zheng He's treasure ship), *Chuan shi yanjiu* (Studies of shipbuilding history), 2(1986). *Huai chi* and *Ming gong bu chi:* Chen Yenhang, personal correspondence, March 17, 1993.
80. Auspiciousness of "four": Wolfram Eberhard, *Dictionary of Chinese Symbols*, Singapore, Federal, 1990, 115–16.
80. Earlier large ships: Zheng Hesheng and Zheng Yijun, "Dui Zheng He baochuan de tantao" (Discussion of Zheng He's treasure ships), in *Zheng He xia Xiyang lunwen ji* (Collection of essays on Zheng He's voyages to the Western Oceans), Beijing, Renmin jiaotong, 1985, 54.
81. The treasure ship's low length-to-width ratio (2.4) has been verified in recent archeological finds. In 1973 a Song dynasty ship was unearthed in Quanzhou, Fujian, that was 79 feet long by 30 feet wide for a length-to-width ratio of 2.6. Committee for compiling the preliminary report on the excavation of a Song period oceangoing ship in Quanzhou Bay, "Quanzhou wan Songdai haichuan fajue jianbao" (Preliminary report on the excavation of a Song period

oceangoing ship in Quanzhou Bay), *Wenwu* (Cultural Artifacts), 10(1975), 1–34; Donald H. Keith and Christian J. Buys, "New light on medieval Chinese seagoing ship construction," *The International Journal of Nautical Archaeology and Underwater Exploration,* 10:2(1981), 119–32.

81. Balanced rudder: Needham, IV:3, 655–56.
81. Types of ships in the treasure fleet: Luo, chap. 15; Zheng (1), I, 204–206. In calculating the sizes of the smaller ships in the fleet, I am using a *chi* of 10½ inches.
83. Signals: Chen, "Zheng He bao chuan fuyuan yanjiu."
83. Makeup of the crew: Zheng (1), I, 144–50; Ma Huan, 31–32.
84. Rewards: Zheng (1), I, 151–52, citing *Taizong shi lu,* chap. 78.
84. General supplies for fleet: Zheng (1), I, 220, citing Gong.
84. *Kesi:* Michael Sullivan, *The Arts of China,* Berkeley, University of California, 1984, 213.
84. Export porcelain: Sullivan, *The Arts of China,* 222.
84. Ironworks: *Xuanzong shi lu,* chap. 54.
84. Orchards outside Nanjing: Zheng (1), I, 211, citing *Hongwu jing cheng tu zhi* (Illustrated history of the capital during the Hongwu period) [compiled ca. 1385], section entitled "Yuan pu" (Orchards and gardens).
85. Corruption story: Zheng (2), 161–62, citing *Huang Ming wen heng* (Records of the imperial Ming) [1527], 96.

5. Destination: Calicut

87. Zheng He's ability to command the fleet: Zheng (2), 25–26, citing Luo.
88. Calicut: A. Sreedhara Menon, *A Survey of Kerala History,* Kottayam, Sahitya Pravarthaka Co-operative Society, 1967, 60, 176–184.
88. "Now all within the four seas . . .": Zheng (1), I, 92, citing *Taizong shi lu,* chap. 12.
88. "Let there be mutual trade . . .": Duyvendak (2), 357–58, citing Tan Xisi, *Ming da zheng zuan yao* (A compilation of important government policies of the Ming court) [1619].
89. Banquet before the voyage: Zheng (2), 197–201.
89. Worship of Celestial Goddess: Interview with Yong Canlin, head of the Cultural Foundation of Tianfei, Beigang, Taiwan, April 1990.
90. "Our one fear . . .": Duyvendak (2), 352.
90. "As the divine swirling smoke rises . . .": *Shun feng xiang song,* 23–24.
92. Compass: Needham, IV:3, 563, 576.
92. Liujia and Taiping: Interviews with local Fujian officials, May 1990.
93. Yang water: *Shun feng xiang song,* 25.

96. *Qianxingban* ("star-taking" or celestial navigation boards): Sun Guangqi and Chen Ying, "Shilun Zheng He qianxingshu zhong de Alabo tianwen hanghai yinsu" (A preliminary discussion of the elements of Arabic nautical astronomy in Zheng He's technique of celestial navigation), *Zheng He Yanjiu* (Zheng He Studies), 14(May 1992), 21–26.
96. Zheng He's sailing charts: *Wu bei zhi.*
97. Champa: Kenneth R. Hall, *Maritime Trade and State Development in Early Southeast Asia*, Honolulu, University of Hawaii, 1985, 192.
98. Cham trade goods: Ma Huan, 81.
98. Javanese attack: O. W. Wolters, *The Fall of Srivijaya in Malay History*, London, Lund Humphries, 1970, 49–76.
99. Devil worshipers: Ma Huan, 93.
99. "Each time he [the performer] unrolls . . .": Ma Huan, 97.
99. Javanese jousting contest: Ma Huan, 94.
100. The king 'proved arrogant . . .' ": Pelliot (2), 283–84, translation of *Taizong shi lu*, chap. 77. Controversy over the date of Zheng He's visit to Ceylon: Duyvendak (2), 368.
100. Ceylon's holy mountain: Ma Huan, 127–28. Ceylon was a center for Theravada Buddhism. Ma Huan reported the folklore related to Adam's Peak (altitude 7,353 feet) on a visit there during the fourth voyage of the treasure fleet.
100. "The people are very honest . . .": Ma Huan, 140.
101. "In such and such a moon . . .": Ma Huan, 141.
101. "There is a traditional story . . .": Ma Huan, 139.
102. Naval battle with Chen Zuyi: Zheng (2), II:2, 1563–67, citing *Taizong shi lu*, chaps. 51, 71. Weapons: Zhang Tienlu, "Zuzhi yanmi zhuangbei jingliang de haishang jing lü" (A well-organized and powerful armada), *Zheng He Yanjiu* (Zheng He Studies), 12(May 1991), 30–31.
103. "At dawn, look to the southeast. . . .": Zheng (2), 135, citing Zhang Xie, *Dong xi yang kao* (Study of the Eastern and Western Oceans) [1618].
103. "Suddenly, there was a magic lantern . . .": Tablet to Tianfei, erected at Songjiang, Jiangsu province, by Zheng He, March 14, 1431. Translated in Duyvendak (2), 345.
104. Hu Ying: Zheng (1), II:2, 1566–67, from *Ming shi*, chap. 169.
105. "Alas, tributary king! . . .": *Ming shi*, chap. 325.
106. Siamese men: Ma Huan, 104.
106. "Though the journey . . .": Ma Huan, 138.

6. The Strange Kingdoms of Malacca and Ceylon

107. "very warlike man": Wolters, *The Fall of Srivijaya,* 117.
108. Legend of the naming of Malacca: "Malacca—the city of living history," *Malaysian Digest* (January 31, 1980), 4.
108. Malacca's patrol boats: Paul Wheatley, *The Golden Khersonese,* Westport, Conn.: Greenwood, 1973, 308.
108. Zhu Di's tablet inscriptions: Wang Gungwu, "Early Ming relations with Southeast Asia: A background essay," in John K. Fairbank, ed., *The Chinese World Order,* Cambridge, Mass., Harvard University, 1968, 56–57.
108. Malaccan stele erected by Zheng He: *Taizong shi lu,* chap. 47:

> We think the great service sagacious and virtuous rulers render for heaven and earth is that their governance defines and aids the working of heaven, earth and humanity, assists the forces of nature, and molds the myriad things so that the sun, the moon, and the stars shine, and so that the cycle of the seasons and the course of the year are completed; thus, heaven is able to be heaven and earth to be earth, each taking its proper place in peace, while the myriad things thereby evolve and grow. That they can achieve these things is because the workings of their one mind and the wonderfulness of their arrangements are greater even than heaven and earth, being such that they cannot be expressed in words.
>
> Formerly, my deceased imperial father, the Supreme Ancestor, sagelike and divine in his civil and military conduct, reverent and illustrious in creating the destiny of the dynasty, of exalted virtue and accomplishment, the realm unifier and great filial august emperor, assuming the position of a sage because he had the virtue of a sage, was the supreme lord of heaven and earth and mankind, regulating the cosmic forces, protecting and uniting all that was ever created and transformed in the world. Extending through the universe and encompassing heaven and earth, his wisdom was all pervasive and his actions always in accord with those of the divinities. It has been four decades and more since all living things between heaven and earth have without exception benefited from him unawares, and have been living and growing ignorant of his virtue.
>
> We have inherited from him this great enterprise, and we respectfully pursue his grand plan. Having received such good fortune and felicity, with good intentions we meet the ten thousand countries. So it was that in the ninth month of the third year of the reign of Yongle (Everlasting Joy), you, king of Malacca, dis-

patched an envoy to come and pay court and fully expressed your intentions, saying that your domain was in harmony and unity, your people living in peaceful happiness, its products abundant, its customs pure and harmonious, and that, cherishing benevolence and admiring righteousness, you wished it to be treated as a subject domain of the Middle Kingdom so that it could excel and be distinguished from the barbarian domains and forever be a region of the imperial domain, year upon year offering tribute and taxes, paying us the utmost obeisance and asking for our commands. Your sincerity is worthy of commendation. In truth, it is our deceased imperial father's overflowing favor and good blessings reaching unto your lands that have caused this to come about.

Thinking back to the ancient sage kings' enfeoffing of mountains, offering of libations to domains, giving out of seals, and bestowing of feudatory guards for the establishment of fiefdoms and to their expression of favor and distinction to the ten thousand countries through written proclamations and public orders, all to express far and wide that none are excluded from the imperial realm, let the western mountain of the kingdom of Malacca be enfeoffed as the Guardian Peak of the Kingdom. A commemorative poem is herewith bestowed to be engraved on everlasting stone, forever to show your descendants and the people of ten thousand generations to come that this bond with the Middle Kingdom shall be there like heaven unto the end of time.

The poem reads:

The vast southwestern sea reaches unto the Middle Kingdom,
  its waves cresting high as the heavens,
  watering the earth, the same way for countless eons.
Washed by sunlight, bathed in the moonlight,
  its luminous seascape is harmonious. Rain-swept crags
  and dewy rocks in its midst luxuriate with vegetation.
Golden ornaments and precious filigrees [from these lands]
  are resplendent with reds and blues.
  And in such a place people live in harmony.
Its righteous king, paying his respects to imperial
  suzerainty, wishes his country to be treated as one of
  our imperial domains and to follow the Chinese way.
He comes and goes in the midst of a retinue, rows of
  parasols unfurled around him. In performing rituals,
  his demeanor and dress are pious and reverent.

So here writ large on everlasting stone we do proclaim
your loyalty; your country's western mountain shall
forever be enfeoffed as a Guardian Peak.
The lords of the mountains and earls of the seas
shall all join its retinue, when the spirit of
our deceased imperial father descends from on high.
Posterity will smile upon your deed as time passes;
and your sons and grandsons will have
limitless good fortune.

—translated by
CHU HUNG-LAM AND JAMES GEISS

109. Chinese entrepôt in Malacca: Ma Huan, 113–14.
110. Malay textile patterns: Richard Winstedt, *The Malays: A Cultural History,* Singapore, Graham Brash, 1981, 162–64.
110. Malay spirit beliefs: Winstedt, *The Malays,* 7.
110. "The head eats . . .": Ma Huan, 84.
111. "black tigers . . .": Ma Huan, 113.
111. Pregnant women: Hajid Abul Majid, "Some Malay superstitions," *Journal of the Malayan Branch of the Royal Asiatic Society,* 4:4(1928), 42.
111. "Ho! mighty Brahma . . .": "Malay charms, Kelantan" collected by Anker Rentse, *Journal of the Malayan Branch of the Royal Asiatic Society,* 9:1(1931), 146.
111. Siamese mahogany: Kong, 152.
112. Epidemics: *Ming shi,* chap. 25.
112. Medical purpose of the voyages: Chen Yachang, "Chutan caiban fanyao shi Zheng He xia Xiyang de zhuyao jingmao huodong" (Preliminary discussion on the collecting of foreign medicines as the primary commercial activity of Zheng He's voyages), *Zheng He Yanjiu* (Zheng He Studies), 13(1991), 40–48.
113. "His Imperial Majesty, Emperor . . .": Needham, IV:3, 522–23.
114. "In Lanka, O lord . . .": Evelyn F. C. Ludowyk, *The Story of Ceylon,* London, Faber & Faber, 1967, 37.
114. Importance of the possession of the tooth relic: Garrett C. Mendis, *The Early History of Ceylon,* New York, AMS, 1975, 39, 73.
114. Alakeswara's refusal to pay tribute: Edward W. Perera, "Alakeswara: his life and times," *Journal of the Malayan Branch of the Royal Asiatic Society,* 18:55(1904), 291.
115. Chinese account of Ceylon fighting: Zheng (1), II:2, 1577, quoting *Taizong shi lu,* chap. 77.
115. "Straight-away, their dens and hideouts . . .": Yang Rong, *Yang Wenmin gong ji* (The collected works of Yang Rong) Jianan, Yang shi chong kan ben [1515], chap. 1.

116. Singhalese history of Chinese fighting in Ceylon: Perera, "Alakeswara," 291–95.
117. "The tooth shone . . .": *Ming bei ben ta Tang Xiyu ji* (Ming northern Tripitaka edition of the Record of the Western Regions in the Tang) [1440], taken from Sun Zongwen, "Zheng He xia Xiyang hongfa shiji" (Achievements in spreading Buddhist doctrines during Zheng He's voyages), *Zheng He Yanjiu* (Zheng He Studies), 13 (November 1991), 58–59.
117. "For the Tooth-relic of the Sage . . .": Edward W. Perera, "The age of Sri Pakakama Bahu VI," *Journal of the Ceylon Branch of the Royal Asiatic Society,* 22:63(1910), 17, translation from the *Mahavansa,* 91.
118. End of tribute trade with Ceylon: Perera, "The age of Sri Pakakama," 19.
118. Chinese procedures for handling tribute: *Ming hui dian,* chap. 109.
119. Market: *Ming hui dian,* chap. 108.
119. Introduction of eyeglasses into China: Duyvendak (3), 6–15.
119. Glassblowers: Kong, 153, citing *Zheng zi tong* (A complete guide to the correct orthography of characters) [1685].
120. Gifts to Parameswara: *Ming hui dian,* chap. 111.
120. *Jiu lou* and *guan ji:* Zheng (1) II:2, 1337–39, citing Jiang Nan, *Rong tang shi hua* (Poetry talks at the hibiscus pool) [mid–sixteenth century].
120. Archery contest: *Taizong shi lu,* chap. 140.
121. Cost of pagoda: *Zheng He shiji wenwu xuan* (Selected historic objects and sites of Zheng He), Beijing, Renmin jiaotong, 1984, 13.

7. Emissaries of the Dragon Throne

123. "that future generations . . .": *Huang Ming zu xun lu* (Ancestral injunctions) [1395], 5–6; cited in *Ming chao kai guo wen xian* (Documents from the founding of the Ming dynasty), Taibei, Xuesheng, 1966, III, 1588–89.
124. Horse markets: Morris Rossabi, "Two Ming envoys," 5.
125. Yishiha's tablet, written in Chinese, Jurchen, and Mongolian, is in the Vladivostok Museum, according to the *Dictionary of Ming Biography,* 685.
125. "lord of the realms . . .": Joseph F. Fletcher, "China and Central Asia, 1368–1884," in Fairbank, ed., *The Chinese World Order,* 211, citing a translation of the Persian text of the Yongle emperor's letter in 'Abd al-Razzāq Samarqandī, *Maṭla'-i sa'dayn wa majma'-i baḥrayn,* ca. 1475, 2:1, 130.
126. "thief and a bad man": *Narrative of the Embassy of Ruy González de Clavijo to the Court of Timour at Samarkand, A.D. 1403–6,* trans. Clements R. Markham, New York, Burt Franklin, 1970, 133–34.

126. Zhu Di's relations with Shāhrukh: Rossabi, "Two Ming envoys," 15–17, 26–29.
126. Arughtai: Dreyer, 178–82.
127. Zhu Di's letters to Shāhrukh: Rossabi, "Two Ming envoys," 26, translation of Chen Cheng's diary and record. Also, *Taizong shi lu*, chap. 143.
128. Trade needs of the Mongols: Henry Serruys, "Sino-Mongol relations during the Ming: The tribute system and diplomatic missions (1400–1600)," *Mélanges chinois et bouddhiques*, Bruxelles, Institut Belge des Hautes Études Chinoises, 14(1967), 19, 21, 249, 267–69, 279.
128. Post houses: *A Persian Embassy to China—Being an Extract from Zubdatu al-Tawārīkh of Hāfiz Abrū* [1423], trans. K. M. Maitra, New York, Paragon, 1970, 27–35.
129. Burden of Mongol missions: Serruys, "The tribute system," 383–84.
129. A Ming copy of the *Illustrations of tribute-bearing people* has not survived, but one exists from the Qing dynasty, and navigation charts in the *Wu bei zhi* include information based on these interviews.
129. Karmapa's birth: Nik Douglas and Meryl White, *Karmapa: The Black Hat Lama of Tibet*, London, Luzac, 1976, 61.
130. Buddhist symbols: *Catalogue of the Tibetan Collection and Other Lamaist Artifacts in the Newark Museum*, Newark, 1950, 27–28, 32.
130. Miracles: H. E. Richardson, "The Karma-pa Sect. A historical note," *Journal of the Royal Asiatic Society*, 2(1959), 1–6, translation of a scroll given to the fifth karmapa by the Yongle emperor.
130. *Dakinis* and *vajra:* Antoinette K. Gordon, *Iconography of Tibetan Lamaism*, New York, Columbia University, 1939, xxix and 80.
131. Yongle's offer to unify competing Buddhist sects: Douglas and White, *Karmapa*, 62.
131. Eunuch's role: Mitamura, 111–12. Abortion drug *ling hua: Jin ping mei jianshang cidian* (Phrase dictionary for the appreciation of *The golden lotus*), Shanghai, Guji, 1990, 932, citing Miao Xiyong, *Ben cao jing shu* (Marginalia to Shen Nong's treatise on materia medica) [sixteenth century].
133. Korean tribute relations: *Cambridge History of China*, VII, 268–69.
133. Conception of children: R. H. Van Gulik, *Sexual Life in Ancient China*, Leiden, E. J. Brill, 1974, 274–75, 333.
133. Sex to preserve a man's vital essence: Van Gulik, *Sexual Life*, 193–94, 197, 206, translation of Sun Simo, *Qian jin yao fang* (Important prescriptions worth a thousand gold pieces), section entitled "Fang nei bu yi" (Healthy sex life) [seventh century A.D.]. Women's vital "yin" essences were referred to as "jade fountain" or "jade fluid" (saliva); "peach of immortality" or "white snow" (breast milk); and "moon flower" (vaginal secretions): ibid., 283.
135. "I withdraw from the battlefield . . .": Van Gulik, *Sexual Life*, 279,

translation of Lu Dongbin's *Chun yang yan zheng fou you di jun ji ji zhen jing* (True classic of the complete union of the all-assisting lord of the yang force) [Song dynasty].

8. The Auspicious Appearance of the Celestial Animals

138. "a fine city . . .": H. A. R. Gibb, translator, *The Travels of Ibn Battuta, 1325–1354,* Millwood, N.Y., Kraus Reprint, 1986, 400.
138. "If the world were a ring . . .": Sir Percy Sykes, *A History of Persia,* London, Macmillan, 1921, 186.
139. Succession of king of Semudera: Zheng (1), II:2, 1593, citing *Ming tong jian,* chap. 16.
139. Maldive Islands: Ma Huan, 147–51.
140. Hormuz: Ma Huan, 165–72.
140. *Qilin* mythology: Charles S. Williams, *Outlines of Chinese Symbolism and Art Motifs,* Shanghai, Kelly & Walsh, 1932, 409–11.

   The special affection of the Chinese for giraffes continues to this day. When Kenyan President Daniel arap Moi visited China in October 1988, he brought along two giraffes as a symbol of friendship between the two countries: "Kenya to get Shs 230M loan from China govt," *The Standard* (Nairobi, Kenya, October 5, 1988), 24.
141. "In a corner of the western seas . . .": Duyvendak (2), 404, quoting Shen Du's poem accompanying his court painting of the *qilin,* dated the ninth month of the twelfth year of the Yongle reign (1414).
142. "If formerly, when the scholars . . .": Duyvendak (2), 405, citing *Ming shi,* chap. 326.
143. "This event is due . . .": Duyvendak (2), 405, quoting *Ming shi,* chap. 326.
143. "Mountain ridges in endless layers . . .": Kathy Liscomb, "The eight views of Beijing: Politics in literati art," *Artibus Asiae,* XLIX ½(1988/9), 139, translation of Wang Fu's poem accompanying his painting *Juyong die cui* (Layered shades of green at Juyong Pass) [1414].
144. Workforce for the Forbidden City: Wan-go Weng and Yang Boda, *The Palace Museum: Peking,* New York, Harry N. Abrams, 1982, 78.
145. Cochin tablet: *Taizong shi lu,* chap. 183:

   The kingly culture resonates everywhere with heaven and earth, and that all under heaven and on earth are included in its molding process is an embodiment of the benevolence of nature. There being no two principles under heaven and no two hearts in mankind, how can the same feelings of sorrow, grief, joy and pleasure and the same desires for peace, ease, satiety and warmth not be shared because of distance? He who is entrusted with the duty of ruling the people should strive to his utmost to treat the people like his children. The *Classic of Poetry* says:

The royal domain of a thousand leagues
Is where the people rest; but
There commence the boundaries that reach to the four seas . . .

And the *Book of Documents* says:

On the east reaching to the seas;
On the west extending to the moving sands;
To the utmost limits of the north and south;
His fame and influence fills up all within the four seas.

WE rule all under heaven, pacifying and governing the Chinese and the barbarians with impartial kindness and without distinction between mine and thine. Extending the way of the ancient sage emperors and enlightened kings so as to accord with the will of heaven and earth, we desire to have all distant countries and foreign domains each achieve its proper place under heaven. And there is not only one place that has heard of our customs and admired our culture.

The kingdom of Cochin is situated far off on the shores of the vast southwestern sea. Far more than any other foreign country, it has admired China and been familiar with the kingly culture for a long time. When our imperial orders arrived, its officials received them with their arms raised and their knees bent midst pounding drums. Submitting and adhering to us like people returning to their homes, they all looked up to heaven and then bowed, saying: "How fortunate we are that the teachings of the sages of China have benefited us. For several years now, we have had abundant harvests in our country and our people have had houses to live in, have had the bounty of the sea to eat their fill of, and have had fabrics enough for their clothing. Our old are kind to the young, and our juniors respectful to their seniors; all lead happy lives in harmony, without the habits of oppression and contention for dominance. The mountains lack ferocious beasts, the streams are free of noxious fish, the seas yield rare and precious things, the forests produce good wood, and all things flourish in abundance, more than double what is the norm. Violent winds have not arisen, torrential rains have not fallen, pestilence and plagues have ceased, and there have been no disasters or calamities. Truly this has been brought about by the kingly culture."

WE being meager in virtue, how could this be so? Is it not indeed brought about by the leader of the people there? Accordingly, we enfeoff Koyili as the king of the country and bestow on him a seal of office, so he might govern his people in peace.

WE further enfeoff a mountain in the kingdom as the Guardian Peak of the Kingdom, on which will be erected a stele to stand for ages to come. The inscription to be engraved reads:

Majestic that lofty mountain,
Guardian of the maritime country,
Dispersing mists and generating clouds,
Bringing great grace and favor to the kingdom beneath.
Make timely the rain and the sunshine there;
Silence the troublesome pounding storms there;
Help grow those crops in abundance;
Dispel those demonic hazes;
Protect the people there;
So they may be free from disasters and diseases,
To live with joy in their houses and homes,
And be so throughout the year.
High the mountain,
And deep the sea!
Let this inscription and poem be engraved,
And remain standing there forever with them.

—*translated by*
CHU HUNG-LAM AND JAMES GEISS

147. "The Imperial envoy . . .": Duyvendak (2), 381, translation of the tablet at Cemetery of the Sacred Tombs of the Sages, Quanzhou.
147. Yongle tablet inscription outside Quanzhou's Ashab mosque: *Quanzhou Yisilanjiao shike* (Islamic inscriptions in Quanzhou [Zaitun]), Chen Dasheng, compiler, Quanzhou, Fujian Jenmin, 1984, 11.
148. Baiqi's early navigators: Interview with Baiqi official Guo Xiangpeng, May 1990.
149. "At the king's [sultan's] palace . . .": Ma Huan, 155.
149. Swahilis' sense of themselves as *uungwana:* Derek Nurse and Thomas Spear, *The Swahili: Reconstructing the History and Language of an African Society 800–1500,* Philadelphia, University of Pennsylvania, 1985, 25.
150. "Every soul shall taste death. . . .": Arab tomb inscription, Jumba La Mtwana mosque, Kenya.
150. Possible cool reception of Chinese in Africa: Duyvendak (3), 18, referring to Luo, chaps. 72, 77, 78.
151. "craning their necks . . .": Duyvendak (2), 382–83, translation of a poem by Jin Youzi in Yan Congjian, *Shu yu zhou zi lu* (Comprehensive record of information about foreign places) [1574], chap. 9.
151. "There is no darkness . . .": Duyvendak (2), 409, translation of a *qilin* poem by Jin Youzi in *Shu yu zhou zi lu,* chap. 9.
151. Mogadishu: Foccardi, translation of *Xing cha sheng lan,* 71, 73.
152. Ceremony celebrating the opening of the Forbidden City: Interview

with Xu Qixian, director of the library at the Forbidden City, Beijing, June 1990.

152. "The Chinese porcelain that I use . . .": *Taizong shi lu,* chap. 53.
152. "*Tian bai*" and blue-and-white porcelains: *Imperial Porcelains of the Yongle and Xuande Periods Excavated from the Site of the Ming Imperial Factory at Jingdezhen,* Hong Kong: The Urban Council, 1989, 65–66, 71–73, 76.

9. Fires in the Forbidden City

155. "He who offends . . .": Legge, *The Chinese Classics, Analects,* III:13, 159.
155. Empress Xu's influence: *Dictionary of Ming Biography,* 567–68.
156. Palace massacre: Ellen Felicia Soullière, *Palace Women in the Ming,* doctoral dissertation, Princeton University, 1987, 290; Shang, 345, citing *Chosŏn wangjo Sillok* (Veritable records of the Korean court) [1400–45].
157. Emperor's riding accident: Shang, 270–71, based on a Persian account of the story in Ghiyās al-Dīn Khwand Amīr, Ḥabīb al-siyar (Beloved companion of the traveler) [fifteenth century].
157. "The ambassadors . . . are in no way . . .": *A Persian Embassy to China,* 104–5.
157. In the Manchu Qing dynasty (1644–1911), the names were changed to Taihe dian (Hall of Great Harmony), Zhonghe dian (Hall of Central Harmony), and Baohe dian (Hall of Perserving Harmony).
157. Palace fires: *A Persian Embassy to China,* 113–15.
158. Legend of Hu's prediction: Shang, 214.
158. "The God of Heaven is angry . . .": *A Persian Embassy to China,* 115.
158. "If a ruler's words . . .": Legge, *The Chinese Classics, Analects,* XIII:15, 269.
158. "My heart is full of trepidation. . . .": Shang, 214–15, citing *Taizong shi lu,* chap. 236.
159. Fujian epidemics and widespread starvation: *Taizong shi lu,* chaps. 116, 124, 162.
159. Annamese rebellion: *Cambridge History of China,* VII, 231.
159. "Those who responded to your edict . . .": Shang, 216, citing *Ming shi,* chap. 149.
159. Mongol campaigns: Dreyer, 180.
160. Supply figures: Shang, 218, citing *Taizong shi lu,* chap. 246.
160. "If all the people around me . . .": Shang, 346, citing Zhang Xuan, *Xi yuan wen jian lu* (Record of observations in the west garden) [1632], 102.
161. Zhu Di's views on health and medicine: Shang, 342–43, citing *Taizong bao xun* (Precious injunctions of the emperor Taizong) [1430],

1, and Cha Jizuo, *Zui wei lu* (Apologetic record of misdemeanors) [ca. 1670], 32:1, "Yongle yi ji." The opinion that he suffered from paralysis and took Daoist elixirs: *Cambridge History of China*, VII, 272–73.

161. "Yuanji loved me": *Dictionary of Ming Biography*, 533.
161. Death and burial of the Yongle emperor: Interview with Wei Yuqing, historian at the Ming tombs northwest of Beijing, April 1990. Also, Shang, 347. Sacrifices were held for Zhu Di at the Ming tombs by his descendants twice a year until 1924.
162. Young Zhu Gaozhi: *Dictionary of Ming Biography*, 338.
163. "All voyages of the treasure ships . . .": *Renzong shi lu*, chap. 1.
164. "Relieving people's poverty . . .": *Dictionary of Ming Biography*, 338.
165. Zheng He in Nanjing: Interview with three of his nineteenth-generation descendants—Zheng Ziqiang, Zheng Mianzhi, and Zheng Zhihai—at the Zheng He Institute, Nanjing, May 1990.
165. "I have reigned . . .": Ann Paludan, *The Imperial Ming Tombs*, New Haven and London, Yale University, 1981, 71.

10. The Last Voyage

167. Matching verses: *Taizong shi lu*, chap. 140.
168. "After only three turns . . .": *Dictionary of Ming Biography*, 283.
169. "The new reign of Xuande . . .": Zheng (1), II:2, 1621, citing *Xuanzong shi lu*, chap. 67.
169. "Is this the way to protect . . .": Zheng (1), II:2, 1622, citing *Xuanzong shi lu*, chap. 76.
170. Changle tablet [1431]: Translated in Duyvendak (2), 349.
170. Five parts of India: *Ming tong jian* [1873 reprint], Beijing, Zhonghua shuju, 1959, 874–75.
171. Reception in Jidda: K. N. Chaudhuri, "A note on Ibn Taghrī Birdī's description of Chinese ships in Aden and Jedda," *Journal of the Royal Asiatic Society of Great Britain and Ireland*, 1(1989), 112, translation of Abu'l-Mahāsin Ibn Taghrī Birdī, *History of Egypt 1382–1469* A.D., vol. 4, 1422–38 A.D.
171. Imported drugs: Needham, IV:3, 530–1; Hong-yen Hsu, *Oriental Materia Medica: A Concise Guide*, Taiwan, Oriental Healing Arts Institute, 1986, 88, 650–51, 656, 782.
171. Medina and Mecca: Ma Huan, 174–77.
172. Possibility of Zheng He's death at sea: Interviews with nineteenth-generation descendants of Zheng He at Zheng He Research Institute, Nanjing, April 1990.
172. *Ghaib* service: H. J. de Graaf and T. G. T. Pigeaud, *Chinese Muslims in Java in the 15th and 16th Centuries*, North Melbourne, Ruskin, 1984,

17, translation from *Malay Annals of Semarang and Cerbon* [ca. eighteenth century].

173. "I do not care for . . .": *Xuanzong shi lu,* chap. 105.
173. Death of Sumatran envoy: *Xuanzong shi lu,* chap. 108.
173. Death of Wang Jinghong: *Dictionary of Ming Biography,* 1365; *Yingzong shi lu,* chap. 4.
173. Events of 1436–38: Zheng (1), II:2, 1631–34, excerpts from *Guo que* (Assessments of the state) [ca. 1653], chap. 23; *Yingzong shi lu,* chaps. 31, 38, 45.
174. Increase in smuggling and nongovernment trading: *Yingzong shi lu,* chap. 113; Tian Peidong, "Lun Zheng He xia Xiyang zhongzhi de yuanyin" ("On the cause of the end of the voyages of Zheng He"), *Zheng He yanjiu* (Zheng He Studies) (May 1991), 12, 32–35.
174. Decline of Ming navy: Needham, IV:3, 326–38; Lo Jung-pang (2).
175. Increased power of eunuchs and grand secretaries: *Cambridge History of China,* VII,, 286–88.
175. Eunuch Wang Zhen: *Dictionary of Ming Biography,* 1347–49.
176. Tumu battle: Frederick W. Mote, "The T'u-mu incident of 1449," in Fairbank, ed., *Chinese Ways in Warfare,* 243–72.
178. Ming area measure: *Cambridge History of China,* VII, xxi: 1 *qing* = 100 *mou;* 1 *mou* = .14 acre.
179. Zheng He logs: Duyvendak (2), 395–598, from Gu Qiyuan, *Ke zuo zhiu yu* (Idle talk with guests) [1617], 1; Su Wangxiang, "Zheng He Xiyang dang'an wei Liu Daxia shaohui shu zhiyi" (Doubts about the reporting of Zheng He's logs being burned by Liu Daxia), *Zheng He Yanjiu* (Zheng He Studies) (November 1990), 11, 39–43.
180. "[The Chinese] have found by experience . . .": Juan González de Mendoza, *The History of the Great and Mighty Kingdom of China* [1585], trans. R. Parke, New York, Burt Franklin, 1970 reprint, 92–93.

11. The Sultan's Bride

183. Story of Princess Hang Libo: Malay primary school readers and an interview with Mrs. Charlie Chua, retired schoolteacher, Malacca, April 1990. In some versions of the story the princess is named Hang Liu.
183. Marriage of the second sultan of Malacca: Victor Purcell, *The Chinese in Malaya,* Kuala Lumpur, Oxford University, 1967, 20, citing *The Commentaries of the Great Afonso Dalboquerque* [1774], trans. Walter de Gray Birch, London, Hakluyt Society, 1880, 3.
184. Chinese merchants in Tumasik: Purcell, *The Chinese in Malaya,* 16.
184. Chinese in northern Malaysia: Purcell, *The Chinese in Malaya,* 14.
184. "The Chinese fled . . .": Zheng (1), II:2, 1463, citing *Ming shi,* chap. 324.

184. The Chinese in Siam: Zheng (1), II:2, 1574, citing *Taizong shi lu,* chap. 66.
184. "Gift" of thirty-six families: Chang Pin-tsun, "The first Chinese diaspora in Southeast Asia in the 15th century," paper contributed to the Symposium on entrepreneurs, emporia, and commodities in Asian maritime trade, 15th–18th centuries, Universität Heidelberg, Heidelberg, August 31–September 3, 1989, 21–22.
185. Bad treatment of Chinese in Luzon: Zheng (1), II:2, 1913, citing *Ming shi,* chap. 323.
185. Bandit-monk Xu Hai: Charles O. Hucker, "Hu Tsung-Hsien's campaign against Hsu Hai, 1556," in Fairbank, ed., *Chinese Ways in Warfare,* 280.
186. Hui'an women: Interviews with local women in Hui'an prefecture, June 1990.
186. Ming calendars: *Ming hui dian,* chap. 223.
186. Reinstatement of civil service exams: Zheng (1), II:2, 1946, citing *Taizu shi lu,* chap. 52.
187. Calendars to Vietnam: Zheng (1), II:2, 1940, citing *Taizu shi lu,* chap. 47.
187. "Poetry and writing are the means . . .": Zheng (1), II:2, 1949–50, citing *Yingzong shi lu,* chap. 279.
188. Zhu Yuanzhang's refusal to send weapons to Champa: Zheng (1), II:2, 1952, citing *Taizu shi lu,* chap. 67.
188. Scene from Ming play about Zheng He: *Feng tianming San Bao xia Xiyang* (Obeying the emperor's orders, the Three-Jeweled [eunuch] goes out to the Western Oceans), anonymous [1615], in *Xia Xiyang zaju* (Plays concerning going to the Western Oceans), Singapore, Shijie shuju, 1962, Interlude between Acts II and III, 38–40.
188. Zheng He play performed as puppet theater: Liu Ruoyu, *Zhuo zhong zhi* (A record of thoughts about life in the imperial palace) [ca. 1638], chap. 16.
189. Comparison of Luo Maodeng's novel to *The Divine Comedy:* J. J. L. Duyvendak, "A Chinese 'Divina Commedia,' " *T'oung Pao,* 41(1952), 255–316.
189. Journey to the underworld: Luo, chaps. 87–93. Partial translation in Anne Swann Goodrich, *Chinese Hells,* St. Augustin, Monumenta Serica, 1981, 88–96.
191. "The place where the honorable San Bao . . .": I. W. Young, "Sam Po Tong," *T'oung Pao,* 9(1898), 93–102.
192. Festival at San Bao Dong: Kong Yuanshi, "Yinni Sanbaolong de Sanbao miao huaren" (The Chinese and the Samboo Temple in Sambaolong, Indonesia), *Zheng He Yanjiu* (Zheng He Studies), 12(May 1991), 16–22.
192. "To us, Zheng He was a great man . . .": Interview with Chan Suat

Lian, daughter of the caretaker of the Zheng He temple, Malacca, April 1990.

Epilogue: A People Called Baijini

195. Baijini links to Chinese: P. M. Worsley, "Early Asian contacts with Australia," *Past and Present,* 7(April 1955), 1–11.
195. Collecting trepangs: Ronald M. Berndt, "External influence on the aboriginal," *Hemisphere,* 9:3(1965), 5.
195. Baijini anchors: A. P. Elkin and Catherine and Ronald Berndt, *Art in Arnhem Land,* Chicago, University of Chicago, 1951, 89. Chinese adze anchors from the late Han: Needham, IV:3, 657.
195. "Cooking rice on the fire . . .": Jennifer Isaacs, ed., *Australian Dreaming—40,000 Years of Aboriginal History,* Sydney, Landsdowne, 1980, 268.
196. "Thunder Man": Isaacs, *Australian Dreaming,* 261–62.
196. Early Baijini camp sites: Ronald M. Berndt and Catherine H. Berndt, *Arnhem Land, Its History and Its People,* Melbourne, F. W. Cheshire, 1954, 15.
196. Early Chinese knowledge of stars: Wei Juxian, *Zhongguoren faxian Aozhou* (The Chinese discovery of Australia), Hong Kong, Weixing, 1960, 1–6. Also, Needham, III:274.
196. "At the south corner of the far West . . .": A. C. Graham, trans., *The Book of Lieh-tzu* [ca. 380 A.D.], New York, Columbia University, 1990, 67–68.
197. Chinese trepang trade: Needham, IV:3, 537.
197. *Lun dao: Sui shu* (Official history of the Sui dynasty) [636 A.D.], chap. 82. *Shuti: Shan hai jing* (Stories of mountains and seas), Zhou and Han dynasties, section "Da huang nan jing" (The great beyond to the South). Drawings, based loosely on oral traditions, came into later editions.
197. Early European exploration of Australia: O. H. K. Spate, "Terra Australia—Cognita?" *Historical Studies of Australia and New Zealand,* 29:8(November 1957), 19.
198. Early Chinese contact with Australia: C. P. Fitzgerald, "A Chinese discovery of Australia," in *Australia Writes,* ed. T. Inglis Moore Melbourne, F. W. Cheshire, 1953, 81, 85.
198. Habu'er: *Dictionary of Ming Biography,* 199.
198. "very rich silk cloths . . .": Freeman-Grenville, *The East African Coast,* 142.
199. Asian elements in Pate culture: Interview with coastal archeologist James de Vere Allen in Nairobi, Kenya, October 1988.
199. "a physical type absolutely . . .": Anthropological studies of Bajuni,

N. Puccioni, *Giuba e oltregiuba (The Juba River and beyond)*, Florence, 1937, 110.

199. Famao clan: Howard Brown, *History of Siyu*, doctoral dissertation, Indiana University, Bloomington, 1985, 73, 77.
200. Washanga folklore: Interviews with Bwana Omar Bwana Fumo Mshanga, 90, the head of the Washanga clan; his sister, Esha Bwana Fumo; and other members of the clan on the Kenyan coast, October and November 1992.
200. "Yājūj" and "Mājūj": Al-Masûdî, *Kitâb at-tanbîh wa'l-ischrâf* (The book of advertisement and revision) [tenth century], *Bibliotheca geographorum Arabicorum*, VIII(1967), 24, 26, 32.
201. "This island [Zanzibar] has . . .:" Al-Idrīsī, *Opus geographicum*, Neapoli-Romai, Instituto Universitario Orientale di Napoli, 1970, 7, 62.
201. "women and children who were . . .": François Valentyn, *Beschryvinge van de Kaap der Goede Hoope met de zaaken daar toe Behoorende* (Description of the Cape of Good Hope with the matters concerning it) [1726], ed. Dr. E. H. Raidt, trans. Maj. R. Raven-Hart, Cape Town, Van Riebeeck Society, 1973, 61.
202. Thc name "Bajuni": V. L. Grottanelli, *Pescatori dell'Oceano Indiano* (The fishermen of the Indian Ocean), Rome, Cremonese, 1958, 12.
202. Aboriginal word *darabu:* Brendt, *Arnhem Land*, 36.
202. Kiswahili word *darabu:* Interview with Washanga clansmen (see note above).

Acknowledgments

When I first started this project in September of 1988, I visited British sinologist Joseph Needham, author of the *Science and Civilization in China* series, at his research institute at Cambridge University. Soon after we started talking late one afternoon, he interrupted himself abruptly.

"Much has happened since I wrote about Chinese navigation twenty years ago," he said. "Why don't you stay here for a few days and go through the correspondence and files I have kept on the subject?"

I stayed. And Dr. Needham, in a generosity of spirit and openness rare in academia, set me on a truer course in my research than might otherwise have been the case.

During those days at Cambridge, I also had the good fortune to meet Dr. H. T. Huang, a collaborator of Dr. Needham's and now deputy director of the Needham Research Institute, who greatly assisted me in my fieldwork in Malaysia. My conversations with his brother, Peter H. H. Huang, and also with John N. Miksic, Ernest C. T. Chew, Liaw Yock Fang, and Ng Ching-keong of the National University of Singapore were extremely helpful in understanding the maritime history of Malacca. I thank Charlie Chua Seng Kee and his family for my wonderful days in Malacca getting to know the Chinese community through their eyes, and also Chan Suat Lian for her insights at San Pao Gong. My knowledge of China's interaction with southeast Asia was also greatly enhanced by several long and interesting interviews with Wang Gungwu of the University of Hong Kong.

In my investigation of Swahili culture on the East African coast, I am grateful to the late British coastal archeologist, James Kirkman, and to the late James de Vere Allen of Kwale, Kenya. Both died in recent years, which is a great loss to Swahili studies. John Sutton of the British Institute of East Africa has taken many scholars under his wing, and I thank him for his immeasurable help and good fellowship on my behalf. My thanks to Richard Wilding, formerly of the Fort Jesus Museum, to Howard Brown of St. Lawrence University, and also to Mark Horton of Oxford for my fascinating days on site at his Pate excavation. My work with the Washanga, however, would have been impossible without the assistance of Ahmed Sheikh Nabany. I hope that someday we can finish the studies that will establish definitively these peoples' link to China.

In the spring and early summer of 1990, I traveled to the People's Republic of China as a visiting scholar with the Johns Hopkins University–Nanjing University Center for Chinese and American Studies. It was a tense time in China, and many cultural exchange programs had been canceled. This one weathered the storm, largely through the efforts of the directors at the time, William Speidel and Richard Gaulton, and I'm grateful that they both supported me and this far-flung project.

In Nanjing, my special thanks to archeologist Luo Zong Zhen, Wang Ying of the City Museum, and Kong Lin Ren of the Zheng He Research Institute. The institute has become a magnet for Zheng He scholarship around China and I drew on its published papers in my research. For sharing with me their family historical records, and for their warmth and encouragement during my stay in Nanjing, I thank Zheng Ziqiang, Zheng Mianzhi, and Zheng Zhihai, nineteenth- and twentieth-generation descendants of Zheng He's adopted nephew. The book is dedicated to them and to all of the descendants of Zheng He in Nanjing and in Kunming, in hope that the achievements of their ancestor may become better known in the West.

I am grateful for the long conversations on Ming history with Zhou Shaochuan, Wang Yichuan, and Shang Chuan of the Chinese Academy of Social History in Beijing. I have translated and excerpted portions of Shang Chuan's excellent recent book on the Yongle emperor, the first to synthesize accounts in the official histories. I thank Yang Boda, Xu Naixiang, Shan Guoqiang, and Yu Zhouyun for assistance in the Forbidden City; Wei Yuqing for help at the Ming tombs; Kong Xiangxing, Li Zefeng, and Liu Ruzhong for graciously seeing me under the most difficult of circumstances at the Chinese History Museum.

My sincere thanks to Li Guo Qing, director of the Museum of Overseas Transportation History in Quanzhou for his assistance in understanding Fukanese junks and shipbuilding, and to his wife for her help with translations. The museum's Yuan dynasty junk recovered from Quanzhou harbor is a rare find. My thanks also to Guo Xiang Peng of Baiqi, to Abdullah Huang Qiu Lun of the Fujian Islamic Association, to Han Zhenhua of Xiamen University, and to Xu Gongsheng of Fujian Teacher's College. In my travels in China, I worked with Karin Malmstrom. Her grace and good humor and command of Mandarin enabled us almost always to find the man with the key, and my research benefited enormously from her persistence.

I also spent several weeks at Academica Sinica in Taibei, and I want to express my gratitude to Chang Pin-tsun for his insights into the Chinese diaspora, to Gene J. Y. Chang for his advice on Mongolian matters, and to Julie Kung-shin Chou of the National Palace Museum for all her assistance in securing illustrations, and for her innumerable kindnesses. My sincere thanks to English teacher Pal Bjerkmann in the town of Beigang on the Taiwanese coast, and to his knowledgeable friends, Lin Yongcun, K. Y. Wang, and Cai Weibin.

Most of the research and writing of the book was done in Washington, D.C., where I had a study facility at the Library of Congress and was able to obtain most of the Ming manuscripts and other research materials I needed. I was continually amazed at the breadth and depth of the library's resources in every department and feel privileged to have been able to work there, thanks to the support of Bruce Martin and Victoria Hill. For their patience and encouragement throughout my years of research, I'm indebted to Robert Dunn, David Hsu, and Wang Chi of the Asian division. I learned from all of them. I also wish to thank Susan Meinheit, the Tibetan expert; George D. Selim and Christopher Murphy of the Arab section; Yoshiko Yoshimura in the Japanese department; and James Armstrong and Ellis

Gene Smith, two of the library's field officers, who were very helpful with African and Indonesian materials.

For the long and difficult task of translating Mandarin and classical Chinese source material, I relied principally on Chu Hung-lam, James Geiss, Scott Pierce, Wu Weiping, and Zuo Huanqi. I worked—together with Wu Weiping or Zuo Huanqi, Chinese linguistics scholars at Georgetown University—for the better part of two years, spending hours at a time at the library, editing and transcribing their loose, oral translations. The work would have been even more difficult without Zheng Hesheng and Zheng Yijun's multivolume collection of source material related to Zheng He, *Zheng He xia Xiyang ziliao huibian* (1980–89). The father and son, devoted Zheng He scholars, spent ten years gleaning Ming documents to produce this four thousand–page collection of excerpts. It is a rich repository that will, I'm sure, assist Ming scholars for years to come. I have benefited as well from a steady correspondence with Zheng Yijun in Qingdao, Shandong, through the course of my research and am indebted to the knowledge he brought to my queries.

I decided to transcribe Chinese characters into pinyin, the official romanization system in the People's Republic of China and many international agencies, which has largely supplanted the earlier Wade-Giles system. Thus, Nanking, Cheng Ho, and Yangtze become Nanjing, Zheng He, and Yangzi. Confucius and Mencius have not been changed because their names are so well known by their conventional spellings.

For the last six months of the project, I worked with James Geiss, a Ming historian and author of a forthcoming text on classical Chinese. Dr. Geiss, together with his colleague Dr. Chu Hung-lam, reviewed much of the previous work and tackled the translations of the official tablets and prose poems cited in the text. They are both poets in their own rights and, through them, the voices of the Yongle emperor and Daoist priests speak to us eloquently through the centuries. In addition, Dr. Geiss fielded my last and often unanswerable questions, tempering a journalist's judgment and adding immeasurably to the integrity of this work. I thank professors Kausalya Hart, David Keightley, Frederick Mote, Herbert Phillips, and John Wills for their comments on the manuscript. Whatever errors and lacunae might remain are mine.

Simon & Schuster and my editors there—Allan Mayer, Alice Mayhew, Marie Arana-Ward, Rebecca Saletan—supported me and this adventurous project faithfully and generously. My thanks particularly to Denise Roy and Jay Schweitzer for seeing the manuscript through production. I'm grateful to my agent, Carol Mann, for her confidence in the idea, which alone fueled my first year of research, and to Amanda Vaill Stewart for her critical guidance. Artists Kinuko Craft and Jan Adkins have done an extraordinary job creating images of the Yongle emperor and the treasure fleet that appear here.

And, for emergency assistance halfway round the world and immediate advances of cash and kindness when all my accounts were overdrawn, I'm indebted to my family and friends: Peter G. and Christine Levathes, Peter C. Levathes and Mary Kirby, Janet Adams Nash, Michael Lovendusky, Bryan Hodgson, and Mark Perkins. They were my copyeditors and confidants, my buoys in the storms. This is their book as well.

Index

Aaron, 101
Aden, 149, 151, 171, 172
Africa:
envoys from, 151
Chinese knowledge of, 37–38
Chinese settlers in, 198–203
Portuguese exploration of, 20–21, 180
slaves from, 37–38
Swahili culture in, 149–50
treasure fleet's voyages to, 19–21, 149–50, 151, 171
Alakeswara (Nissanka Alagakkonara), 114–16, 117, 118
Allah, 100, 113
Altan Khan, 179
Analects (Confucius), 33
anchors, 81
Annam, 54
Chams' conflict with, 97, 188
Chinese conflict with, 105, 124, 159, 160, 163, 168, 169, 179
Antarctic Ocean, 198
Arab traders, 20, 37, 39, 41, 43, 49, 147
Arabia, 35, 149, 170, 171
Arnhem Land (Australia), 195–96, 202–3
Arughtai, 126, 128, 160, 161
astronomy, 36, 83, 96, 97, 144
Atjeh, 98, 148
Australia, 195–98, 202–3
Baijini in, 195–96, 202–3
Chinese knowledge of, 196–197
migration of southern Asians to, 23–24
possibly visited by treasure fleet, 197–98
Austronesians, 23

Baijini, 195–96, 202–3
Baiqi, 148
Bajun Islands (Lamu Archipelago), 198–200
Bajuni, 198–200, 202–3
banquets, for foreign envoys, 120
bao chuan (treasure ships), 19, 21, 79–82
Bao Liang, 153
Bao Shan (Treasure Mountain), 93
Bao'en Temple complex, 165
bark cloth, 26–27
bartering rituals, 100–101
Basalawarmi, 57
Bebshin Shegpa (Halima), 129–131
Beijing (formerly Beiping or Daidu), 54, 58, 164, 167
capital moved to, 138, 143–45, 151–53, 159, 160, 163
Forbidden City in, 144–45, 151–152, 153, 155, 157–58, 159, 161, 162, 168
Beixi zi yi, 41
Bengal, 118, 138
giraffe presented to Zhu Di by, 140–42
Berndt, Ronald M., 202
Bismarck Archipelago, 25

Bo Juyi, 38
Bo'a'erxintai, 126
boats and ships:
amenities on, 44, 82
bao chuan (treasure ships), 19, 21, 79–82
canoes of early Pacific seafarers, 25, 28
communication at sea between, 83
construction of, 76–78
flat-bottomed river barges, 177, 178
fuchuan, 79, 80, 81, 82
Han, 30–31
ke zhou (guest ships), 80
long chuan (dragon boats), 80
lou chuan (castle or deck ships), 30
Mongol, 49–50
Pacific sailing rafts, 25–26
paddle-wheel ("flying tiger warships"), 45–46, 47
of Persian traders, 35–36
qiao chuan (bridge ships), 30–31
"sea falcons," 44
shachuan (sandboats), 78, 82
shen zhou (spirit ships), 80–81
size of, 80–81
Song, 43–45, 49, 80–81
Tang, 80
terms for, 25
Xihu zhou chuan (West Lake ships), 81
Borneo, 23, 197
Brawa, 140, 149
bridge ships (*qiao chuan*), 30–31
Brunei, 104–5, 109
Buddha, 93, 100, 112–13, 114
sacred tooth of, 114, 116–18
Buddhism, 59, 130, 147, 163, 189
in Ceylon, 100, 114
cultural exchange and, 187
in Malay Peninsula, 110
Mayan civilization and, 40–41
mistakenly believed to have originated in India, 170
Mongols and, 125
in Tibet, 129, 131
bulwark compartments, 81–82
Bureau of Merchant Shipping, 38–39
burial customs, for Ming emperors, 161–62
Burma, 35, 57, 176

calendars, 186, 187
Calicut, 140, 145, 180
bartering rituals in, 100–101
envoys from, 102, 118
Old Testament tale heard in, 101
treasure fleet's voyages to, 88, 100–102, 103, 105, 106, 114, 149, 170, 171, 172
zamurins of, 100, 101, 103, 106
Cambodia, 184
canoes, of early Pacific seafarers, 25, 28
Cape of Good Hope, 180
castle ships (*lou chuan*), 30
Cathay, 180
celadon, 84
Celestial Consort, *see* Tianfei
Ceylon, 36, 49, 172
civil war in, 114–18
gemstones in, 100
legend of founding of, 113–14
sacred tooth of Buddha in, 114, 116–18
strong religious undercurrents in, 100, 113–14
treasure fleet's voyages to, 100, 112–18, 138, 140, 149, 170
tribute demanded from, 114–15, 118
trilingual tablet taken to, 112–13, 114
Champa, 187
Annam's conflict with, 97, 188

treasure fleet's voyages to, 93, 96–98, 107, 138, 148
Chang'an, 34–35
Chavin culture, 28
Chen Cheng, 126–27
Chen Chun, 41
Chen Zuyi, 98, 102
Chongming Island, 78
Christianity, 111, 170–71
Chu, Mistress, 186
Chunqiu (Spring and autumn annals), 60
civil service examinations, 186
Cizhou, 84
Clavijo, Ruy González de, 125–126
clothing:
dress requirements and, 187
foreign influences on, 38
Cochin, 88, 100, 109
envoys from, 118, 172
sovereignty of, 145–46
treasure fleet's voyages to, 114, 149
Cocotin, Lady (Kuka Chin), 79
colonialism, 146, 180–81
Columbus, Christopher, 180
compasses, water, 92, 93–96
Confucian advisers, 88, 155, 168, 179
tension between eunuchs and, 72, 163, 164, 165, 175–77, 180
Confucianism, 80, 144, 189–90
filial obligations and, 33, 60, 133
foreign wars discouraged in, 163, 168, 179
in Han dynasty, 33–34
intimate relations and, 133
profit-making and, 41, 55
and rationale for tribute system, 36
resurgence of, after death of Zhu Di, 163–64, 165, 167–68
resurgence of, under Zhu Yuanzhang, 58
trade and foreign travel and, 33, 34, 36, 41, 54–55, 88, 164, 165, 175, 179, 180
in Yuan dynasty, 49, 54–55
Confucius, 33, 34, 36, 60, 64, 155, 158, 164
qilin and, 141
Cook, James, 197
corruption, 85, 178

Da xue yan yi (Zhen Dexiu), 60
Daidu, *see* Beijing
Daoism, 59, 148, 152, 161, 198
sexual behavior and, 133–135
Daoyan, 68–69, 70, 73
deck ships (*lou chuan*), 30
Dehua, 84
Deli, 98, 102
Dhufar, 171, 172
Dias, Bartolomeu, 180
dragon boats (*long chuan*), 80
dress, *see* clothing
drydocks, 77, 81
Duan Chengshi, 37

Eastern Yi, 27
Egypt, 149, 171
epidemics, 112
eunuchs, 57–58, 63–64, 167
as emissaries to frontier regions, 124, 125
imperial harem and, 131–32
tension between Confucian advisers and, 72, 163, 164, 165, 175–77, 180
treasure fleet supervised by, 83, 85
Zhu Di's rebellion and, 70, 72
Europe, 142
Chinese commercial relations with, 186
Chinese knowledge of, 20
colonialism of, 146, 180–81
explorers from, 180
firepower of, 177
see also specific nations
eyeglasses, presented to Zhu Di, 119

Fang Bin, 160
Fangzhang, 29
Fan Ji, 179
Fei Xin, 110, 111, 150, 151, 183, 198
Feng tian ming san bao xia Xiyang (Obeying the emperor's orders, the three jeweled [eunuch] goes out to the western oceans), 188–89
Fiji, 25
fire weapons, 47, 50–51, 52, 102, 177
"flying tiger warships," 45–46, 47
foot binding, 38
Forbidden City (Beijing), 153, 161, 162, 168
  construction of, 144–45, 159
  description of, 151–52
  festivities honoring completion of, 151, 152, 155
  fires in, 153, 157–58, 159
foreign envoys:
  banquets and entertainments for, 120
  daily rations for, 129
  guest house in Nanjing for, 118
  information collected from, 129
  post house system for, 128–129
  procedures for presentation of tribute by, 118–19
  trade conducted by, 119
  transported by treasure fleet, 19, 102, 103, 105, 140, 142, 145
foreigners:
  within borders of Tang dynasty, 34
  Confucian suspicion of, 33, 34
  discriminatory laws and, 39
  tribute demanded of, 36–37; *see also* tribute
  Zhu Di's opening to, 88
Fu Youde, 57, 58, 61
Fuchai, King, 79
fuchuan, 79, 80, 81, 82
Fujian, 32

Gama, Vasco da, 20–21, 180
Gao Zong, Emperor, 41, 42
Genghiz Khan, 48, 62
geomancers, 92
giraffes, presented as tribute, 140–43, 149, 151, 153, 172–173, 200
Goto Archipelago, 185
Grand Canal, 54, 55, 70, 138, 144, 177, 185
Gresik, 184
Gu jin lie nü zhuan, 163
guan du shang ban ("government supervision and merchant operation"), 55
Guangdong, 32, 84, 123
Guangzhou, 62, 89
  foreigners residing in, 39
  monitoring of trade in, 38–39
guest ships (*ke zhou*), 80
gunpowder weapons, 47, 50–51, 52, 102, 177
Guo Qi, 126

Hafiz, 128
Hāfiz-i-Abrū, 157
Halima (Bebshin Shegpa), 129–131
Han dynasty, 29–32, 92, 195, 196
  boats in, 30–31
  Confucianism in, 33–34
Hang Libo, Princess, 183
Hangzhou, 41, 42, 48, 84
Hanlin Academy, 163, 175, 179
Hasan, 138
He Baiquan, 184
herbs:
  of immortality, 29–30, 31–32
  medicinal, 83, 112, 128, 133
Hinduism, 40, 99–100, 101, 110
Honduras, 40

Hong Bao, 171
Hongwu emperor, *see* Zhu Yuanzhang
Hongxi emperor, *see* Zhu Gaozhi
Hormuz, 137, 138, 140, 171, 172
Hou Xian, 106, 107, 129
Hu, 158
Hu Tun, 52
Hu Ying, 104
Huang Chao, 39
Huang Huai, 168
Huang Huaixin, 77
Huang Yan, 133
Huang Zicheng, 68, 71
Hui Shen, 40
Hui Tong Hall (Nanjing), 118, 119, 121
Hui yao fang (Pharmaceutical prescriptions of the Muslims), 171
Hui'an Peninsula, 186
Huizong, Emperor, 80–81

Ibn Battūtah, 49–50, 138, 171
ice age, 23, 24
Idrīsī, al-, 200–201
Ilkhans, 138
import duties, 38–39
India, 35, 40, 49, 108, 110, 200
  religions mistakenly believed to have originated in, 170–171
  treasure fleet's voyages to, 114, 138, 170
  see also Calicut; Cochin
Indian Ocean, 21, 22, 25, 35, 41, 78, 198, 200
  China's dominance in, 121, 173
  Malacca as gateway to, 109
Indonesia, 31, 88, 89, 108
  Chinese residents of, 99, 192, 202
  conflict in, 98–99
  evidence of early Pacific seafarers in, 25
  migration of southern Asians to, 24
  possible exoduses from, 27
  treasure fleet's voyages to, 98, 99–100, 111–12
  vestiges of contact between New World and, 26–27
  see also Java; Sumatra
ironworks, 84
Islam, 126, 171, 191, 199
  in Africa, 149–50
  in Ceylon, 113, 114
  mistakenly believed to have originated in India, 170
  practiced by Zheng He, 147, 172
  Yongle emperor's protection of, 147–48

Japan, 88, 109, 153, 187
  Chinese families sent to, 184–185
  Chinese trade agreements with, 123
  Mongol invasion of, 50–54
  wako pirates of, 20, 89, 175, 181, 185–86
  Xu Fu's expedition and, 31
Java, 23, 35, 54, 104, 107, 145, 187, 197
  Chinese residents of, 99, 184
  envoys from, 118, 174
  Hindu practices in, 99–100
  jousting contests in, 99
  Palembang's conflict with, 98–99
  temple to Zheng He in, 190–92
  treasure fleet's voyages to, 98, 99–100, 138, 148, 170
  wayang performances on, 99
Java la Grande, 197
Jesus, 170
Jianwen emperor, *see* Zhu Yunwen
Jidda, 171
Jimmu Tenno, 31
Jin dynasty, 46–47, 48
Jin Youzi, 151, 168
Jing Hai Temple (Nanjing), 116, 117, 137

jousting contests, 99
Jurchens, 125, 128

Kaifeng, 41, 48
kamikaze, 54
ke zhou (guest ships), 80
Kerqueland Island, 198
kesi ("cut silk"), 84
Khmers, 23, 97, 105
Khubilai Khan, 54, 57, 81, 116, 170
  Japan invaded by, 50–54
  Song defeated by, 48–49
  trade conducted by, 49
Korea, 78, 119, 186
  Han and, 31
  Tang and, 34, 35, 36
  virgins from, sent to imperial harem, 37, 131, 132, 133, 135
  Zhu Di's relations with, 124, 132–133
Kuang Yu, 112

lacquerware, 19, 152, 153
Lamu Archipelago (Bajun Islands), 198–200
La-sa, 150
Le Loi, 159, 168
Li family, 34
Li Shaochun, 29–30
Li Shimian, 159
Li Ta, 127
Li Xian, 127
Liang shu (History of the Liang dynasty), 40–41
liangtianchi, 96
Liao, 46
Liao Yongzhong, 179
Lie nü zhuan (Biographies of heroic women), 187
Ling wai dai da (Information on what is beyond the passes) (Zhou Qufei), 37, 44
Linggu temple (Nanjing), 130
Liu Cheng, 48
Liu Daxia, 179–80
Liu Qiu, 176
Liujia, 92–93
Lo Jung-pang, 177–78
long chuan (dragon boats), 80
Longfellow, Henry Wadsworth, 121–22
Longjiang shipyards (Nanjing), 75, 76–80, 87, 89, 173
lou chuan (castle or deck ships), 30
Lou Maotang, 82
Lu, dukedom of, 60
Lu Chen, 142
Luo Maodeng, 150, 189–90
Luzon, 185

Ma, Empress, 59, 60–61, 121, 130
Ma Hajji, 61–63
Ma He, *see* Zheng He
Ma Huan, 100, 101, 106, 110, 111, 137–38, 139, 149, 171, 172
Ma Shun, 177
Ma Wenming, 62, 63
Macao, 186
Macassans, 195, 196
Madagascar, 25, 37, 54
Magellan, Ferdinand, 180
Majapahit, 184
Malacca:
  Chinese entrepôt established in, 109–10
  Chinese population of, 183
  emmisarial missions from, 102, 111, 118, 173
  founding of, 107–8
  religious and folk beliefs in, 110–111
  Siamese relations with, 107, 109, 145, 169
  sovereignty of, 107, 108–9, 145
  temple to Zheng He in, 192–193
  treasure fleet's voyages to, 107, 108–11, 148–49, 170
  tribute from, 119
Malay Archipelago, 27
Malay Peninsula, 23, 89, 98, 138
  Chinese population of, 184
  migration of southern Asians to, 25

see also Malacca
Malays, 198
ancestors of, 110
religious and folk beliefs of, 110–111
Malaysia, 88, 192, 202
Maldive Islands, 138, 139–40, 149
Malindi:
giraffes given to Zhu Di from, 140–43, 200
treasure fleet's voyages to, 19–20, 149, 171
Mamelukes, 149
Manchuria, 34, 124–25
Manchus, 179
Manila, 186
Mansūr Shah, Sultan, 183
Mao Kun map, 94–95, 96
Masudi, al-, 200
Mayan civilization, 31–32, 40–41
measurement systems, 187
Mecca, 149, 171–72, 189
Medina, 149, 171
Melanesia, 24, 110
Mencius, 64
Mendoza, Juan González de, 180–181
meteorology, 102–3
Mexico, 28, 40
Mayan civilization in, 31–32, 40–41
Mimat, 183
Ming bei ben ta Tang xi you ji (Ming edition of "Travels to the western regions during the Tang"), 116–17
Ming dynasty, 57–181
burial ground for emperors in, 161–62
civil war in (1398–1402), 66–74, 124
decline of navy in, 173, 174–79
downfall of, 179, 188
early, persecution of Muslims in, 148
emigration in, 183–86
eunuchs in court life of, 63–64, 131–32
fiscal problems in, 159, 177–178
instruction of princes and court officials in, 60
Mongols defeated by, 57–58, 59, 64–66
notion of semidivine emperor in, 145, 146
peak in influence of, 142
population rise in, 112
rituals of, 186–87
royal bedchamber in, 131–32, 133, 135
trade in, 19–20, 73–74, 84, 85, 88–89, 98–99, 100, 104, 105–106, 109, 119, 121, 123, 125, 128, 137, 138, 140, 142, 149, 174, 177, 184–85
treasure fleet in, *see* treasure fleet
tribute in, 88, 98, 105, 114–16, 118–20, 123, 125, 126, 128, 133, 140–43, 149, 151, 152, 156–57, 168, 172–73, 174, 176, 177–78, 185, 186–87
Ming shi, 185
Ming shi lu, 115
Ming tong jian, 73, 170, 171
Ministry of Revenue, 83, 119
Ministry of Rites, 83, 118–19, 120, 129, 142, 172–73, 187
Mo Ji, 43
Mogadishu, 140, 149, 150, 151
Mohammed, 170
Mōko shūrai ekatoba, 50–53
Moluccas, 25
Mombasa, 149, 150
Monclaro, Father, 198
Mongolia, 34, 160
Mongols, 48–55, 116, 144, 148, 168, 186
conquest of Japan attempted by, 50–54
emissarial missions of, 128–29
increased threat from (late Ming period), 178–79, 185
Ming defeat of, 57–58, 59, 64–66

Mongols (*cont.*)
navy of, 48, 49, 50–54, 81
Song defeated by, 48–49, 54
tribute from, 125, 126, 128–29, 156–57
Zhu Di's campaigns against, 159–161, 167
Zhu Di's stabilization of relations with, 124–29
Zhu Qizhen captured by, 176, 177
see also Yuan dynasty
Moses, 101
Mu Jing, 160
music, 187, 199
Muslims, 165
of Quanzhou, 147–48
see also Islam

Naghachu, 64–66
Nanjing:
capital moved from, 138, 143–45, 151–53, 159, 160, 163
capital returned to, 164, 167
Longjiang shipyards in, 75, 76–80, 87, 89, 173
Nanjing campaign (1402), 70–71, 73
navigation:
astronomy and, 36, 96, 97
latitude readings and, 96
Song innovations in, 43
soundings and, 96–97
water compasses and, 92, 93–96
Nayira'u, 65–66
Neolithic peoples, 22, 23, 24
New Guinea, 23, 24, 37, 197
New World, pre-Columbian contacts between Asia and, 22, 24, 25–27, 28, 31–32, 40–41
Ningbo, 123
Nissanka Alagakkonara (Alakeswara), 114–16, 117, 118

Oceania, 22, 25
Oirats, 125, 126, 129, 160, 161
Old Testament, 101
Olmecs, 28
Otomi tribes, 26–27

Pacific Ocean, 21, 22, 31
paddle-wheel boats, 45–46, 47
Pagoda of the Three-Peak Temple, 93
Pahang, 148
Palembang, 148, 162, 170
Java's conflict with, 98–99
Parameswara's departure from, 107–8
pirates of, 98–99, 102, 106, 184
Parameswara, 107–9, 111
eyeglasses presented to Zhu Di by, 119–20
Pate Island, 198–200, 201–2
Peng Bailian, 85
Penglai, 29
Persia, 35
Persian Gulf, 35
treasure fleet's voyage in, 137, 138, 140
Persian traders, 37, 39, 41
porcelain route and, 35–36
Peru, 25, 28
Philippines, 25, 185, 186, 192, 196
pirates, 82, 89, 185–86
of Palembang, 98–99, 102, 106, 184
Song navy's defeat of, 45–46
wako, 20, 89, 175, 181, 185–86
polar regions, Chinese knowledge of, 196
Polo, Marco, 42, 49, 54, 79, 180, 197
Polynesia, 24, 110
porcelain, 19, 35, 82, 84, 85, 98, 150
Bao'en pagoda built of, 121–22
trade route for, 35–36
Zhu Di's interest in, 152–53, 167
Portugal, 20–21, 111, 121, 142, 180, 183, 185, 186, 198
post houses, 128–29

Qi Tai, 68, 71
Qian Yi, 163
qianxingban, 96
qiao chuan (bridge ships), 30–31
qilins (sacred animals), 140–43, 149, 153, 151, 172–73, 200
Qin dynasty, 28
Qing dynasty, 131
Qingbai, 84
Quan shu (Exhortations), 163
Quanzhou, 62, 123
  Muslims of, 147–48
  treasure fleet docked at, 146–148
Qui Nhon, 170
Quilon, 100, 102, 114

rafts, Pacific sailing, 25–26
Rasulid dynasty, 149
religious beliefs:
  of Malays, 110–11
  see also Buddhism; Christianity; Daoism; Hinduism; Islam
Ricci, Matteo, 171
river barges, flat-bottomed, 177, 178
rudders, balanced, 81–82
Ryūkyū Islands, 173–74

Saifu'd-Din, 140
Saint Elmo's fire, 103
San Bao Gong (Semarang), 190–192
San Bao taijian Xiyang ji tongsu yanyi (Lou Maotang), 82
sandboats (*shachuan*), 78, 82
"sea falcons," 44
Sekander, 139, 142
Semudera:
  civil war in, 139, 142
  envoys from, 102
  treasure fleet's voyages to, 98, 111, 139, 148, 151, 170
sexual behavior:
  Daoist views on, 133–35
  importation of Korean virgins and, 37, 131, 132, 133, 135
  in royal bedchamber of Ming court, 131–32, 133, 135
shachuan (sandboats), 78, 82
Shadi Khwaja, 157
Shāhrukh, Mirza, 156, 157
Shāhrukh Bahadur, 126, 127–28
Shan hai jing (Stories of mountains and seas), 197
Shang kingdom, 27, 28, 34
Shanga, 201–2
Shanghai, 93
Shen Du, 141–42
shen zhou (spirit ships), 80–81
Shi Jing (Book of poetry), 60
ships, *see* boats and ships
Shou Lao, 198
Shu Jing (Book of documents), 60
Siam, 88, 98
  Chinese residents of, 184
  emissarial missions of, 174
  mahogany of, 111–12
  Malacca's relations with, 107, 109, 145, 169
  treasure fleet's voyages to, 105–6, 169
silk, 19, 35, 82, 84, 98, 198
Sinbad legend, 40
Singhalese, 114–15
Siyu, 198–200
slaves, 37–38, 39, 89, 97
Somalia, 35, 37–38
  see also Mogadishu
Song dynasty, 38, 40–48, 202
  boat design in, 43–45, 49, 80–81
  change of outlook in, 41–42
  Jin attack on, 46–47
  Mongol defeat of, 48–49, 54
  navy of, 42–43, 44–48
  trade in, 41, 43–44
Song Lian, 60
soundings, 96–97
Spain, 25–26, 125–26, 185, 186
Spice Islands, 180
spice trade, 49, 88, 89, 98, 108
spirit ships (*shen zhou*), 80–81
Sri Parakrama Bahu VI, 116, 117–118

star maps, 96, 97
storytelling, 99
Strait of Malacca, 98, 102
Sui dynasty, 34
Sui shu (History of the Sui dynasty), 197
Sulawesi, 23, 25, 26–27, 195, 196
Sumatra, 23, 49, 170
  disputes on, 139, 142, 162
  envoys from, 102, 172
  Palembang pirates of, 98–99, 102, 106, 184
  Parameswara's departure from, 107–8
  treasure fleet's voyages to, 98, 111–12, 138, 139, 148, 151, 170
Surabaja, 170
Suzhou, 75, 84
Swahilis, 149–50, 200, 201

Taiping, 93, 107
Taiwan, 23, 25
Tamerlane (Timur), 125–26, 157
Tamils, 113, 114
Tang dynasty, 34–39, 133
  boats in, 80
  Chang'an court in, 34–35
  establishment of, 34
  familiarity with Africa in, 37–38
  fondness for foreign objects in, 38
  trade in, 35–36, 38–39
  tribute in, 36–37
Tartars, *see* Mongols
Temasek, 107, 108
Tenavarai-Nayanar, 113
Thailand, 192
  see also Siam
Tianfang, 170, 171, 189
Tianfei (Celestial Consort), 192
  legend of, 89
  prayers and sacrifices offered to, 89–90, 91, 92, 93, 103
  tablets erected to (Changle), 169–170
  temple to (Meizhou), 103
  temple to (Nanjing), 89
Tianshun emperor, *see* Zhu Qizhen
Tibet, 35, 40
  Zhu Di's relations with, 124, 129–131
Timor, 198
Timur (Tamerlane), 125–26, 157
Timurids, 125–26, 127–28
  tribute horse from, 156–57
Toghon-temur, 59
trade:
  adventure tales of, 39–40
  bartering rituals and, 100–101
  in Chang'an market, 35
  Chinese dominance of, 121
  Chinese vs. European concept of, 146
  Confucian views on, 33, 34, 36, 41, 54–55, 88, 164, 165, 175, 179, 180
  eunuchs' continual involvement in, 177
  at guest house for foreign envoys, 119, 121
  with Japan, 123, 184–85
  Malacca's practices in, 108
  in Ming dynasty, 19–20, 73–74, 84, 85, 88–89, 98–99, 100, 104, 105–6, 109, 119, 121, 123, 125, 128, 137, 138, 140, 142, 149, 174, 177, 184–185
  with Mongols, 128
  monitoring of, 38–39, 55
  in Persian Gulf, 137, 138, 140
  piracy and, 20, 45–46, 82, 89, 98–99, 102, 106, 175, 181, 184, 185–86
  porcelain route and, 35–36
  private, ban on, 185, 186
  in slaves, 37–38, 97
  in Song dynasty, 41, 43–44
  in Tang dynasty, 35–36, 38–39
  thievery or smuggling and, 174
  Zhu Di's liberalization of, 88, 123
  Zhu Yuanzhang's restriction of, 88–89, 98–99, 112, 123

treasure fleet, 19–21, 73–118, 124, 144, 159, 160, 165
  first expedition of (1405–7), 87–103, 137
  second expedition of (1407–9), 88, 103, 104, 106, 137
  third expedition of (1409–11), 107–18, 137
  fourth expedition of (1413–15), 137–42
  fifth expedition of (1417–19), 19–20, 145, 146–51
  sixth expedition of (1421–22), 151
  seventh expedition of (1431–33), 168–73
  Bao'en Temple complex built with revenues from, 121–22
  cessation of, 20, 163–64
  Chinese culture spread by, 186–187
  Chinese people dispersed throughout southeast Asia by, 183, 184, 186
  command structure of, 83
  commander in chief appointed for, 87
  communication between boats in, 83
  construction of, 76–78
  craftsmen assembled for building of, 76–77
  decoration of boats in, 82
  emergency replacements for, 111–112
  eunuch supervision of, 83, 85
  fictional accounts of, 188–90
  fire weapons of, 102
  foreign envoys transported by, 19, 102, 103, 105, 140, 142, 145
  launching of, 87–88, 89–92
  legacy of, 183–87
  loss of life due to, 189, 190
  loss of Zheng He's logs from, 179–180
  medical staff of, 83–84, 112
  navigation methods of, 93–97
  personnel in, 83–84
  pirates and, 98–99, 102, 106, 184
  shipbuilding innovations in, 81–82
  size of ships in, 80–81
  southern hemisphere possibly visited by, 198
  tablets documenting achievements of, 169–70
  trade goods commanded for, 84, 85
  types of vessels in, 82–83
  weather forecasting and, 102–3
  Zheng He relieved of command of, 164
  Zhu Di's motivations for, 88
  Zhu Yunwen sought by, 73, 88, 104
treasure ships (*bao chuan*), 19, 21, 79–82
tribute, 54, 82, 88, 98, 105, 123, 140–43, 149, 151, 152, 168, 172–73, 176
  civil unrest and, 142
  decline of, 174, 177–78, 185
  demanded from Ceylon, 114–15, 118
  elaborate procedures for, 118–119
  housing arrangements for bearers of, 118, 128–29
  imperial banquets and, 120
  from Mongols, 125, 126, 128–29, 156–57
  and spread of Chinese culture, 186–87
  in Tang dynasty, 36–37
  see also foreign envoys
Tuban, 184
Tumasik, 184
Turks, 34, 62

Uriyangqads, 124, 128, 160–61

Valentyn, François, 201
Vietnam, 25, 170, 184, 186, 187
  see also Annam; Champa
Vijaya, 113–14
Vijaya Bahu VI, 116, 117, 118

wako pirates, 20, 89, 175, 181, 185–186
Wang, Madame, 155–56
Wang Fu, 143
Wang Jinghong, 106, 107, 169, 173, 190–91
Wang Min, 189–90
Wang Shen, 71
Wang Zhen, 175–76, 177
Wang Zhi, 179–80, 185–86
Washanga, 199–200, 202
water compasses, 92, 93–96
wayang performances, 99
weapons:
  fire or gunpowder, 47, 50–51, 52, 102, 177
  restrictions on trade in, 187–188
weather forecasting, 102–3
were-tigers, 111
West Lake ships (*Xihu zhou chuan*), 81
Willandra Lakes people, 24
Wu, Emperor, 29, 30
Wu bei zhi (Records of military preparation), 94–95, 96, 97
Wu Zhong, 160
Wu's Head, 93

Xia Yuanji, 159, 160, 161, 163, 168, 169
Xiao Yi, 159
Xihu zhou chuan (West Lake ships), 81
Xing cha sheng lan (Marvelous visions from the star raft) (Fei Xin), 110
Xu, Empress, 155, 161, 163
Xu Da, 58, 155
Xu Fu, 29, 31
Xu Hai, 185–86
Xuande emperor, *see* Zhu Zhanji
Xuanzong, Emperor, 36

Yan Zhen, 73
Yang Fanchen, 36
Yang Mao, 153
Yang Min, 138, 140, 141
Yang Pu, 163
Yang Rong, 157, 163
Yang Shiqi, 168, 179
Yangzi River, 48
  piracy at mouth of, 185–86
  shift in course of, 24
  in Song defense network, 42, 43
Yao peoples, 57
Yellow River, 196
Yellow Sea, 78
Yi Pangwon, 132–33
Yi peoples, 23–28, 110, 196
  legacy of shipbuilding tradition of, 32
  legend associated with, 27–28
  migrations of forefathers of, 23–25
  New World cultures and, 25–27, 28
  Shang kingdom and, 27, 28
Yiben Deguang Gong, 148
Ying yai sheng lan (The overall survey of the ocean's shores), 171
Yingzhou, 29
Yishiha, 125
Yongle emperor, *see* Zhu Di
Yoshimitsu, 123
Yu Shiji, 132
Yu Yunwen, 47
Yuan dynasty, 48–55, 148, 186
  Confucianism in, 49, 54–55
  establishment of, 48–49
  fall of, 57–58, 59
  grain transports in, 54–55
  influx of Muslims in, 62
  see also Mongols
Yue peoples, 23
Yunnan campaign (1381–82), 57–58
Yuyang za zu (Miscellany of Yuyang mountain) (Duan Chengshi), 37

zamurins, 100, 101, 103, 106
Zanzibar, 200–201
Zayd, Abu-, 39
Zhang Cheng, 153

Zhang Degang, 153
Zhang Heng, 31
Zhang Xuan, 48, 54
Zhang Yi, 42
Zhejiang, 32
Zhen Dexiu, 60
Zheng Haozhao, 165
Zheng He (formerly Ma He), 17, 20, 21, 73, 82, 103–4, 124, 160, 162, 183, 184, 197–98, 202
appointed commander of treasure fleet, 87
in campaign against Mongols, 64, 65
in civil war, 70, 72–73
death of, 172
education of, 63
family background of, 61–63
as fictional cult hero, 150, 188–190
legacy of, 183–87
loss of logs of, 179–80
Malaccan entrepôt established by, 109–10
Muslim beliefs of, 147, 172
name Zheng bestowed on, 72–73
Nanjing home of, 164–65
as patron saint for expatriate Chinese, 190–93
physical appearance of, 64, 87
pirates fought by, 102, 106
relieved of treasure fleet command, 164
sailing charts of, 94–95, 96
stone tablets erected by, 169–170
taken prisoner, 57–58
in treasure fleet's first expedition (1405–7), 87–103, 137
in treasure fleet's third expedition (1409–11), 107–18, 137
in treasure fleet's fourth expedition (1413–15), 137–40, 142
in treasure fleet's fifth expedition (1417–19), 19–20, 145, 146–151
in treasure fleet's sixth expedition (1421–22), 151
in treasure fleet's seventh expedition (1431–33), 169–72
Zhengtong emperor, *see* Zhu Qizhen
Zhiguang, 129
Zhou dynasty, 27, 141
Zhou Man, 151
Zhou Qufei, 37, 44
Zhu Bo, 67, 68
Zhu Di (Yongle emperor, formerly Prince of Yan), 58, 59, 61, 63, 64, 93, 165, 174, 176
as able soldier, 64
ambition and megalomania of, 124, 137, 144
armies sent abroad by, 123–24
Bao'en Temple complex built by, 121–22
burial of, 161–62
in campaign against Mongols, 64–66
capital moved by, 138, 143–45, 151–53, 159, 160, 163
Ceylon's rulers and, 115, 116, 117, 118
Chinese culture spread by, 187
Chinese emigration and, 183, 184
Cochin sovereignty and, 145–146
concubines and consorts of, 131, 133, 135, 152, 155–56, 157, 162
eunuchs' aid to, 70, 72
eyeglasses presented to, 119–120
fiscal problems of, 159
giraffes presented to, 140–43, 149, 151, 153, 172–73, 200
Heaven's signs of displeasure with, 155–59
illness and death of, 161
Islam and, 147–48
king of Brunei's visit and, 104–105
Malaccan sovereignty and, 107, 109, 111, 145

Zhu Di (*cont.*)
Mongol campaigns of, 159–61, 167
Mongol relations stabilized by, 124–29
porcelain and lacquerware as interests of, 152–53, 167
purges of, 156
rebellion of, 66–74, 124
reign name chosen by, 72
as semidivine emperor, 145, 146
Semudera's civil war and, 139, 142
successor to, 162–63
thrown by tribute horse, 156–57
Tibetan relations improved by, 124, 129–31
trade policies liberalized by, 88, 123
travels of, 145
treasure fleet and, 73–74, 75–76, 78, 81, 82, 84–85, 87, 88–89, 124, 137, 138, 144, 145, 151, 159, 183
Zhu Yunwen's escape and, 73, 88, 104
Zhu Zhanji and, 167, 168
Zhu Gaoxu, 163, 168
Zhu Gaozhi (Hongxi emperor), 162–164, 165, 167, 168
Zhu Qing, 48, 54
Zhu Qizhen (Zhengtong emperor; Tianshun emperor), 175–76, 177
Zhu Yuanzhang (Hongwu emperor), 58–61, 68, 76, 109, 124, 125, 130, 141, 143, 144, 145, 146, 155, 164, 179, 188
Chinese culture spread by, 186–187
concubines and consorts of, 59, 60–61, 66
Confucianism and, 60
legend of vermilion chest of, 71
Mongol defeat and, 57, 58, 64, 66
palace eunuchs and, 63, 64
paranoia of, 59, 61
purges of, 61, 69, 72
religious beliefs of, 58–59
restrictive trade policies of, 88–89, 98–99, 112, 123
successor of, 61, 66–74
temper of, 60–61
tomb of, 66, 81
Zhu Yunwen (Jianwen emperor), 61, 66–72
reputed escape of, 71, 73–74, 88, 104
Zhu Zhanji (Xuande emperor), 84, 167–69
death of, 173
and tension between eunuchs and Confucian advisers, 175
treasure fleet and, 168–69, 172–173
unsuccessful campaign against, 168
Zi zhi tong jian (Comprehensive mirror for aid in governance), 36
Zu xun lu (Ancestral injunctions) (Zhu Yuanzhang), 123, 124
Zubdatu't Tawarikh (Hafiz-i-Abru), 157